A
BROKEN
PROMISE

Hilda M. Perry

Born at Eastmere Farm, Tottington, 1912,
much of this book is autobiographical,
concerning her reminiscences about life in that village.
She now lives in Hethersett, Norfolk.

TOTTINGTON

A LOST

VILLAGE IN

NORFOLK

*by Hilda Perry
and Edmund Perry*

Edmund G. Perry

Educated in Norfolk at Wymondham College; studied at Keele University and the London School of Economics; taught at several schools in Norfolk and Suffolk; presently Head of Economics at Sir John Leman High School, Beccles. Whilst this book is the result of collaborative writing, he has been responsible for the historical and genealogical research, creating the maps, collating the photographs, arranging the layout, editing and proof reading the text.

© Copyright Hilda and Edmund Perry 1999
First published 1999
Reprinted 2000

ISBN 0 900616 56 3

Printed and published by Geo. R. Reeve Ltd.
9-11 Town Green, Wymondham, Norfolk NR18 0TT.

'It was one of our great poets who said that the tender grace of a day that is dead will never come back to us . . it is only valuable for the lesson it affords.

But the simple story which our forefathers have handed down to us is a precious inheritance and one which we regard with thankfulness and a deep sense of responsibility, for our "present" will be the "past" to those who come after us.

The past history of a country village is so rarely written down in book form that to many, I feel sure, it would not be uninteresting to learn how life was lived in a little Breckland parish'.

The Land of the "Babes in the Wood"
by Charles Kent (1910)
Merton Rector

CONTENTS

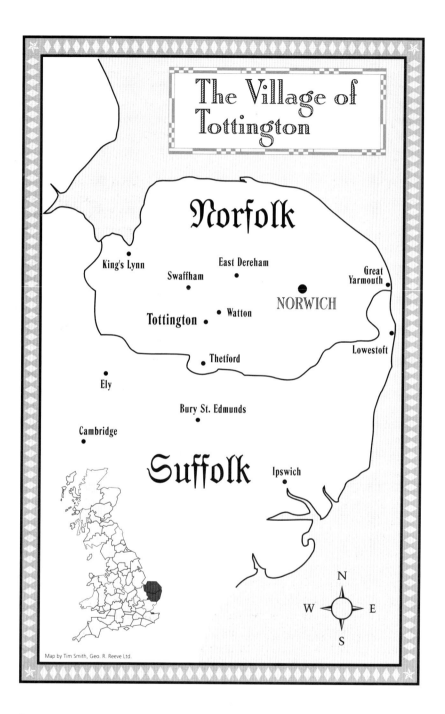

The Village of Tottington

Norfolk

King's Lynn

Swaffham

East Dereham

Great Yarmouth

NORWICH

Tottington

Watton

Lowestoft

Thetford

Ely

Bury St. Edmunds

Cambridge

Suffolk

Ipswich

N
W — E
S

Map by Tim Smith, Geo. R. Reeve Ltd.

PREFACE

On 19th July 1942, Tottington, a small village in South Norfolk ceased to exist as a community. Along with many others its two hundred inhabitants were forced to leave their homes by the War Department which created a Battle Area in the Breckland as a training camp for the Army. Those families have never been allowed to return; their homes either fell into decay or were destroyed.

Imagine a village, where your ancestors have lived for generations and most of your neighbours are relatives. A small, quiet, peaceful community where people work, loyally supporting their country's war effort. One day the military turns up, calls a meeting and gives everyone a week (later extended to a month) to pack up and leave. Such a scenario might not seem out of place in Nazi Germany or Soviet Russia: European history abounds with examples of towns and villages destroyed, lives lost, inhabitants made refugees, never to return. Even parts of Scotland and Ireland have suffered from forced depopulation but such cases in England are few. Our example may not be so grave, there was no loss of life, yet the destruction was equally as real as you would find in a deserted village in present day Bosnia. That in itself makes Tottington an important and interesting issue especially since its original inhabitants were given a promise of return after the Second World War had ended. Sadly that promise was never kept; indeed it was broken deliberately.

Tottington is 'lost'; physically in that there is little or nothing to return to, and spiritually, in that it has no reality except in the memories of an ever diminishing number of souls. Apart from the ruin of St. Andrew's Church, there exist a few empty council houses in Church Lane, and brick shells which used to be the old shop and the school house. Previous inhabitants might recognise trees and hedgerows but the fields are overgrown and nothing remains of the dwellings except mounds and foundations covered in grass and bracken.

In part, this is the story of how that destruction came about, how the promise of prosperity failed to materialise, of how and why Tottington ceased to exist. More importantly it is a resurrection of those who lived there, and simply saw it as 'home'. In attempting to rediscover a 'lost' village this book blends local history with autobiography, to draw attention to those aspects which gave Tottington its own rural identity.

TOTTINGTON VILLAGE

Towards the bridge over the River Wissey into the village.

Towards St. Andrew's Church out of the village.

INTRODUCTION

Many settlements in England have a long recorded tradition and most well-known towns and villages have had local histories written. However, certain small hamlets remain obscure with only a passing reference to their origin and development found in some manuscript or local study. Time passes, events fade from memory, structures remain but those who made and lived in them are forgotten. Places have disappeared for one reason or another over the centuries; villages have decayed or been depopulated. Their individual sites remain, witnessed by a mound, a ditch, a ruined wall, or etched into the landscape as dark lines on an aerial photograph. Numerous examples exist in Norfolk: at least seventeen deserted medieval villages in the North-West area alone, particularly Egmere and Waterden near Little Walsingham, as well as Alethorpe and Thorpland near Fakenham; the Breckland has more than twenty such sites, most notably Panworth, near Ashill, Houghton-on-the-Hill and Caldecote. Some of these villages disappeared long ago as with Ringstead Parva, totally destroyed by the Black Death during the 14th century. Others were abandoned because of the consequent economic hardship. Indeed, often it was more profitable for landowners to run estates as sheep-farms for wool than to rely on rents and profits from tenant farmers on the poor sandy soil. The process of desertion was piecemeal and gradual, and the villages were always small, numbering at most a few dozen households. This was true of three closely related places: *Buckenham Tofts, Langford and Sturston,* in the Wayland Hundred north of Thetford in Norfolk.

In 1332 the village of *Buckenham Tofts* had only fourteen taxpayers; in 1428 fewer than ten householders and in 1603 only ten adults. Writing his *'Essay towards a Topographical History of the County of Norfolk'* in the 1730s, Blomefield declared, "there is nothing left of this village but the Hall and the miller's house." (The Census of 1801 recorded four houses and a population of twenty-four, but by 1901 this had risen to forty-two). Of *Langford*, a mile to the east, he noted "only the Manor House standing. . . . to which was a Park adjoining." *Sturston* had been all but destroyed in 1597 by the local lord, Edmund Jermyn who pulled down the houses in the village leaving only the Hall and the Rectory. He ploughed up the boundaries, dug ditches and enclosed the commons. No doubt this was so he could enjoy his estate more privately but it also fulfilled a prophetic legend.

Miss. Lucilla Reeve recounts the story in her book *'The Earth No Longer Bare'*. In March 1550, during the reign of Elizabeth I, a violent storm shook the village and a old woman on her death bed cursed it and the local landowner, a Catholic Recusant named Sir Miles Yare: *"Not one stone shall remain on another. . not one stone of the village shall stand. . . You shall perish and woe to your land - cursed be you. . . not one stone. . not one stone. "* Nevertheless in 1739 the manor house still stood as did the church of the Holy Cross. According to White's Directory 1845, Sturston had a population of 47, one farm of 1802 acres and a rabbit warren of 800 acres but the church was a ruin.

In his book *'The Breckland Wilds'*, W. G. Clarke referred to Sturston as a "lost" village. Such a description applies equally to its close neighbours; the Breckland villages which have been depopulated and deliberately destroyed in the past half-century. This is the story of one of those villages - *Tottington* - and of the people who lived there, from the perspective of someone whose relatives populated the dwellings for nearly two hundred and fifty years.

For the author there will always be some nostalgia: re-living a childhood, remembering places, possessions, names and faces of those nearest and dearest, recalling some distant past which beckons daily. Perhaps there is a whiff of that rosy sentimentality with which some town dwellers view the countryside and which so often one reads in books about the traditional English village. If so, then it runs much deeper, being more personal and emotional than anything experienced by rural commuters let alone the occasional visitor. It involves all the senses of sight, sound, smell, taste and touch, deeply implanted in the memory. It is an intimacy born of belonging; the village was home, an extended family, a way of life. For those who lived and worked there its essence was about relationships: between friends and relatives, labourer and farmer, worker and employer; between village and surrounding countryside and with the nearest town. Above all it was a relationship to the land and to all that grew upon it -a field of wheat or barley, a garden of flowers and vegetables, hedgerows down the lanes, woodland and well-trodden paths.

However, this story doesn't try to present a 'Constable Cottage' picture, the romantic illusion of a gentle, happy rural landscape. There is no desire to perpetuate that myth of a golden past which offered a more ethical, spiritually uplifting, lifestyle. Tottington was hardly a rural idyll; it bore no resemblance to those perfectly preserved 'chocolate box' images which pander to the tourist voyeur. It wasn't quiet and lifeless like so many places one drives through in Norfolk and

Suffolk today. The village was not about dead physical structures to be viewed and admired: old fashioned buildings, a medieval church, a pond and a green. It was a living organism vibrant with economic and social activity, with personal and family interaction, which created an attitude and a way of thinking, a spirit of belonging, an undefined continuity between family, friends and ancestors, between the quick and the dead. That state of being resided in a life regulated by nature and the rhythm of the seasons, tempered by religious belief, ordered by daily routines and local traditions. It was a personal and family calender of shared events like Easter, and Harvest, Christmas and New Year, attending Church, Village Fetes, weddings, baptisms and burials. It involved time-honoured practices, the ritual of unwritten rules and regulations, the common use of old-fashioned words and phrases, familiar sayings often quoted, and a deeply imbued deference to class and power.

It was a harsh environment, not so much a contrast in extremes but an unending sequence of struggle against the elements. The flat open Brecklands were well known for dusty and windy conditions, rain and snow could be bitter, dirt and mud affected everything. Living conditions were bad: no piped hot and cold water, no electricity, no mains drainage, few home comforts, little entertainment and culture, above all a lack of money even for necessities. It was not a life for the weak or the faint-hearted. Village folk had a stoical approach to such difficulties: their's not to reason why, neither to complain nor make excuses. Their's was a noble endurance; not to 'flinch' had a special significance - from pain, from hardship, from responsibility. Their's was a pride, in hard work and thrift, in well learned skills, in a man's ability 'to plough a straight furrow' - all of these were badges of self-respect. Honesty, good humour and kindness acted as a shield against the worst aspects of deprivation and human suffering. Those who survived the tribulations had an unsentimental approach to the landscape. Any concern for the environment was usually selfish and accidental; their thoughts were not so much for the landscape but for the type of soil in each field, its lightness or heaviness, whether easy or difficult to work, what it was best used for - wheat, barley, clover, sugar- beat, or pasture.

Nowadays we see the countryside as an opportunity for freedom, open spaces, fresh air, peace and quiet - a chance to escape the din and clamour, the congestion and pollution of city life, but in the nineteenth and early twentieth centuries, drawbacks to the daily existence of propertyless countryfolk resulted in discontent and disaffection. To a large extent rural life was circumscribed by boundaries of class, distance, and tradition. Family background, lack of education, poverty and unemployment restricted social mobility; the Parish wrapped villagers in a comfort zone because people hardly travelled ten miles from home; religion and superstition inhibited freedom of thought and independence; the past illuminated the present but in doing so it controlled so many aspects of daily activity. This straight-jacket of a tight-knit, hierachical social order with its claustrophobic differences and distinctions, often stifled the creative energy and intelligence of ambitious men and women. To them the village was an 'open prison', a place and a condition to escape from. Admittedly the grinding poverty, sickness and famine forced the exodus of many but those who emigrated to the great Metropolis or to the northern cities, or further afield to America and Australia, wanted freedom, the opportunity of a better life. Yet, where some men, like John Herring and Judd Macro from Tottington, succeeded, many others failed. Not everyone wanted, or was able, to leave. For those who, for one reason or another, stayed, the village remained a haven if not a sanctuary. Many who left went to other similar villages or returned regularly to visit friends and relatives. If not their physical residence, the village remained their spiritual 'home'.

Memories of the Victorian age and vestiges of its daily life lingered but the hallmark of rural existence was slow, pervasive change, accelerated by the effects of the First World War, altered by technological progress, affected by social and cultural development. The physical reality continued since Tottington altered little in appearance: the fields, woods, commons, heathland survived; farm buildings remained standing; some new machinery appeared but much of the old was retained; fewer horses were used but they were the mainstay of local transport. Yet, between the World Wars, the pace of change and development quickened promising a better standard of living for those families who stayed behind and who saw their future as bound up with the village.

It wasn't about turning the countryside into a nature reserve nor accepting it as a wasteland; the village wasn't to be preserved as a museum let alone a ruin for tourists to visit. Whilst few could have foreseen the influx of 'foreigners' who buy holiday homes or crowd the new rural housing estates, even fewer would have imagined their village 'disappearing' altogether. After all generations had lived there maintaining a strong link with the land and with a shared past, a collective memory of people, places and events. That heritage was continued by the families living in and around the village. To someone like the Merton Estate Agent, Miss Lucilla Reeve, such continuity also meant the fruition of all that effort put in during the nineteenth century to reclaim marginal soil, not just for forestry and shooting but as productive farmland for crops and animals, something which was coming true in the 1930s with the duck farming at Eastmere near Tottington. It was the promise of a future based upon the land which created wealth and a decent living for those villagers who worked it. She never lost faith in its possibility even when abruptly halted during that fateful Summer of 1942; after all the Government promised the land would be returned once the war had ended. Sadly it was 'a broken promise' in every respect.

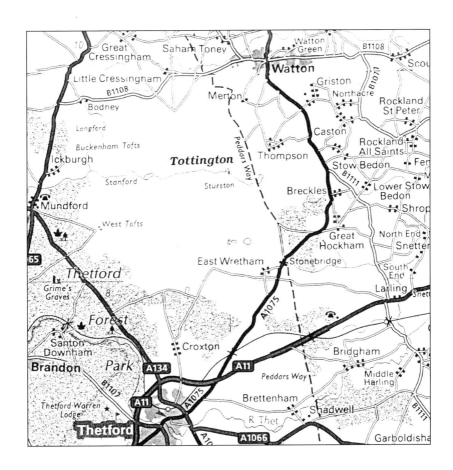

A SHORT HISTORY

"Tottington - where's that?" - you may well ask. "In the Breckland in Norfolk", one might reply. Yet there are two generations of people born in East Anglia since the last War who have scant knowledge about either, so anyone from outside the area is unlikely to know where or what Tottington was. But then that remained true of the village for most of its long history since it never numbered more than 400 souls and wasn't the birth place of anyone famous. Nor is it the site of a major battle even though the locality is known as 'The Battle Area', - a blank patch on a Norfolk road map where thin white lines go nowhere and the few small specks of blue stare back in isolation.

   " *Tottington is a small irregular village in the hundred of Wayland, deanery of Breccles, and archdeaconry of Norwich, and lies on the road between Thetford and Watton, distant eight miles from the former, and four from the latter. The parish is bounded on the north by Threxton, Little Cressingham, and Merton; by Merton and Thompson on the east; on the west by Stanford; and on the south by Wretham and Sturston.* "   Gentleman's Magazine January 1819, page 24.

   Nevertheless the area does have a lengthy history and numerous remains have been found: notably huge numbers of flint tools from the Stone Age (the Neolithic flint mines at Grime's Graves are only ten miles away from Tottington), and burial mounds or barrows from the Bronze Age such as 'Mill Hill' to the east of Keymer's Plantation, Tottington. It was the heartland of the British Iceni tribe: the tumuli which exist along the Wretham road going towards Thompson Watering were treated with reverential respect. Children were not allowed to walk or play on these mounds which were considered to be the burial grounds of Queen Boadicea's warriors who died fighting the Romans. The latter were responsible for the Peddars Way which cuts across the heaths and plantations dividing Tottington from the neighbouring village of Thompson. No major Roman settlement has been discovered but their artifacts have been found and they did introduce sheep which continued in importance throughout the Saxon-Norman period.

   Unravelling the history of an obscure village like Tottington would be impossible without the assistance of certain reference works; much of the following is abridged from Blomefield's *Topographical History of Norfolk*. Originally most of the villages in the area received their titles from the Angles and Saxons. Tottington was named after a chief

16

called Tota; Buckenham Tofts after someone called Bucca (tofts being a smallholding, hence West Tofts); Stanford is a 'stony ford', and Langford is a 'long ford'; Sturston after a man called Styr; and Merton after the water found there.

In the eleventh century, during the reign of Edward the Confessor, Tottington was owned by Alwi, a Saxon, but after 1066 William the Conqueror gave it to Robert Bigot. At the time of the Domesday Survey, when Ralf Herlewin held the village, it was four miles long and two miles wide, had four carucates of land, three of which were demesne, and paid 15d to the geld; there was a wood for 30 swine, a walk for 137 sheep and 24 goats plus 15 mares although there had been 63 during the Confessor's survey. The manor was worth 80s but afterwards it fell to 60s. Tottington gained fame as the birth place in 1132 of the celebrated Abbot Samson, of Bury St. Edmund's. According to his friend, the monk Jocelin de Brakelonde, Samson, *"lying uneasily in his crib at Tottington, saw the arch enemy in person. . . shrieked desperate to St. Edmund for help."* (in *Past and Present* by Thomas Carlyle). His Mother dedicated him to St. Edmund and left him at the Abbey ; he became Abbot in 1182 and his remains are buried in the grounds.

In the reign of King Stephen, Hugh Bigot divided the land giving part to the Prior of Thetford - 'Thetford-Monks' Manor' - and the other part to John le Strange; plus a small area to Roger de Reymes who conveyed it to Warner or Warin de Tottintona (who gave the tithes of his estate as a pension to the Priory of the Virgin Mary and St. Andrew at Thetford - hence the name of the village and its church). Had Tottington been called 'Bigot' or 'Strange' then like other odd sounding places, it might have had lasting distinction. However, these families had more important possessions elsewhere and neither name continued. The family which took its title from the village was still around in 1286 when John de Tottington released nine acres of his land to Vincent, the Prior of Thetford but kept a free-tenement or Manor; and an Alexander de Tottington became the 23rd Bishop of Norwich (1407-1413). However, in 1402, the estate passed from Thomas de Tottington to Sir John Fitz Ralf who held it from another John le Strange.

The local landowners were really 'farm tenants'. Of these Manors, *Tottington or Mortimer's, Strange's, Stanford's, Campesse, Thetford-Monk's and Bokenham's or Macham's,* were the most important. Many disputes arose over boundaries and inheritance as the lands were parcelled out amongst relatives. Tottington is mentioned in a well-recorded land dispute of 1195 between Robert de Mortimer of

Atilburgh and John le Strange of Hunstanton. Eventually Robert released the whole to John who then rented it back to Robert except for the church, together with rents and services, which were confirmed on Mary Felton, the Prioress of the nuns at Campesse in Suffolk, in 1196. This *'Strange's Manor'* continued in that family until the son and heir, Sir John le Strange, in the reign of Henry V, confirmed it to Alice Corbet, Prioress of Campesse and her successors.

In 1244, William de Mortimer was lord of *Mortimer's Manor* which sometimes became synonymous with Tottington and a farm with this name continued right up to the Second World War. In 1339, Constantine de Mortimer and his wife Sybil, held Strange's Manor, along with Scoulton and Stanford. In 1390 Sir John le Strange of Hunstanton gave his estate at Tottington in trust only to Sir Robert Ufford. Evidently the Mortimer's Estate was divided so that Strange's Manor along with Atilburgh and Scoulton passed to Sir John Fitz Ralf, who held the manor of Tottington in 1402.

After the dissolution of the monasteries during Henry VIII's reign, land belonging to the religious orders devolved to the crown. In 1530 the patronage of the vicarage was given to Sir Richard Southwell (who belonged to a family living near Norwich) and in 1531, *Campesse Manor* was given to him and his heirs for an annual farm rent. His brother, Sir Robert, had a son Sir Thomas Southwell who sold the vicarage in 1583 to Thomas Hall and the land thereabouts was farmed by Francis Windham. In about 1600, Sir John Southwell sold the tenancy to a John Hall. Part of this Manor included the Vicarage and nearby fields. According to Bloomfield's *Topographical History,* Gonville College Cambridge, had owned a tenement in Tottington since 1480 and for some reason when the Vicarage lapsed King James I gave it to Trinity College, Cambridge, to maintain a professorship of divinity. Sir Thomas Southwell then appears to have acquired these leases and sold their property rights to Henry Best working for Samuell Harsnett, Archbishop of York, who endowed his free schools at Chigwell in Essex with the tithe revenue, from 1629 onwards.

Thetford-Monk's Manor was granted to Thomas, Duke of Norfolk, who sold it to the Southwell's in 1541. This family also bought Strange's Manor from a Ralf and Elizabeth Chamberlain in 1544 and Stanford's Manor from the Wyndham family. So by 1558 nearly all the land of the manors in Tottington, Stanford, Little Cressingham, Thomson, Sturston and Threxton were held under the old name of *Mortimer's Manor* by Sir Richard Southwell. Thereafter, in 1572 the land passed to his daughter Elizabeth, wife of George Heinage, and to his brother, Sir Robert Southwell, who sold *Strange's Manor* to Edward Coke. In the reign of Charles I, **Campsey Manor** was sold to Thomas Garrard, Knt, who also owned Strange's Manor at that time. It passed to Sir Nicholas Garrard of Langford, Bart, who died in 1727, leaving it to his widow, who sold it to Sir William de Grey.

Stanford's Manor, was held by the De Ware family for much of the twelfth and thirteenth centuries, then by the Wyndham's and the Southwell's joined it to Mortimer's Manor. However, in 1345, Thomas de Ware had settled half of Stanford's Manor on Hugh de Bokenham which by 1402 was held by Thomas de Tottington. It came down to the Salter's who were an important family in the village for over two hundred years, as the memorials in the church testify. William Salter, a yeoman, held land here in the reign of Henry VIII, 1539, as did his son and grandson both named Thomas. Edmund Salter was lord of this small *'Bokenham's or Macham's Manor'* in 1629. About 1714 it was sold by Edmund son of Robert Salter to a Mr. Evesdon. The sale included the site of the rectory next to the churchyard and an area four hundred yards north-west of the church where, in the early nineteenth century, there was a barn, surrounded by a moat with a good fishery.

During the second half of the eighteenth century these various tracts of land were unified under the 'de Grey' family which owned the **Merton Estate** nearby. They had a noble ancestry, having come over with William the Conqueror, and inherited the site of the old Merton Hall from Ralf Baynard who died without male issue so that his daughter carried it to her husband Sir Thomas de Grey in 1337. The family name is infamously connected to the "Babes in the Wood" legend, associated with Wayland Wood on the edge of Merton Estate near Watton which gave its name to the Anglo-Saxon 'hundred' and to the larger modern administrative district of Wayland. The "Babes", Thomas and Jane, were placed in the charge of their Uncle Robert, after their parents, Edmund and Elizabeth de Grey, had died of sickness. According to popular story, Robert stood to inherit everything if the children died, so he hired two ruffians to take the children into the forest and kill them. One of the men was so enchanted by the youngsters that he wanted to let them go. He argued with the other who died in the resulting fight. The murderer led the children deeper into the forest and left them hoping someone would find them. Tired of waiting, Thomas and Jane wandered about eating some berries and then lay down under an oak tree to sleep. They died that night from cold and hunger and were buried by a robin covering them with leaves. The villain was caught for another crime and sentenced to hang, whereupon he confessed to the Babes' deaths. The oak tree, where the children were found, was marked in Wayland Wood but lightning destroyed it in August 1879 leaving only a stump which is still visible.

Standing half-a-mile to the south-east of Wayland Wood is an Elizabethan Manor House, Griston Old Hall, part of the de Grey property which, until one hundred years ago, contained a large Tudor overmantel carved with a representation of the Babes in the Wood. This suggests that the legend is much older and current before Robert's time; it is unlikely that he would keep an ornate reminder in his own home if he were guilty of such a crime. The story was published by Thomas Millington in 1585, since when a ballad, "The Children in the Wood" has become a favourite subject for Christmas pantomines. Whether legend is fact is another matter. Robert was thirty-six years old when he inherited the Merton Estate in 1566 but suffered great misfortune as a result: his cattle died, his crops did not ripen, his barns burned down, his two sons died on their way to Portugal and he was forced to sell some of his land to pay his debts.

Wayland Wood nearly disappeared during the sixteenth century. Robert de Grey was an obstinat Roman Catholic, a 'Papist' who refused to acknowledge Queen Elizabeth as Head of the Church of England. After 1578 penal laws against Catholic recusants were enforced with increasing severity; agents were employed to persecute them and sequester their estates. These Commissioners feathered their own nests by returning lower rents than they received from the farmers and villagers. They pillaged the estates, by letting houses fall into ruin and by felling timber. Robert was imprisoned in 1584 for failing to attend the Anglican services and for not paying the cumulative fines. He forfeited his goods and chattels and two-thirds of the estate revenues to the Crown. His estate was taken over by a Crown Commisioner called Thomas Felton and his lessee John Cotch. They hired a gang to fell Wayland Wood but a friend of Robert's, named Francis Woodhouse of Breckles, warned him of their intent. Robert paid his fines, bailed himself out, collected his employees together, armed them with forks and staves and, backed by men from the neighbouring village of Griston, forced Felton's men to withdraw.

The record of the subsequent inquiry shows that Felton complained of "threatening speech" by Robert, and also of the loss of much of the timber felled. Robert had to return to gaol eventually being released in 1598. Before dying in 1601 he set himself to rebuilding Merton Hall and cultivating the land. This work was continued by his son Sir William de Grey, who, although a Protestant, had much difficulty in exempting the Estate from paying the arrears of his Father's fines amounting to £1780 - a huge sum at that time. Nevertheless he was wealthy enough to build a Jacobean mansion of red brick, finished in 1613, and additions were made to the Hall from then onwards.

The de Grey family grew in power and prosperity during the seventeenth century and by the eighteenth they were in a position to acquire and control the nearby villages like Tottington. Sir William de Grey, Lord Chief Justice of the Common Pleas, set about buying up individual plots of land. This process was consoliated by the second Lord, Thomas (1748 - 1818) and George (1776 - 1833) and Thomas (1778 -1839) the fourth Lord Walsingham. Land acquisitions were:

	1754	from Mrs Gallant, Mrs Duffield, Mr. Rolfe, Mrs Briggs, Thomas Warner and George Salmon.
December	1761	from Jonathan West after Robert West, a farm, the farmhouse and sixteen-and-a-half acres of land for £500
January	1763	from Susan Machin (widow)
January	1767	from Henry Spooner to Thomas de Grey.
July	1770	from Matthew Lusher (after John Balls in 1757, the Manor of Macham)
	1771	from Jacob Thomas Speidell, the Rectory, to Sir William de Grey
August	1774	from Sarah Barton (84 acres) previously held by Elizabeth Knopwood
	1774	from Mrs Mary Duffield (widow) 39 acres in 33 different pieces for £1100. 'to live in her house for the rest of her life'
April	1776	Thomas to William de Grey, transfer of the Madhouse area.
June	1792	from Lord Walpole

Thus began a process of Enclosure described by Thomas as *"bringing forth a ragged, dirty parish to neatness and cultivation"*. In a letter to his brother William he wrote *"Tottington is now what Merton was when I came to it, one great Sheep's walk starv'd all the rest of the parish"*. In 1774, during the reign of George III, Sir Thomas de Grey asked Sir Edward Astley to present a Bill to the House of Commons: ' *for dividing and inclosing the Common Fields, Half-year lands, Common Pastures, Common Meadows, Commons, Commonable Lands, Lammas Meadows, Heaths and Waste Grounds, within the*

Merton Hall – Home of the De Grey family.
This beautiful building stands behind Merton church but is now in ruins after two serious fires. In the early part of this century it was let to shooting syndicates, later became a school and then service flats.

parish of Tottington, in the county of Norfolk.' This became an Act of Parliament agreed to by the smaller landowners: Thomas Levett (5 acres); William Tooke (42 acres); Peter Dent (9 acres); John Frost and Daniel Neale. It left the Rectory Glebe (7 acres) plus six acres of Common for the Parishioners of Tottington and Thompson to walk on and a Common called Lammas Meadows (30 acres). The total area was 3039 acres, and by 1819 *"the whole parish except the Glebe and one cottage now belongs to his Lordship."* (George de Grey, 3rd Lord Walsingham, 1776 - 1831). There was a piece of land, a charitable bequest called Chandler's Pightle (about one acre), which the parish officers let to Lord Walsingham, for 4s a year:

the rent of this piece of land (5s. per ann. 1777) was formerly received by the overseers; and instead of being given to the "industrious poor" went towards paying the expenses of the town meetings! . . . is now let, , , , to Samuel Chilvers, who pays the rent to his Lordship's steward. Gentlemans Magazine 1819

In 1801 Tottington only had 26 houses and 40 families, consisting of 104 males and 94 females, altogether 198 people. There were about 3000 acres of land in the parish; a mere, north-west of the church, which in rainy seasons covered seven acres of land; and two public-houses known by the signs of the Cock and the Green Man. Not much to show or record for over a thousand years of continuous settlement. Still it had fared better than the nearby village of Sturston which had all but disappeared.

The question to ask is why so little development and lack of prosperity? In general the Breckland was an impoverished area and Blomefield records that villages like Santon and Bodney were depopulated in the 18th century. Sheep grazing had brought about a major degradation of the soil which was already poor; it was made worse through the rabbit which had been introduced by the Normans and extensively reared in warrens ever since, both for its skin and to supplement the diet. To those who wanted to farm the land rabbits were a menace, destroying cereals and young trees and close cropping the thin vegetation on the dry Breckland. This loosened the light surface sand which drifted away with the wind.

Blomefield, writing about the Breckland in 1739, felt that the rabbits were excellent and, " *renders that which would otherwise be of no use, to be of equal value with much better land.*" In 1745 the Rev. Dr. Stukely, travelling over the Western part of the Breckland wrote: "*we passed through an ocean of sand. Scarce a tree to be seen in miles, or a house,. . . . This country abounds with rabbits of an excellent sort.*" He called it *"this vast Arabian desert"* . William Gilpin touring in 1769 declared, *"Nothing to be seen on either side but sand and scattered gravel without the least vegetation; a mere African desert."* All the travellers commentated on the inhospitable nature of the Breckland at this time - its sandiness, its dryness, the absence of trees - and huge sandstorms were frequent. Yet it had a remarkable fascination; *"this terra ignota throws a mysterious spell . . . like the Great Sahara it is always calling you to return."* (The Rev. Charles Kent). The Duc de la Rochefoucauld, travelling in 1784, recorded:

"In some of the valleys watered by a stream I saw fine trees, houses and cultivated lands but all in small numbers. . . . A large portion of this arid country is full of rabbits, of which the numbers astounded me. We saw whole troops of them in broad daylight; but they were not alarmed by the noise and we could almost touch some of them with our whips." The Warrens were big business; *"there was an immense warren which brought in 200 guineas a year to the owner . . . . Nor can*

they be caught, since the penalty is so disproportionate to the prospect of gain that no one would be willing to take the risk. In the eyes of the law, rabbits in a warren are as sacred a piece of property as the land itself, and to transgress the laws of property is a capital offence . . . . to risk being hanged!"

In 1813, at Thetford, two young lads named Rush Lingwood (aged 18) and Robert Plum (aged 22) were indicted for entering the Warren of Thomas Robertson of Hockwold and taking one coney. Lingwood received two years in prison but Plum was transported to Australia for seven years! Tottington was surrounded by rabbits: to the north was Tottington Warren; to the west was Bodney; to the south west, Sturston, where my Gt. Grandfather worked as a Warrener at the turn of this century, and another at Santon where there is Warren Wood; and to the south-east, Blackrabbit Warren where stands Warren House. Breeding and skinning rabbits was a major industry. In the 1890s, A. W. Julnes, *'The Poor Man's Friend'* , Coal and Coke Merchant of Watton, who dealt in rags and skins, carried an advertisement *"Notice to hawkers. Wanted 100,000 dozen Rabbit Skins."* Even between the two World Wars, furs from rabbits were being sent to a felt factory in Brandon employing seven hundred workers.

The Duc de Rochefoucauld didn't believe it would ever be possible to cultivate the land, *"poor quality soil . . little chance of agricultural prosperity . . covered with heather . . . not a shrub, not a plant . . . no trees, no cultivation, everywhere sand, everywhere little clumps of reeds and bracken."* In 1797 William Kirby wrote that the Breckland was *"an ocean of sand producing little besides nettles and brakes, with here and there an islet of firs."* However, enclosure led to the planting of trees like Scots pine or spruce fir to partition the open spaces and shelter the new fields which were fenced in; holdings were unified into large estates, and higher prices made it profitable to plant wheat and barley even though yields were relatively low.

At the begining of the nineteenth century, land to the south-west of Tottington was virtually uninhabited until one reached the small hamlet of Stanford with its two farms, a pub and a church and about one hundred villagers. Some shelterbelts had been planted during the Napoleonic Wars when high food prices brought a resurgence in agriculture and both wheat and barley were grown. Still there remained a great sweep of breck across Mortimer's, Waterloo and Mousehill, the three farm houses built around 1817/18 to commemorate those who fell at the Battle of Waterloo. Most of the land was allocated for sheep-walk but seldom trod by human feet.

Prosperity declined rapidly after the Napoleonic Wars with commodity prices falling drastically (wheat sold for 126s 6d per quarter in 1812 but fetched only 38s 6d in 1851). High taxation, the tithe burden, a fall in demand for labour coupled with a considerable population increase, caused great distress, especially in the countryside. Both outdoor relief and the Speenhamland system (which subsidized low wages out of the rates on a scale related to the price of bread and the number of children in a family) were unable to deal with the increased rural poverty. From 1780s onwards Workhouses were been built for the aged, sick and disabled. The Poor Law Amendment Act 1834 prohibited outdoor relief and restricted it to these Workhouses, the conditions of which were often so dreadful and feared (strictly enforced rules, harsh punishments, complete segregation of the sexes) that people risked prison through crime rather than face such a fate.

At this time, Thomas, 4th Lord Walsingham, began a process of afforestation of the great expanse of bracken and heath by setting Frogshall Plantation on Deadon Hill in 1835. When the Rt. Hon. Thomas de Grey, 5th Lord Walsingham, inherited the Merton Estate in 1839, he adopted an approach of self-help and had workmen dig out the numerous pockets of clay and chalk to scatter on the land. Such 'marling' had been done in pre-Roman times but went out of fashion during the Middle Ages. The many 'pit-holes' like the one at Eastmere bear evidence to his industry. Rent allowances were given for this work because it was so time-consuming and expensive. Farm leases stipulated how much marling the tenant was expected to do - up to 80 loads an acre - and twenty years later another 30 loads had to be deposited. This wasn't always successful:

Marling seemed to make the land unhealthy for sheep tenants complained that lambs were dying of a disease called 'warping'. This was put forward as a reason for not paying rents. Mr. Deforges, who rented 212 acres on the Walsingham Estate around Stanford "has lost this season nearly two hundred lambs being warped in consequence of claying land". Norfolk: A Changing Countryside 1780-1914 by Susanne Wade-Martins

Thomas had the land fenced round, planted mustard, ploughed it in, then grew barley and turnips. He built farmhouses and cottages of brick and flint, put tenant farmers in and gave them sheep to walk over the breck in summer; in Winter these were folded on turnips, mangolds and clover. During the 'hungry forties' rural distress was terrible, people were out of work and starved but Thomas brought the local unemployed together and put them to work on the land to earn some sort of living wage. He was responsible for major works of construction including laying a new drive from Merton Hall to Tottington and making Stanford Water out of the mere in 1847 as well as Thompson Water, both 40 acres in extent and used for duck shooting and the fishing of perch, tench, rudd and eels. He created a seven acre garden at Merton Hall, its seedbeds and nursery lines used for the new plantations like the fine oaks in Prince Albert Plantation which was set in 1839. Thomas invested in the land and the Estate, making the farms of *Mortimer, Sturston, Waterloo, Bagmere, and Mousehill* food producing areas, and laying the foundations of a sporting Park for the shooting of pheasants and rabbits. Such activity virtually transformed the Merton Estate.

During this period there was a growth in the rural population of villages like Tottington. It can be seen from the Parliamentary Returns and Census counts from 1801 to 1851; despite a typhus epidemic in 1824, and the bitterly cold winter of 1829/30, the population went on rising until the 1850s:

Date	Inhabited Dwellings	Families	Occupations Agric/Trade	Male	Female	Total
1801	26	40		104	94	198
1811	28	47	43 / 4	123	126	249
1821	33	54	46 / 8	143	141	284
1831	34	59	53 / 6	162	151	313
1841	32	55		171	169	340
1851	31	70		180	190	370
1861	30	61		161	147	308
1871		63		155	135	290
1881		62		138	134	272
1891		60		145	142	287

Nevertheless considerable hardship, hunger and poverty was experienced by many families in rural areas during the latter half of the nineteenth century, and the village was seen as an open prison from which escape was sought whenever an opportunity presented itself. It isn't surprising that this led to depopulation by illness and emigration: from 1815-1829 over 300,000 emigrated from Great Britain, and from 1830 to 1855 nearly four million left. The government encouraged it and many of the rural poor were given assistance: between 1835 and 1837, 6403 people were helped to emigrate, two thirds of whom came from East Anglia. Not many Tottington families left to go abroad: from 1801 to 1851 the local population nearly doubled but the Census figures demonstrate a considerable fall during the 'high farming' period, 1850 - 1873, often seen as the 'Golden Age' in nineteenth century agriculture. This coincided with an absolute decline in the rural population of Huntingdon, Cambridgeshire, Norfolk and Suffolk. A mass exodus took place: the Census returns for 1851 show that 31,866 Norfolk born people were living in London increasing to 41,943 in 1861. By then 149,000 'Norfolk' people were living outside the county in other parts of England like the Midlands and the North, particularly Sheffield. Many women worked as domestic servants in large houses and in the fashionable residential districts of St. Pancras, Islington, Kensington and Marylebone; over 27,000 had moved to Middlesex.

By 1853 24,000 people from East Anglia had received assistance to go abroad mainly to Canada and Australia. In that year, the Reverend. Benjamin Drake, an Essex missionary to Tasmania, was sent back to England by the Launceston's Immigration Aid Society which had been formed to obtain a supply of labour from Britain for the colony and to relieve the plight of rural labourers in the Eastern Counties. The fifteen founders each subscribed 100 pounds to pay the deposits for 80 families and 60 single Government Bounty tickets. Those families willing to emigrate were lent money for their fares, to be repaid by instalments after they had become established in Tasmania.

The St. Andrew's Immigration Society in Launceston had already sent a Mr. Joseph Bonney to recruit immigrants - these were the tradesmen of Essex and the farm labourers of Norfolk and Suffolk who sailed on the WHIRLWIND arriving in Launceston 31st March 1855. The Rev. Drake was able to relate the success stories of these Whirlwind immigrants to achieve his target for the SOUTHERN EAGLE which arrived 28th August 1857 bringing 51 single adults and 176 family immigrants, in all 229 souls. The ship's log records Judd Macrow (1830-1908) and his wife Mary Ann Mayne (1828-1898) plus four children as passengers out of Gt. Cressingham and Bodney. Judd was born in Sturston, the third son of Jacob Mackrow (1765-1830) and Elizabeth Gofs (1765-1810) and the Grandson of Thomas Mackrow (buried 1794) and Elizabeth Angel (buried 1793) both from Sturston who happen to be my own Gt. Gt. Gt. Gt. Grandparents.

Like many others leaving Britain in the nineteenth century, Judd Macrow became a successful farmer settling "Mt. Pleasant", a property of 150 acres, at Don, Penguin, Tasmania. There he is buried with Mary Ann and their son, Edward, under a tombstone inscribed, *"Having a desire to depart and lie with Christ which is far better"*. Judd's sister Eliza also emigrated to Tasmania in 1857 as did their cousins, Mary Elizabeth and Harriet Macrow in 1862 on the SOLWAY (a vessel of 946 tonnes owned by James Baines of the Black Ball line): they were the daughters of Jacob Macrow (1798-1846) and Karenhappuch Chilvers (1807-18) from Tottington who later moved to Hockham, whose descendents in Australia, being interested in genealogy, have traced their ancestors back to Tottington and Sturston.

Farm workers were badly paid and very poor, not owning any land or property. Whole families existed for years on home-made food like bread and cheese, horse beans, turnips and swedes, with meat and even potatoes considered a luxury. Naturally the young and healthy wanted to leave for somewhere better. It says something about their courage, or desperate plight, yet one cannot help but admire the spirit of adventure in rural families who made their way to ports like Lynn and Yarmouth and boarded ships either for America or Australia, travelling thousands of miles on an alien sea into an unknown land and an uncertain future. A pity the 6th Lord Walsingham didn't possess the same enterprise and vision. He succeeded to the Merton Estate in 1870 and squandered a fortune; few woods were planted, the land was neglected and the area turned over to annual shoots for the benefit of the rich and famous. Wildlife was plentiful (in medieval times a natural mere near East Wretham was well known as 'Fowlmere') and the area became part of the famous shooting estates of Merton, Buckenham Tofts, Hilborough, Clermont and Lynford.

Thomas the 5th Lord, left the 12000 acres of Merton flourishing and free of debt, plus another 5,590 acres in Yorkshire and 1,075 acres in Suffolk. The estimated aggregate annual value of this inheritance was £16,178. In 1876 the income from the Norfolk Estate alone was £9,695 but these rentals declined alarmingly during the agricultural depression. All over England farming suffered from floods in the Winter of 1878, a wet spring and a cold Summer, which saturated and chilled the soil producing coarse grain and destroyed the finer grasses. Fodder and corn didn't mature properly, mould and ergot were prevalent, fluke produced liver rot in the livestock. During Black '79 three milion sheep died or were slaughtered because of rot in England and Wales. The Winter of 1880-81 was very severe leading to one of the worst harvests of the century. Mechanisation reduced the number of farm labourers and increased the output of crops but, with the application of Free Trade, the urban demand for cheap food was met increasingly by imported grain and frozen meat from the American continent and Australasia. As corn prices were forced downwards, poor soil like the Breckland went out of cultivation and became pasture. A second phase of agricultural depression in the 1890s left more than two million acres of arable land fallow; mainly weeds and rough grass but with no livestock to graze it. Such events had a severe effect upon the marginal lands of the Merton Estate. Two miserably wet years, 1891 and 1892, followed by a drought, were disastrous for the light Breckland soil and by 1894 the price of wheat had fallen to 22 shillings a quarter, half the price of twenty years earlier. In consequence, farm rents were reduced by a third between 1874 and 1894. In 1900 Lord Walsingham admitted to the writer H. Rider Haggard that he *"had no great hope for the future, no prospect of improvement unless prices rose, land would go out of cultivation and husbandry would come to an end"*.

The 6th Baron's attempts to augment his income by turning Walsingham House in London into a Club and Hotel and by speculating on railways failed lamentably. By 1890 there were debts of £14,356. The site in London covering 20,000 feet with frontages to Piccadilly and Green Park was let at a ground rent of £5,110 a year. Yet even this did not help and in 1902 there was a fifteen days sale, in 4788 lots, of the contents of the Hotel in Piccadilly. By 1911 all the valuable assets had been disposed of and even Merton Hall had to be rented out to shooting syndicates with the Family living in a place called "The Hassocks" at the back of Home Farm near Merton school. Where did all the money go to? In an obituary, 9th December 1919, The Eastern Daily Press, referred to his *"charming and courteous personality, his kindness of heart and his considerateness"* - but that isn't how many of his tenants viewed him. The paper went on to describe him as *"perhaps the most versatile man in the Peerage – thrice married and his great nephew recounts how 'his marital infidelities also were remarkable, in an age when infidelity was common place'. . . apart from his sporting and sexual prowess, Lord Walsingham . . was an authority on entomology, Director of the British Museum and High Steward of the University of Cambridge. . but he seems to have lacked business acumen and financial judgement"*.

(from 'Norfolk Landowners Since 1880' by Pam Barnes)

The truth is that the 6th Lord Walsingham was a spendthrift and more interested in his reputation as one of the finest shots in Britain, and in his collection of moths, than he was in the land and villages like Tottington. His passion for shooting and his friendship with the Prince of Wales, led to a profligate lifestyle; he went regularly to

Sandringham, and in turn entertained the future Edward V11 at Merton; it led to insolvency and exile abroad from 1912 onwards. As Rider-Haggard noted *"the majority of these rich men are pleasure seekers, they do not fulfil the conditions which are well-nigh vital to the welfare of rural England . . . their interest for the most part is so often purely selfish and personal"*. Whilst the complex system of imperial taxes and local rates, along with the fall in price of agricultural produce, helped cripple agriculture, the value of sporting land improved and good 'shoots' were easy to let. Capital was not attracted to land which didn't offer a safe or reasonable return, and the rentals of farms fell by a third. The long period of neglect caused a decline in the prosperity of the villages on the Merton Estate. Land was left uncultivated; the worst cottages were abandoned, others fell into disrepair as did the farms; yet, during this time Tottington Church was renovated and the old school plus some new cottages were built.

Farm workers were badly treated and poorly paid: indeed, during the 1870s and 1880s, Lord Walsingham *"was an uncompromising opponent (of Combinations by farm labourers) and set to work to favour the non-uninonist on his estate. he was a keen suppporter of the Farmer's Defence Associations and would have no interference from Unions in disputes betwen master and men"*

Labouring Life in Norfolk villages 1834-1914. (Springall).

No local industry was created to employ people: intelligent young men migrated to the town, found employment on the railways or in the police, entered the army or worked in factories up north, often in Yorkshire; and the young women went into service in the neighbouring towns or in London, and married outside the village. In the Brecklands, labour became scarce: men would not take up piece work or learn skills and the women preferred to stay at home - parents wanted their children to go into trade. By 1881 the population of Tottington had shrunk to 279 and the 3213 acres had a rateable value of £2387. 11s. By 1911 the population was down to 250 and the rateable value had fallen to £1468.

Nevertheless Merton remained an important Estate in Norfolk and a number of farms around Tottington had been developed. Tenancies changed hands regularly and numerous 'outsiders' came and went. The White's and Kelly's Directories of the nineteenth century list several names as 'Farmers': Thomas Buckle from the 1830s to 1860s on thirty acres; Robert Fowler whose widow Hannah still held 70 acres in 1851; William Sutton whose family have prominent gravestones in St. Andrew's churchyard; Robert Chilvers who farmed 50 acres in 1851 as did Richard Webb from Barton in Suffolk who must have prospered because the 1861 Census records him farming 683 acres (Mortmer and Grange Farm) and employing eight men and six boys plus a shepherd; Wiliam Fowler on 54 acres from 1861 to 1871 (probably Church Farm) later taken over by John Elvin until the late 1890s. The 1871 Census records William How farming 1000 acres, employing nineteen men and three boys; also Phillip Pitts, originally from Hingham, farming 340 acres employing four men and two boys until the turn of the century.

Whether all their land was around the village or spread across the whole Merton Estate is another matter but a living was there to be made. By the turn of the century tenant farmers practised a four-course cropping rotation: roots, barley, seeds, wheat or oats. The main

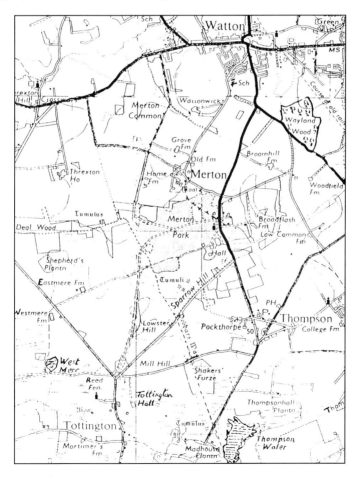

livestock were sheep, Suffolk Blackface crossed with Cotswolds, lambs that were taken in for rearing, plus a few bullocks for fattening. The land wasn't good enough to rear sound horses so colts were sent to the Fenland to mature. In no sense was it a wealthy area and the prospects for agriculture didn't look good but in 1901 a famous writer drove through a large part of Merton estate in the company of Mr. R. P. Harding, the sub-Agent for Lord Walsingham:

At . . . Tottington I saw the best pastures in this district; one . . . of eight acres was so exceptionally good that . . . thirty head of bullocks had been running on it for a while . . . however, the light land had produced very poor crops and the roots were inferior. Still it had enough substance in it to grow good oak and ash, of which I saw many. The cottages, which were built for the most part of clay lump, seemed very fair. The average rent of holdings in this district was about 10s the acre.   Rural England by H. Rider Haggard

This was the situation into which Hilda Perry was born in 1912 at Eastmere Farm in the small village of Tottington, a community of about fifty families, many closely related through birth and marriage. Nearly all her relatives were agricultural labourers living in tied cottages working for farmers who hired their land from Lord Walsingham and the Merton Estate which lay to the south of Watton in Norfolk.

(by Edmund Perry)

Post Office, Tottington

NEAREST AND DEAREST

Family history presupposes a continuity of knowledge about people, places and events. Older relatives are an intimate link with the immediate past but without Family bibles, diaries, letters and other documents, it is frustratingly difficult to research our direct ancestors. Fortunately mine can be traced back for nearly two hundred and fifty years living in and around the village of Tottington. I always had an interest in family affairs and learned much from my parents and Grandparents about the numerous relatives and other people in the village. Over thirty years ago whilst living on the outskirts of Norwich, I became a member of the Church of Latter Day Saints. They are well known for collecting and keeping genealogical records and encouraging members to pursue family trees. By looking at Parish Registers and Census records in the Norwich Library and at Shire Hall, we have been able to establish a long line going back to about 1700 which includes the names of all the major families living in Tottington since that time.

I was christened Hilda Moore Worby; my middle name being that of my Mother Alice Moore whose father was an Edmund Moore (1852-1911) from Coddenham in Suffolk who married a Tottington woman, Maria Macrow (1855-1899) when they worked in Sheffield. My Father was christened Albert Edward Worby but his Birth Certificate has his Father as John Warby and his Mother as Frances Worby. One branch of the family ended up as Worbey. It isn't a common surname in Norfolk although there were several distinct families in Swaffham, Watton, Lopham and Garboldisham. The family name, spelt WARBY, first occurs on the Tottington Register (dating from 1711) in the late eighteenth century. There are three marriages dating from the 1770s:

Mary Warby married William Gee (at Thompson)	31. 5. 1773
William Warby married Elizabeth Oldfield	14. 7. 1774
Sarah Warby married Richard Raven (at Thompson)	8. 4. 1779

Who they were and where they came from isn't known for certain: their births are not recorded on the Tottington Church Register so it seems safe to assume that they moved into the village as labourers during the 1770s when the de Grey Family was consolidating its hold on the village and Enclosing the land into the Merton Estate. They may have come from the nearby village of Hockham since there was a William Warby married (24. 7.1744) to an Ann Reeve who had seven children before he died in 1765. Two children also died and after 1880 there is no trace of the Warby family in Hockham, certainly not in the Register. It may be speculation that this is the same family but the five remaining children were named Elizabeth, Mary, William, Sarah and Henry (born between 1746 and 1764). Of the marriages in Tottington there is no death date for a Mary Gee or a Sarah Raven, and no children recorded, so we may assume they left Tottington to live elsewhere. There is one child recorded for William and Elizabeth:

(1)   William   Warby   10. 4. 1775 - 15. 10. 1839   (aged 64)

No other children are registered; there is no record of Elizabeth Warby's death nor of William remarrying. Yet three births are recorded to a William Warby and Ann Tash:

(2)   Elizabeth   Warby   13. 11. 1787
(3)   Sarah   Warby   4. 1. 1790
(4)   James   Warby   26. 12. 1792 - 18. 7. 1825   (aged 32)

It seems reasonable to assume that this is the same William Warby as previously and that the wedding took place outside of Tottington in the home village of Ann Tash. The Parish Register does record a William Warby buried 14. 7. 1793. (no age is given), yet three more children are recorded later as born to Ann Warby:

(5)   Susannah   Warby   23. 3. 1798
(6)   John   Prig   9. 6. 1804
(7)   Elizabeth   Collin   23. 11. 1807

Unravelling this mystery took some investigative work but there are clues elsewhere. None of the children are recorded as 'base born'; there is no record of any other Ann Warby (she died 9. 8. 1824 aged 64) and the children, John and Elizabeth, took the Mother's married name. Their Father would appear to be a man called John Collin (born in 1856 at Hockham) who in the 1841 Census was recorded (aged 85) as living with his son's family in Tottington, my Great-Grandparents, John Warby and Hannah Oldfield (married 14. 2. 1828) and their six children. His death is recorded in the Register: *17. 1. 1843 John Collin otherwise known as Prig, aged 87*

By 1810 the family was well established with seven Warby brothers and sisters living in Tottington:

(1)   William Warby married Elizabeth Barrett (a widow) on 3rd March 1800; (witnessed by Thomas Tash (1766-1846) and Elizabeth Tash (nee Barrett) (1764-1839). One child is recorded as born to them: Rose Warby 19. 6.1816.

(2)   Elizabeth Warby married George Oldfield 9th December 1817; (witnessed by Susannah Warby) without issue.

(3)   Sarah Warby - no marriage recorded.

(4)   James Warby married Margaret Barrett 26th October 1813. They had one son, William Warby born 22. 5. 1814.

(5)   Susannah Warby married James Macrow 16th November 1818 (witnessed by George Oldfield) and had three children.

(6)   John (Prig) Warby married Hannah Oldfield 14th February 1829 (witnessed by George Oldfield) and had eleven children.

(7)   Elizabeth Collin Warby married Christmas Hunt 15th February 1828, went to live at Thompson and had a very large family.

Since the numerous descendents inter-married over the following hundred years, I grew up in a village where most of the agricultural labourer families were related to one another over a number of generations. For instance, my Great, Great Grandmother, on my Mother's side, Susannah Warby (who married James Macrow) was the sister of my Great-Grandfather John Warby, (9. 6. 1804 - 1. 5. 1861) on my Father's side, an agricultural labourer who married Hannah (8. 7. 1808 - 1. 5. 1861) the daughter of John Oldfield (1784 - 1815) and Hannah Lake (1781 - 1860) both from Tottington.

My *Great-Grandparents John and Hannah Warby* had eleven children:

James	16. 6. 1825 - 18. 7. 1825	died aged one month.
James	27. 1. 1827 - 15. 3. 1910	married Elizabeth Quantrill.
William	14. 3. 1830 - 19. 1. 1912	married Rebecca Lake.
Ann	18. 11. 1832	
George	22. 2. 1835	
Henry	26. 3. 1837	married Mary Elizabeth
Charles	4. 8. 1839	
Hannah	28. 7. 1841	
Sarah Ann	3. 3. 1844 - 13. 10. 1844	died nine months.
John	10. 7. 1847 - 27. 3. 1933	married Frances Ann Williams
Sarah Ann	11. 6. 1849 - 4. 5. 1904	married John Wright.

My *Grandmother Frances Williams* was one of eight children born to George Williams (1823 - 1900) , and Maria Howling (1824 - 1894):

Henrietta	15. 12. 1849	married James Coates
William John	8. 6. 1853	married Ann Macrow
Frances Ann	15. 5. 1856 - 11. 9. 1936	married John Warby
Eliza	15. 7. 1859 -	married Henry Oldfield
Caroline	15. 7. 1862 - 28. 12. 1933	married William Hancock
George	12. 11. 1865 - 1. 7. 1926	married Elizabeth Quantrill
Herbert James	7. 1. 1869 - 18. 11. 1878	
Anne Marie	31. 8. 1871 -	married Alfred Reynolds

Hence the Warby family became related to those of Quantrill, Lake, Williams, Wright, Coates, Macrow, Oldfield, Hancock and Reynolds. Strangely enough at this time the family name began to be written as WORBY which is the spelling I have adopted for my parents and Grandparents.

GRANDFATHER JOHN WORBY was a warrener for Lord Walsingham on Merton Estate. A dear old man who nearly always dressed in a heavy keeper's jacket with large pockets, and breeches with khaki putties (long pieces of cloth wound, like bandages, around the legs from the knees downwards). Sometimes he wore leather buskins done up with buckles and straps, or corduroy gaiters which buttoned up at the side. All the keepers and warreners dressed this way to keep their legs warm and dry whilst walking in the woods and across the fields. I never saw him in an ordinary suit. He kept Spaniel dogs and ferrets and was up at 4 a.m. to catch rabbits. His cart and black horse often passed us on the road with rabbits hung on poles. They went to the Estate but he also caught some for baking, boiling or rabbit pie. Grandfather could not read or write but he could count his rabbits! We ate a lot in those days before mexamatosis was introduced to kill them off in large numbers. Rabbit and mole skins were sold for about 6d each to gypsies who called to sell pegs, etc.

Grandad wasn't as tall as his sons (my Father Albert was six feet and Uncle John was taller) but he did have large hands and lots of dark hair as well as a long, thick, square beard which made him appear ancient to me. Unfortunately he went rather deaf as he grew older. Sometimes I would call in after going to church on a Sunday and Grandpa would be sitting shelling peas on a seat beneath the kitchen window next to his favourite red rose bush.

Grandfather John Worby with wife Frances (Williams), daughter Blanche and youngest son, John (about 1908).

GRANDMOTHER FRANCES WILLIAMS was a large stout woman who kept her hair straight off her face with a little bun at the back. She wasn't very tall and always dressed in black and usually wore a half-apron of black alpacka. She never seemed to ail anything but I cannot remember her doing much work either, except for wiping up and preparing the vegetables, but I think she was the boss. She had a passion for runner beans and often ate so many that they caused her gall-stone problems, and for a number of years, each September, she was rushed off to hospital because of this.

There were always members of the other families at Granny Warby's which made it an interesting household so I didn't like it very much when my Mother took me to see her relatives instead. My Mother had two sisters and a brother in Yorkshire but her Aunt Elizabeth Alice Macro lived in Tottington, and had married William Field in 1906. She was well known in the village having been the teacher at the Old School. Mother was a little in awe of my Father's family; his sisters didn't think the wives of their brothers were good enough, and treated them shabbily. However, children were made very welcome and we just used to lift the catch and walk in. During my late teens I often visited and sat between my Grandparents in front of the fire. I cannot remember ever sitting on Grandmother's knee but then again she had

Worby Family: Alf Simpson (son-in-law), John (son), Gertie (daughter),
Albert (son), John and Frances Worby, Frank Hunt (grandson),
Kenneth Simpson (grandson), Percy Worby (grandson), Edmund Worby.

so many Grand-children who visited her regularly. My cousin Hilda
Nash, who lived with them after her Father died, was frightened stiff of
Grandmother. She always knew when Grandmother was going out
because the hat box would come down from upstairs.

Grandfather John Worby died in 1933 at the ripe old age of 86, three
years before his wife Francis. I remember coming home one day from
London with Uncle Jack and his wife Doll in their Austin Seven whilst
Grandfather lay dying. He had been ill for some time and my Father sat
up with him on several nights. The night he died my Father would not
let Grandmother or Aunt Blanche enter the room and I felt this was
most unkind, but Grandfather had a hard death; he didn't want to let go
and they had to restrain him and hold him down. This I could never
understand but remembering that today lots of people are deeply
drugged as they are dying, I suppose it was the right thing to do as in
those days there was no such assistance. Grandfather's body was laid
out in the parlour for the family to view. His Grand-daughter, Hilda
Nash, about seven years old, peeped inside the coffin and received such
a shock, causing her to run out of the room and to remember the
incident for the rest of her life. My Father and Uncle John were pall-

bearers and my brother Edmund looked so smart and impressive dressed in the red jacket and black busby of his Grenadier Guards uniform. Being in domestic service down in London I was unable to attend the funeral, nor that of Grandmother Frances who died in September 1936. Most people of the village - the families of Spragg, Williams, Hancock, Oldfield, Simpson, Jones, Jeeves, Hunt , Wolsey, Wright and Worby - attended both funerals and there was a large reunion with food and drink back at the house.

The Worby sons: Frederick, Albert, and John (seated).

John Worby and Frances Williams had eleven children:

Florence Louise
       26. 9. 1878 - 3. 3. 1962 married Thomas Spragg
Rose Alice   13. 12. 1879 - 11. 6. 1967 married Arthur Hunt
Frederick Ernest
       15. 5. 1881 - 24. 10. 1915 died in W. W. I
Albert Edward 12. 12. 1883 - 5. 3. 1963 married Alice Moore
Henrietta Elizabeth
       8. 7. 1885 - 19. 7. 1930 married William Jones
Blanche Annie-Marie
       29. 9. 1886 - 11. 2. 1975 marriedWalter Wolsey
Emmeline Frances
       15. 9. 1888 - 1. 8. 1965 married Herbert Jeeves
Gertrude Mary 17. 1. 1890 - 7. 12. 1946 married Alfred Simpson
Mabel Hilda 8. 6. 1892 - 14. 3. 1947 married James Nash
John George 7. 11. 1896 - 18. 8. 1956 married Martha Hawkes
Herbert   died as a baby,
                             no record found.

ALBERT EDWARD WORBY my Father, the second son, met Alice Mary Moore, when she came down from Sheffield to stay with her Grand-mother, Mary Macro. It seems likely that Albert worked on Grange Farm where Henry and Mary Macro lived; evidently Alice used to help with the milk pans, etc, and her hands were terribly sore, so once my Father walked four miles into Watton to fetch her some ointment. They were married in Tottington Church on Christmas Day 1909, he was 26 and she was 23; my Mother told me she wore a brown costume for the occasion. They went to live on the meadows near the Church, in a thatched building containing three dwellings. My brother, Edmund, was born at the Meadows on 2nd February 1911. The next door neighbour was Mrs Bone who became a very good family friend and my Godmother. Mother and Father were Godparents to her second son, Reginald; we were christened together in 1913. As a young man Father went to London to try and get into the police force but he was rejected on the grounds of having flat feet and a weak heart; which is why he wasn't taken by the Army for the First World War. When a vacancy came up at Eastmere Farm for a Teamsman my Father moved there and stayed for the next thirty years until turned out by the military; Farmers and farm hands always changed hands at Michaelmas (October), and I was born the following 31st December 1912.

Early photo of Father Albert Worby and Mother Alice Moore.

Father looked a tall, strong man but as a child he had pneumonia and this weakened his heart and lungs. Wintertime was very bad for him; invariably he went down with bronchitis or heavy colds and would be off work. In 1918 (and again in 1921) he had pneumonia and Mother had a bad dose of the flu at the same time: one has to remember that in those days both conditions could be fatal, and many people died from influenza after the First World War, so it was potentially very serious for the family. Aunt Blanche came up to see and look after my Father; she kept a bottle of whisky in the bedroom to give Dad but Mother didn't get any. As usual Mum didn't matter and I can remember her lying on the sofa asking me to fetch her a glass of water. Dad, as I called him, nearly always had a bad head on a Sunday (he used to call it a "thick skull"). Maybe it was because he got up later but this went on for years and he still suffered from these migraines after he left Tottington. We had to be quiet because it was so bad he went back to bed and couldn't eat anything. He took Sedletz powders - two packets, one in the blue wrapping was put into a glass of warm water and then the other white one was added causing the water to fizz like Epsom Salts, whereupon it was drunk immediately - and Beacham's pills, but later when aspirin was available these proved to be more effective.

Dad never had any Sunday lunch but about three o'clock he would get up and have some tea and then walk down to the village to Grandmother's and Mother would go to see her Aunt. We children always went to Church and joined our parents afterwards. During the Summer, Mother would cycle to Aunt Field's on a Sunday afternoon and if Father felt well enough he would go to Grandmother's in the morning and meet up with all his relatives, and in the evening Mum and Dad would go for a walk with the dog. Unfortunately to make matters worse Dad developed a hernia which caused him a lot of pain. An operation was fixed up for him in about 1928 but he wouldn't go. He often wished he had for it was a real nuisance wearing a truss the rest of his life. In 1937 he went into Wayland Hospital for an operation on his hammered toes which did help him to walk better.

My Father worked very hard, and was up at four in the morning to fetch the horses off the meadows for grooming and feeding; he was out as soon as it was light in the Winter time. He walked miles each day either behind two horses and a plough, or behind the rake, the harrow or the roll with three horses, in all sorts of weather; no wonder the men had bad feet, piles and hernias! When haytime or harvest came they did manage a ride on the grass cutter or the binder, but there was always a lot of walking to do. Usually the farm implements were left out on the side of the field ready for use next day and the horses taken to them. Dad had names for his brown farmhorses; I recall two , 'Boxer' and 'Depper' - the latter died from a poisoned foot as a result of a horse-shoe nail. Dad's favourites, 'Bunny' and 'Short', wore large wooden collars with two spikes on which their feed bags were carried as well as the farmhands' coats and food bags (often just a piece of sack divided in two). Dad wasn't able to come home for dinner because he couldn't leave the horses so Mum would pack up thick slices of bread and a huge lump of cheese and an onion. Dad loved a piece of fat pork and mustard and always had a bottle of sweetened tea without milk. When tractors arrived these saved his poor old feet with their hammered toes, and he could come home to dinner sometimes.

In general Dad was a poor eater; for breakfast he often had two oxo cubes in hot water and a slice of bread or sometimes he would make himself toast on the open fire. Oxo cubes or Bovril took the place of what people called 'Sop'. This was bread soaked in hot water or milk with either salt or pepper or sugar added plus a nob of butter. Even nursing Mothers had this sop. When he became Foreman on Eastmere Farm, Dad was able to come home for a proper breakfast about 8.30 a.m. In late afternoon he always had a cooked tea, arriving back about the same time as we did from school. Unlike the Gentry who had an evening meal about eight our family had supper at about ten o'clock; the table cloth was spread with bread and cheese, cake and later meat. I remember having a thick slice of bread with cheese, pickled onion or picalilli, with tea or cocoa. We didn't drink much coffee, certainly there was no instant only the black 'Camp' liquid coffee from a bottle. Everyone looked forward to tea on a Sunday. Most families would have a tall tin of salmon with a cucumber (if in season). The latter was cut up with a small onion and covered with vinegar during the afternoon so that it would be ready by teatime. There was a large fruit cake and all the other things made on a Saturday; sometimes Mother made her own bread. Tomatoes weren't eaten a lot then but we did have lettuces from the garden.

Farm labourers worked long hours, including Saturday until 12 o'clock, but they weren't paid that well although Dad earned a little extra, more than ordinary farm workers. In 1923 they were paid sixpence an hour for a fifty hour week; this increased to 28 shillings and sixpence in 1926; by the time Dad was foreman in 1936 he earned more. It doesn't sound much money by modern standards but then one must remember that food, clothing and household items cost a lot less.

Albert Worby with his horses

Dad gave his wage packet to Mum and once a week she bought him an ounce of Digger Shag tobacco from a shop cart that called (it was a long, round, white packet with a negro wearing a cap on his head and smoking a pipe). When they were better off Dad would have another ounce on a Friday night when the papers were brought from the shop in the village.

Gardening was one of my Father's pleasures, as it was for many of the villagers. In a sense it was their mark upon the land, a statement of their own personality, and they were rightfully proud of the fruit and vegetables grown which were an essential addition to the family diet. We grew all our vegetables - potatoes, carrots, beetroot, cabbages, celery, parsnips, sprouts, onions and especially pumpkins on the farm manure heap at the back of our cottage. Father liked to dig the garden himself and make the holes for the potatoes whilst we followed behind dropping them in, then he would walk back and fill in the holes drawing his foot along the trench. Everyone helped with the garden: Mother was very keen on her flowers and my brother Eddie, being a big strong lad, had his own patch of ground.

Father and Ted Williams used to go into the forest to cut down old trees and broken branches but weren't allowed to touch the good wood. On a Saturday afternoon they took the long cart or a wagon to fetch the

Albert Worby in his garden

wood home and share it out. When he was old enough my brother, Eddie, accompanied them and sometimes Mother and I went along to help. All the brushwood was made into faggots for kindling but the rest was sawn into logs for the fire. On a moonlit night we went outside after tea, sawed wood and stacked it in the shed to keep it dry away from the rain and snow. I always collected Father's kindling and left it ready for him with a shovel of coal (when we could afford it) to start the fire. In the Winter time Dad fetched the kindling in before tea and took two pails, which stood on a bench in the kitchen, across to the pump to fetch water - until Thornber's took over the Farm in 1936 when water was laid on to a tap in our yard but not into the cottage. Dad lit the sitting room fire in the mornings but the one in Mum's bedroom was only lit if we were ill or when he swept the sitting room chimney. The house had a central chimney stack and sweeping this was a messy business which he got fed up with so one Saturday afternoon he shoved a gorse bush up the chimney and set fire to it. It created a terrible blaze which sent smoke billowing across the meadow and could be seen for miles; it looked as if the house was on fire! The new Lord Walsingham came over from Westmere; he was none too pleased, as the cottage was his property, and told my Father never to do that again! We had a good laugh about it afterwards but at the time it caused some anxious moments. Dad also used to burn the rubbish in the garden and dampen down the heap for the night. On one occasion the flames broke through and as it was just outside the bedroom window it frightened the life out of all of us; we thought the end of the world had come!

Entertainment was rather limited and Dad wasn't a person for going out unless he had to. For one thing there wasn't the money to spend and he didn't frequent the pub which was four miles away. In his younger days he was captain of the village cricket team, went bell ringing and regularly played quoits (throwing horse shoes at a small peg in the ground) on the little meadow behind the blacksmith's shop. When older he preferred his garden or a quiet walk, whereas Mother was the exact opposite. Once, when I was home on holiday from London in 1930, we took my Father to Wayland Hall in Watton which had been made into a Picture House (later on a new cinema was built near the station but after television became popular it didn't pay so was turned into a 'Hammer's' clothes factory). The old cinema was dark inside as we entered and sat down. Dad looked ever so funny in his seat towering above everyone else, watching the film. He hadn't realised that the seats folded down and not until the lights went up did we realise what had happened. He was so cross and fed up and wasn't coming to that 'duzzy' place again, and of course we had a jolly good laugh. It took a long time for him to live that one down and he never went again. We travelled to Norwich by bus one Saturday with the Bone family. The women went shopping and the menfolk went off to the football match. Dad developed an awful headache which put paid to him ever repeating that trip!

Dad didn't have many clothes although he kept a black suit and a hard hat for funerals as he often acted as a pall bearer. He kept them in a old tin box but the house was so damp that everytime we opened the lid it smelt of mildew and mothballs. For work he generally wore corduroy trousers with khaki puttees to keep his legs warm and dry. His boots were made of strong, heavy leather which laced up at the front; the soles were full of hob-nails set in rows with steel toe-clips and heel-cleats. On a wet day, or if Dad stepped into a water-filled hole, the water would seep into the puttees and fill up the boots, which would have to be stuffed with newspapers and placed in front of the fire at night to dry them. The only trouble was that by morning the boots would end up as hard as rock and difficult to put on. This didn't do his feet any good but then the same thing happened to everyman working on the land. What a difference when rubber boots became common. In those days all the men wore caps but Dad kept his on inside the house as well. We used to say it was why he went bald so early!

Mother never could knit, she always dropped the stitches, so when I was old enough, I used to knit Dad socks. He often sewed on buttons and mended his workday clothes, and liked doing such work. He always ensured that our bicycles were safe to ride and fixed the punctures, something I found difficult to do. He also mended our boots and shoes on an iron foot stool which had three different sized feet on it, for men, women and children. This saved us lots of money as did the making of rag mats and then wool ones; Mum and Dad made me a lovely blue one as a wedding present. In fact that we never wasted anything including string which was picked up, unknotted and put away tidily. I still do the same plus saving the plastic bags, picking up rubber bands and today's silly little pennies which people drop on the paths. Nowadays people throw away so much that we would have kept had it only been available; the more one has the more one wastes. Uncle John was good to Dad and gave him his old police trousers that were very warm, navy- blue serge and lasted for ages. When he went out of an evening and on a Sunday morning, Dad dressed in a heavy smock jacket with huge pockets, something like the poachers wore to put their catches in; when we went 'nutting' he would fill these pockets with chestnuts. He also had a very heavy, long khaki coat which was his 'Old Blokes' coat during the First World War. This was marvellous and he still had it when he died. It was used on the beds in Winter and on cold nights walking home across the fields from Granny's he would let me walk beside him under the coat.

From the things I heard about him, Dad was held a little bit in awe by his sisters who thought the world of him. People often came to him for advice and he had the nickname of 'Doctor'. A spade was a spade with him and we always knew he meant what he said. In one sense he had a very strict manner; a stern look was enough for us to behave. If Eddie and I were misbehaving when he came home, his cap would come sailing across the room. Like most parents in those days he would punish us if we deserved it; I know Eddie received the strap from time to time. Mum was the one who gave me the slaps but I was very provoking at times! In general Dad had much more patience and feeling than Mother. If we had a headache she would say "Oh, go on with you, your tail grows", whereas Dad would bring us brown paper dipped in vinegar. Poor Mum was deaf and didn't always hear us call so Dad saw to our wants at night. He never let us go to sleep unhappy and we could tell him anything and receive good advice. The bedrooms were so damp and cold (no gas or electric fires then) that when small I slept with Mother and Eddie slept with Dad. Saturday was bounty night as I was allowed to sleep with Dad and warmed my feet between his legs. To me it was heaven but Mum thought he spoilt me. He had a good sense of humour and told me some amusing stories: apparently my two Great-Grandfathers were deaf and when they came into the village after work everyone knew because they would be shouting their heads off at one another; once he overheard two women quarrelling and one said to the other, " I suppose you think your 'muck' don't smell like everyone else's ", (swearing was uncommon in the village and I was taught not to say the four letter word she actually used!).

We always had a little oil lamp burning on the chest of drawers throughout the night; it was such a comfort to me as I was scared of the dark. Mum said it was because as a young child I had been taken into a dark tent at a County Fete and screamed all the way home. My brother played all sorts of tricks on me as a result. If I went into a room with a candle Eddie would creep up behind and blow it out but this only happened when Dad wasn't around. Dad was my hero and we spent many happy hours together. My brother didn't seem to find quite the same warmth although they spent a lot of time together. After tea during the Winter my brother went to bed early but Dad would have me on his knee and sing songs or tell me about his family, or we would read and do arithmatic together. The companionship my Dad and I shared never wavered. He was a great friend to me as well as a good Father.

I left school at 14 and after a spell at Westmere Farm went to London. Eddie went into the Grenadier Guards in 1927 so this left Mum and Dad alone quite early in their lives. My Dad said that when I went away he walked up and down the fields with a lump in his throat, but all birds must leave the nest sometime. I came back home in 1929 and Dad said I could stay 'till after Christmas. Luckily the Parish gained a new Rector who needed domestic staff and I went to work at Merton Rectory about three miles away, until 1931 when I returned to London to work in service. During the years before 1939 when I married a Londoner, Mr. Geoffrey Perry , I visited Tottington regularly and kept in touch with my parents but much of the daily village life came to me second- hand through Mother's letters.

In 1936 Thornber's took over Eastmere for duck rearing and Dad was made Foreman on the agricultural side. When the War began my husband was called up and had to report to Nitts Hill Camp in Glasgow, in August 1940 so I returned home to live with my parents. I spent quite a lot of time with Geoffrey at various places such as Long Marston near Stratford-upon-Avon, and between times worked on Eastmere Farm, mainly looking after animals. Dad didn't push me to do hoeing even though this was better paid at 7d an hour; I hated the job. We had lots of grinding to do for fattening bullocks and young calves, then there was the weeding of crops and the harvesting especially since combines were not in use then. I soon settled back into rural life and it was company for my parents. Dad drove one of the three tractors and he had a responsible position breeding the dairy cattle and cultivating extra land for more crops. It was hard but rewarding work which made the 1942 War Office takeover even more of a blow.

After moving to Hingham about fourteen miles to the west of Norwich, Father worked for a Captain Denny until he retired and then went to live in a new coucil house along the Watton road in Hingham. He kept his garden going and since my husband and I lived nearby and ran a shop in the village, we visited regularly. After Mother died in 1957 Dad neglected himself somewhat; he often drank warm milk with an egg beaten in it rather than cook a proper meal, and he used to pour his tea into a saucer and drink it that way. His chest was bad in wintertime and he couldn't go out but spent his time sitting in his large, wooden Windsor chair, in front of the coal fire. He died in the old Wicklewood Hospital in 1963 aged 79 and was buried along with Mother at the front of the new cemetary at Hingham.

ALICE MARY WORBY (nee MOORE) , my Mother, was born in Yorkshire, but her Mother, Maria Macro (born Tottington, 8th June 1855), was the eldest daughter of Henry Macrow (1821 - 1896) and Mary Buckle (1826 - 1903) , who had five other children:

Frederick	9. 10. 1850 - 22. 5. 1896	
Emma	19. 5. 1857 - 24. 5. 1857	
Henry James	24. 4. 1863 - 19. 5. 1882	
Frederick William 31. 3. 1865 -		married Rosie Annie
(emigrated to Australia)		Elizabeth Smith
Elizabeth Alice 14. 5. 1863 - 19. 5. 1882	married William Field (1)	
	married Thomas Buckle (2)	

As a 'Macrow', Maria was related to one of the most prolific Tottington families all descended from a Thomas Macrow (buried 7.1.1795) and Elizabeth Angel (buried 25.8.1793) both from nearby Sturston, whose children and grandchildren intermarried with the Gofs, Cocks, Chilvers, Herring, Reeve, Buckle, Lake and Johnson families. Her own Grandfather was James Macrow (1797-1862), one of thirteen children, who married Susanna Warby (1798 - 1862) sister of my Great-Grandfather John Warby.

Henry Macro and Maria (Buckle)

Maria went to work in Brightside, Sheffield and met Edmund Moore (born 19th October 1852) from Coddenham in Suffolk who was employed in an engineering works. They were part of a general exodus of East Anglian people northwards often going by sea from Lynn or Yarmouth to Hull, staying in Yorkshire or travelling overland to Lancashire. It may be that Maria went to Sheffield because her Father's sister was already living there. This aunt, Ann Macrow, had married a Charles Stannard Nichols from Saham Toney on 13th August 1841. He was working as a Gamekeper at Thelveton before they moved to Grimesthorpe in Yorkshire during the 1870s. In 1881 the Nichols were living at 230 Newhall Road, Attercliffe, a few streets away from where my Grandparents Maria and Edmund were living after marrying on 17th March 1879. Maria had six children two of whom died in infancy; my Mother was the youngest:

Harriet Annie 18. 1. 1890 - 8. 1. 1928 married Frank Williamson
Charles Henry 12. 12. 1881 - 4. 10. 1917 married Rose
Emily Hilda   24. 7. 1884 - 31. 1. 1972 unmarried
Alice Mary   3. 9. 1886 - 11. 10. 1957 married Albert Warby

(interestingly Ann Nichols named three of her sons after her brother Henry - two died in infancy).

Maria was a strict parent but she died aged forty-four in 1899 when Mother was only 13 years old. The eldest daughter, Annie looked after the family whilst Alice came back to Tottington to live with her Grandmother Mary Macrow (nee Buckle) at Grange Farm. Grandmother Mary died on 14th May 1903 and her son, Frederick gave up the farm going to live at Mortimer Farm. Mother went to live with her Aunt Alice and Miss Crawford at the house attached to the Old School. Mother was made to learn music, studying for four years and she played quite well. Paper qualifications weren't so vital in those days but having a town education plus musical ability allowed Mother to become an assistant teacher at the school. After Miss Crawford retired, Aunt Alice continued teaching until the New School was opened in 1910 when she and Mother resigned in the Summer of that year.

Mother's Father, Edmund Moore died in Sheffield 3rd March 1911, but he had a sister called Polly who married a man named George Studd and they lived in Suffolk. My Mother and I visited them in a village called Livermere and Polly was still alive during the Second World War. Mother kept in touch with her sisters and brother's wife in Yorkshire; they often came to visit and we went up to Brightside. Harriet Moore, called by her second name Annie, was a small woman with dark hair and brown eyes. She was very strict and everything had to be just so; my brother Eddie used to say things very quietly but as I always copied him and shouted it out aloud, I got into hot water with Aunt Annie! She was generous too: we enjoyed many a parcel sent by her with lovely mince pies and gingerbread parkin; also pretty dresses some of which were crocheted. Annie married a much younger man named Frank Williamson and had a baby girl who died at birth but afterwards they had two sons, Frank (born 1913) and Clifford (born 1915). Emily Hilda had an accident at birth and became a bit retarded. She too was dark with brown eyes but a taller woman.

They all stayed with us when visiting Tottington, and I remember Frank playing the piano and Clifford the violin. Uncle Charlie was killed in 1917 in France so I never knew him but his wife Rose and their son Charles came down and stayed with Mother's Aunt Alice Field. Visiting Aunt Annie and Uncle Frank in Sheffield was an experience. He was very fond of horses and went to Doncaster Races bringing us back some lovely real butter-scotch. In the bedroom I remember waving the blankets about which put out the gas jets; having known only candles we didn't understand about gas lighting. One year, when I was eight, we stayed over and I had to go to school there

Father Albert Worby, Mother Alice (Moore), and Floss.

Compared to Tottington it was an enormous school with hundreds of children; how I hated it! We had to call out our names every morning to show we were present. I could never recall where mine came and the teacher used to get so cross. I was so upset, Mother had to cut the holiday short and bring us home. Annie died in January 1928 so Emily Hilda had to go in a home where she lived to be over ninety. Gradually we lost touch but Frank used to come to visit and became quite friendly with my childhood friend, Nesta Sculfer who had moved to Mildenhall.

Mother was a robust woman of average height with dark brown hair and merry brown eyes. With her rosy red face she always looked well and healthy; she used to say her looks never pitied her. She had small feet and hands which hardly stretched an octave on the piano. My brother Eddie would say her hands were small but she could hit hard!

She was a very jolly sort of person and would give anyone a friendly push or punch. I don't know if that is a Yorkshire way or just something about her. She was fond of playing a game of hitting one another in fun which used to make my Father angry as he said it always ended in someone being hurt, which in her case it did. I grew up to be a bit taller and while wrestling one day hurt her arm. After that we never played again and I felt so sorry. Dad said "serve her right, perhaps now she will give over" - but she still continued to punch other people in fun! Mother was a good sport and always joined in to play cricket, etc. She liked playing Ludo, Snakes and Ladders, and Dominoes but not Whist. She enjoyed taking long walks and cycle rides and going to Jumble Sales. Mother and Mrs Williams shared a good friendship; they went lots of places together but usually walked as Mrs Williams didn't ride a bike; I never understood why anyone couldn't cycle but I suppose it's a question of balance. At one time when we collected our milk from Westmere Farm, Mother always called in on Mrs Williams for a few minutes and a good old natter.

Mother developed a friendship with the Bishop family who came to live at Eastmere Farmhouse in 1936; Mrs Alice Bishop was from Yorkshire so they shared a common bond. Mother spoke with a broad accent and people loved to hear her talk with a "thee" and a "thou". When she wanted us to stop mucking about she would say "ge-o'er" and use the old-fashioned "lass" and "lad". Sometimes when she got angry she would say "Damn, and that's swearing", but I never knew her to be rude or irreverent.

Her musical talent was much appreciated and she had a good voice. Before I was born, the youngsters in the village all got together and had parties in one another's houses where my Mother played the piano and ended up having a good sing-song. She had a tiny harmonium at home and played the piano at all the dances and social events in the village. As children, we went with her to the Working Men's Club and then walked back home as often the Dances didn't start until 10 p.m. Later we cycled but once Eddie and I left home Mum had to go alone, which was a fair journey late at night and in all weathers. Dad never used to go but whenever I came home I went with her. Mother gave up playing at the village dances in early 1939 when a band was hired. In a way it was a good thing as she cycled two miles there and back again after sitting playing from 7.30 until after 2 in the morning, all for 2/6. In the 1990s at a Battle Area Reunion I overheard people talking and several spoke of Mrs Worby playing the old 'joanna' and the fun they all had. It's good to know mother brought so much hapiness to the village folks.

Mum's piano playing was sizeable achievement considering her deafness. After she gave birth to my brother, her hearing deteriorated a lot and continued to become worse for the rest of her life. She didn't cope well with hearing aids although she bought two and had a health service one. It was a great shame as she was such an intelligent and inquisitive woman who was a great reader of anything she could lay her hands on including childrens' comics. I'm afraid we were often impatient with her and took advantage of her not being able to hear. She asked so many questions and it wasn't easy to shout and make her understand. As Father grew older he wasn't as patient and sometimes lost his temper with her. This could make life difficult for a while but they never disagreed for long and always made up. It is hard to be deaf but also very tedious and stressful to live with someone who cannot hear properly especially if that person has a lively and inquiring nature. Mother loved to go out to see people and places; she remembered the names of everything and never forgot a birthday - she was like a human diary. I inherited this deafness when aged about thirty but I tend to let matters pass me by rather than cause any hassle which means I miss out a lot on what is said and happening. Mother was also fond of gardening and liable to spend a lot of money on flower seeds; she had all the old faithfuls as well as sending away for the latest varieties. I often took a bunch of flowers to school and as soon as I came home the house would be full of them. Mother didn't mind me plucking her flowers, she was proud of them and would drag Dad out to look at her flower beds as they really were a picture. The long light evenings were usually spent in the garden, Mother with her flowers and Father with the vegetables. Often seeds and plants were exchanged with neighbours and Mrs Williams who lived in the other Eastmere bungalow usually had the same species in her garden. We had four large water butts to water the flowers easily but no hoses; I don't remember Father watering the vegetables but everything survived in the poor sandy soil which was heavily fertilized with horse manure.

Normally Mother managed the household budget quite well but one year when her relatives came to stay she bought some extra items from the grocer and of course she fell behind with her bill. Now Father was an honest man and wouldn't owe any money - 'neither a lender nor a borrower be'. Mother was afraid to tell Father and when he did find out he was very angry. His extra harvest money that year had to go on paying off the debt. What we could not afford to pay for we went without. That's how we were brought up and that's how my brother and I always were - honesty in all things.

To be truthful Mother wasn't a 'specially good cook but we always had plenty to eat. Unfortunately she had very little sense of time: my Father had a mere half-hour for dinner but often he came home to find she had just put the vegetables on. Once she was starting to get the dinner ready and decided to have a glass of rhubarb wine and promptly fell asleep! If she made jam she would put it on the oil stove and then start to write letters or maybe pick up a book to read. In consequence the jam was either burnt or boiled so long that it stuck to the saucepan, and suet puddings boiled in a cloth would be so big it was a tug of war getting them out of the saucepans! Nonetheless, Mother was fond of her food especially bananas: neither my brother nor I would eat tomatoes but she ate them like apples. Sometimes, in our younger days, she would have bad billious attacks in the night, but as she grew older these disappeared.

One day Mother accidentally locked herself in the hen house and had to remain there all morning until Dad came home for dinner and let her out. During the War she had several hens which produced lots of eggs. These we often sent by post to friends and relatives, who paid us. We were allowed two eggs per week on our ration books so eggs were seen as precious. They were packed in very strong cardboard boxes with twelve divisions. Each egg was wrapped in newspaper and then in the crinkley cardboard and packed tightly in a division. They arrived safely and were seldom broken. The boxes were returned and used time and time again. The mail was very good in those days with the postman arriving twice a day on his bicycle.

It's strange the memories we store up about our parents; incidents, stories, thoughts and feelings. When I was about four, the postman delivered a letter while Mother was still in bed. She was very upset because her brother Charles had been killed during the War in France; after that whenever she was upset I thought someone had died. At that time cupboards were a rare item of household furniture. so our spare crockery and ornaments were kept in a corner cupboard in the smaller bedroom. Every year this would be spring-cleaned; all the china was placed in a large linen basket but steps had to be used to reach the cupboard. One year I climbed up the steps which fell over with me on top of the basket full of china. Needless to say lots of things were broken and Mum was very upset for a different reason. On one occasion, our dog Floss chewed up her best hat which Mum kept in a box under the bed, and another time Floss ate up the Christmas cake which had been put away for the festive event.

Whilst I was in service in London Mum came to see me on a 5 shillings Sunday trip and wore a brown coat with a light stud fastener on her collar sewn on with green cotton. I took her to see my employers and felt embarassed but I don't suppose they noticed. I was so angry with her but now it causes me to laugh. She had several bad experiences at the dentist so refused to have her teeth out and they became rather decayed. We could never persuade her to have her hair cut and she wore it in an old-fashioned roll at the back.

Leaving Tottington nearly broke my Mother's heart; she had been at Eastmere over thirty years. After many disappointments we found a place acceptable to Mum and moved to Hingham, to Captain Denny's farm but it took her a while to settle down. The house was in a corner of the meadow up a lane off a road about a mile to the south of the

Alice and Albert Worby with Jumbo.

village. Before they left Eastmere my brother gave my parents a wireless but Mum couldn't really enjoy it. At Hingham we had a fire in the middle of the night which we thought started from the accumulator on this wireless. Water had to be fetched from a well in the garden and it was hard work drawing it up by bucket to put out the fire. Luckily I was home at the time since my husband Geoffrey was away in Palestine during the war.

When the Second World War ended Mum and Dad were offered a new council house along the Watton Road in Hingham. Geoffrey returned from the War and I went back to London to live. There my first son, christened James Edward was born 14th March 1947, followed by a second son, christened Edmund Geoffrey 2nd December 1949. My husband wasn't content working for Brooke Bond and I was unwell so we decided to return to Hingham, buying a place called The Coppice in Low Road just outside the village; Geoff set up a grocer's shop opposite the Church. We saw a lot of my parents; Mother spent many happy hours there in her new garden with our lovely old collie called Jumbo. She was so fond of him that when he died it seemed to hasten her own death. In July 1957 on a very hot day Mother was cooking the Sunday dinner and she suffered a stroke at the age of seventy. She did get a little better and was able to carry on a while longer but then had another stroke and went into Dereham Hospital where she died after three weeks. She was buried 16th October 1957 on the front row of the new cemetary at Hingham.

A FARMING COMMUNITY

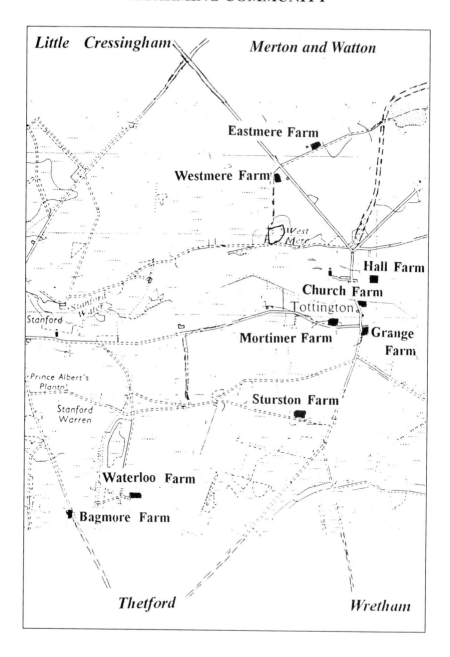

Little Cressingham

Merton and Watton

Eastmere Farm

Westmere Farm

West Mere

Hall Farm

Church Farm

Stanford Water

Tottington

Stanford

Mortimer Farm

Grange Farm

Prince Albert's Plantn

Stanford Warren

Sturston Farm

Waterloo Farm

Bagmore Farm

Thetford

Wretham

EASTMERE FARM

A child could not grow up in a better place than a farm..
A farm is such a carnival of birth and death. Edwin Muir

Farm workers generally gained new jobs on Michaelmas Day, 11th October - the same time as farmers bought or rented the farms. My Father, Albert Warby, moved from the village in the Autumn of 1912 to live and work on Eastmere Farm as a Teamsman. I was born on 31st December 1912, in a small cottage on the little Meadow next to the Farmhouse. Eastmere was my childhood experience and the Farm with which I was most familiar.

Originally it was a part of Westmere Hall to the north of the village on the way to Watton. In 1863 Eastmere Farm consisted of 541 acres let for £400 but by 1907 the rental was down to £145 because of the fall in value of land and its output. From the 1850s up until the 1881 Census, Thomas Palmer from Gayton Thorpe rented and farmed the land, and employed twenty men and two boys. The main crops were wheat and barley. The 1891 Census records Alexander Donovan, a chicken farmer, as renting the property. By the beginning of the this century, Leonard Wace from Carbroke was renting the three farms of Eastmere, Westmere and Sturston from Lord Walsingham, mainly for sheep rearing, as well as another farm called Broadflash the other side of Merton Park. A Farm Steward, Fred Sculfer lived in Eastmere Farmhouse.

There was another small cottage on the Cressingham Road at the bottom of the lane which ran to Merton Park and through the Lodge gates on to Watton four miles away. Here my Father's Uncle, George Williams lived but years later, when his son Ted married Harriot Mace, George moved to another tied cottage on Westmere Farm across the road. As the farms were all rented by Mr. Wace and run by the Steward, this arrangement suited everyone and the various Teamsmen worked on the three farms whenever necessary. However, the cottages were quite small so I have often wondered how Ted and Harriot managed with the five children who were born between 1924 and 1931. At least my parents only had my brother Edmund and myself to worry about.

The farmhouse was surrounded by lawns and possessed a large fruit and vegetable garden. It was brick-built and the outside walls were covered with white mortar and there was a tiled roof. The windows were big and the building was three stories high with attics at the top, no doubt for servants at one time. The house was large enough for two

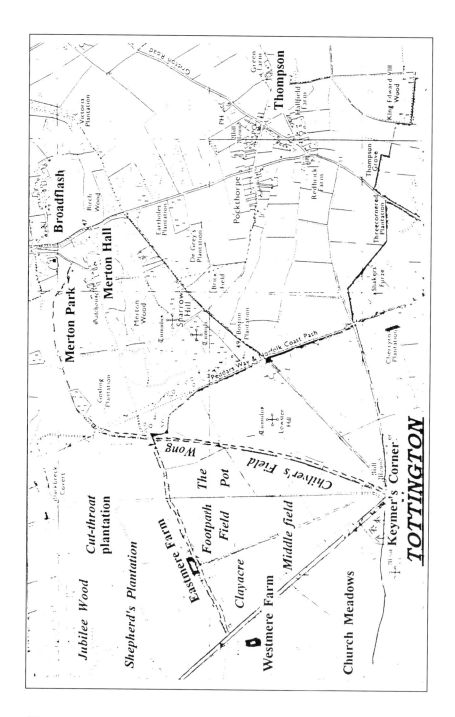

TOTTINGTON

Thompson

Green Farm

King Edward VII Wood

Hallfield Farm

PH

Mill House

Thompson Grove

Victoria Plantation

Threecornered Plantation

Broadflash

Birch Wood

Redbrick Farm

Pockthorpe

Eartholes Plantation

De Grey's Plantation

Shakers' Furze

Merton Hall

Merton Park

Outbuildings

Brick Field

Boston Plantation

Cherrytree Plantation

Merton Wood

Tumulus

Sparrow Hill

Tumulus

49 Norfolk Coast Path

Peddars Way

Gosling Plantation

Tumulus

Lobster Hill

Charbrick Covert

Jubilee Wood

Cut-throat plantation

Shepherd's Plantation

Eastmere Farm

Footpath Field

The Pot

Wong

Chilver's Field

Mill House

Keymer's Corner

Clayacre

Middle field

Church Meadows

Westmere Farm

Gretton Road

Eastmere Farmhouse in 1942

families. It contained a huge room with one window facing the front and another at the side. All the windows had white wooden shutters inside which could be closed to keep out the light and the cold. A nice porch stood in front of the main door behind which was a large hall and a staircase. Passages went off the hall, one to the kitchen a butler's pantry, and another into the dining room, which was used as a sitting room by the Sculfer family. From the dining room there was a dark passage leading to another kitchen which Mrs. Sculfer cooked in, and a huge pantry with other small rooms at the side. The back staircase was in the kitchen and led up to the bedrooms. I never understood why the Sculfers lived in this part of the house rather than in the spacious and lovely rooms on the other side which were left empty. At one time they were occupied by a Mrs. Ray but afterwards, as children we played there.

There were seven Sculfer children: my good friend Nesta being the youngest and the same age as myself; Bessie who became a nurse, Kathleen, Nora and Eileen who became schoolteachers; two boys, John (whom we called Jack) and Joe who became Farmers. Nesta and I shared many happy times; she had a huge rocking horse which five of us could ride at the same time - two on the back, one each side in the rockers and one underneath to help rock it. Behind the house was a

59

meadow with a large chalk pit which we called "The Hills" where Jack kept his bees. It was a favourite playing ground, running up the slopes, sliding down in a bath, and gathering wild flowers. A certain type of very fine grass called 'Ladies hair' grew there; a long sprig with little storks growing out at the sides each with a brown bobble on the end. Strangely I have never seen it anywhere else.

Nesta Sculfer (early 1920s)

As a child, one couldn't wish for a more exciting and interesting place to grow up in than a farm with all the different buildings, strange machinery and tools, various animals, the fields and woods. Here was a fantasy world ready made where imagination could take flight, where there was always something new and enthralling to see or do. Nesta and I spent many delightful hours playing; we were allowed to wander around the buildings and explore, climb in and out of the waggons, slide down stacks, play hide and seek. Of course there were dangers and Father often gave reminders about being careful with this or that - he was a cautious man by nature and would never drive a waggon with children in it. However, we didn't come to any harm. One day when we were about twelve years old, Nesta and I did something very silly. She had more pocket money than me and decided to buy a packet of Jersey Lily scented cigarettes, and I bought the matches. Of all the places we had to choose to smoke our cigs we sat on top of a hay stack. Luckily Nesta's older sister, Eileen came along to find her and saved us from a potential catastrophe. Her other sister Nora broke the lock of a little wooden box to get evidence of the cigarettes. Years later Nesta sold this box for quite a lot of money even though the lock was still broken. Nesta and I laugh about the incident now but at the time it was somewhat embarassing, as we both got into trouble.

By the side of the house was a five-barred gate which opened up into the yard, beyond which lay the farm buildings. On the right, connected to the farmhouse, was a high wall through which a door led into the gardens. The back of the house had two doors, the first being an entrance into the part which wasn't used, the second being an entrance to the Sculfer's kitchen. This door opened into a long, brick-built verander which saved the family getting wet when going to the lavatory at the far end. Near the kitchen was a door used to go out the front way into the fruit and vegetable garden. Mrs. Sculfer grew gooseberries, black, red and white currants, raspberries and strawberries which we helped her pick to make delicious jam. The front garden consisted of a lawn with two lovely beech trees and a thick dog rose hedge next to the lane plus two five-barred gates so you could go in one and out of the other with the cart and later cars. Nesta and I would rush home from school in the Autumn to see if the dog rose hips were ripe. We picked them and ate the succulant skins but not the seeds inside. People wouldn't do this today but it never did us any harm; after all during the Second World War we drank the rose hip syrup which was supposed to be very nutritious.

Mr Sculfer was a nice, calm man who went about his business without any fuss. One night he put his feet in a bath of hot water and promptly fell asleep only to wake up around 3 a.m. with his feet still in the water except by now it was icy cold! Mrs. Sculfer was a meticulous, efficient woman and very particular; she was the sort who made you take off your shoes before entering the house. In the evenings I helped her and Nesta to collect eggs which the hens laid all over the place (Mr. Wace would come in his pony and trap on a Saturday morning to take the eggs back to his home at Carbrooke). When we went into a shed that smelt badly, Mrs. Sculfer would say "Pfha, pfha" which used to tickle me. I was a bit in awe of Nesta's Mother, and never remember her smiling, whereas my own Mum was full of fun and easy going. However, Mrs. Sculfer was kind and generous and would take us anywhere important, in the horse and cart.

She would always fetch our relatives from the railway station when they came down from Yorkshire to stay in the summer. She couldn't get on with their horse called Kruger, a full-sized gelding more like a thickly built racehorse, with a mahogany coloured coat. He was very handsome and strong but had a character of his own and could be stubborn especially when driven by Mrs. Sculfer. Kruger would play her up and sometimes was difficult to catch. Jack, who had to harness him for his Mother, would end up driving the cart. With his nature Kruger wasn't kept with the other horses on the meadows nor was he used for farmwork. I was frightened of Kruger and he knew it. If he was loose on the meadow I was dead scared to cross, as he would come

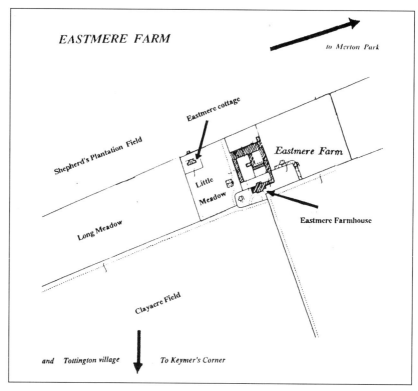

EASTMERE FARM

to Merton Park

Eastmere cottage

Shepherd's Plantation Field

Eastmere Farm

Little
Meadow

Eastmere Farmhouse

Long Meadow

Clayacre Field

and   Tottington village   To Keymer's Corner

over and act threateningly: I soon got out of his way. When Mr Wace
gave up the farms in 1926, I think Kruger went to Broadflash farm; I
never saw him again.

The yard had sheds from the verander to the cowshed door (one cow
was kept for milk but there were no cattle on the farm at that time) after
which stood a high brick wall facing the back of the house. The pump,
with its big iron wheel and two large wooden handles either side, was
built into the wall. Here we collected our water in buckets from the tap
but the pump also fed a large tank behind the wall for the animals in the
horse-yard. Next came the horse-yard and the stables where Kruger
was kept. Here was a huge flat stone, about five feet long and about two
and a half feet high, which the teamsmen used to mount horses from.
The horseyard was quite large with the cowyard and sheds leading off
to the right and further along in front was a door into one side of the
large barn. Another set of doors led to the second horseyard surrounded
by covered food troughs which were used during the Second World
War to fatten bullocks.

62

From the garden of our cottage on the meadow we could see the back of the farm buildings less than two hundred feet away and the house in the distance. The meadow was fenced in by thorn bushes with railings round the stackyard, the cartsheds and the back of the stables. Opposite the cottage stood a large cart shed with its high wagon roof. It held three large waggons with a granary over the top. Two smaller sheds beneath jutted out from the end with their roofs sloping towards the meadow. One was used for chickens to sleep in as they ran loose all over the farm, and the other shed held all the tools like scythes and reap hooks. Men usually had their own favourite implements, especially their hoes. Joining these two sheds and stretching up to the house was the largest structure, the long barn with its wooden double-swing doors fastened down the middle by a thick pole. The doors opened top and bottom so waggons could enter and leave, and there was a high threshold which could be brought out when anything was delivered or removed. The barn was in two sections; on one side all the corn was stored and on the other straw was kept dry and all the grinding was done. The grinder stood about five feet high with an open top into which root crops were placed, and the blades were driven by a winding handle - much like a giant version of the ordinary kitchen meat grinder. Cake for the horses plus mangolds, swedes and turnips were ground up and fell into a skip underneath. Most of the haystacks were in the stack yard next to this barn. A large knife on a long wooden handle was used to cut the hay which was either carted away by tumbril or taken through the barn by pitch fork into the yards and the horse stables or onto the meadows. Along the stable wall was a shed with large doors where the farm cart, which served as the Sculfer's trap, was kept, so we always knew when the Steward's family was going out as the doors would be open.

Originally Eastmere was mainly agricultural for the growing of corn and root crops and the rearing of sheep. My Father was employed as First Teamsman from 1912 to 1936; he and his cousin, Ted Williams, had five large horses each for ploughing, pulling machinery and transport. Tom Spragg, who married Father's eldest sister Florence, was the shepherd and kept about 200 ewes for Mr. Wace until he gave up in 1925. Then George de Grey took over Eastmere and Sturston; the sheep were replaced by pigs and he continued with his dairy herd at Westmere. All the men were kept on except my friend Nesta's Father who had to find another job elsewhere, and Mr. Jock Thompson became the Farm Steward. The Sculfers moved away to Mildenhall but Nesta continued to meet me when I came home from London on

EASTMERE FARM showing barn, stables, cart sheds and Farmhouse at the back. Taken from our garden of Eastmere Cottage.

Teamsman Ted Williams   Joby Hunt and Maurice Wright

holiday. She and I cycled half-way each and met at West Tofts and she
would come back to Eastmere cottage and stay with us. Eastmere
Farmhouse was renovated and a generator for electricity added to pump
water up from the well. Lord Walsingham's sister, Mrs David Bethell
lived there for a while and Miss. Lucilla Reeve, the Estate Agent, had
her office in the large room at the front. Later on Captain Henry Lewis
Selby Moore rented the house with his wife and daughter Betty. A Mr.
Madoc lived there as well and kept bees in the meadow called *The Hills*
at the back of the house; Joby Hunt and Maurice Wright worked in the
barn where the corn had been kept, making the wooden boxes and trays
to put the honey in.

EASTMERE FIELDS: there were about twelve altogether, some were
so large that there would be three different crops growing at any one
time: corn, hay and a root crop of mangolds and swedes. In this way a
crop rotation operated. The soil was sandy with limited fertility and one
had to be careful not to overwork it, but many years of hard toil and
care had improved its texture. However, some fields at Eastmere were
too dry to be cultivated and consequently left fallow, until Mr.
Thornber took over and used them for cattle grazing.

As in most farming communities, fields were known by their
individual names which had been passed from generation to

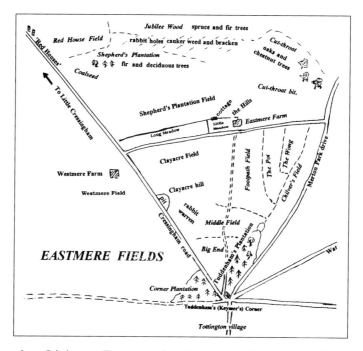

generation. Living at Eastmere for thirty years I can remember names
commonly used on the farm but I don't recall those used elsewhere.
The field area, some 600 acres, was shaped like an old-fashioned kite.
The western boundary was formed by the Cressingham road: Eastmere
Farm went northwards along this road up to a double-dwelling known
as 'Red Houses'; one side was occupied by my Father's nephew, Sid
Jones and his family, whilst the other was lived in by Fred Buckle and
his wife Ethel (nee Williams who was my Father's cousin). Later on,
when Sid Jones went away, a family with the surname Warby came
there to live but they were no relation to us. There was a field named
after these two cottages, which was left fallow for years until 1940
when my Father ploughed it up and managed to cultivate a good crop
of rye. In front of this *Red House Field* was *Shepherd's Plantation*, a
wood of mixed fir and deciduous trees which could be walked all the
way round. A stretch of spruce and fir trees forest called *Jubilee Wood*
formed the northern boundary of Eastmere; my Father always cut our
Christmas tree from this wood which ran from the cottages towards
Merton Park, joining up with *Cut-throat,* a plantation of oaks and
chestnut trees, where supposedly a man committed suicide by cutting
his throat.

66

Between our cottage and these trees were two large fields named after the woods; *Shepherd's Plantation piece* and *Cut-throat bit*. A trackway divided them going from the farm towards to a very deep well and evidence of an old ruin. This well was never used until Miss Reeve discovered water there in 1936 after which Mr. Thornber built ten large brick duck-huts on Shepherd's Plantation piece. A long strip of land about four acres in size, ran in front of Jubilee Wood to separate it from the fields. It was sandy and full of rabbit holes and only grew canker weed and bracken, but made a nice nature walk. This kept the rabbits from burrowing on the cultivated fields. Alongside Cut-throat bit was a piece of land called Merton Field which joined Lord Walsingham's Park. Along the Cressingham road a small field called *Coalseed* was divided from Shepherd's Plantation piece by a small hedge of crab-apple trees. There was one particularly nice tree from which we gathered the sour apples every year, and Mother often made these into wine. The hedgerows had huge blackberry bushes and in my child's mind, it was similar to the place where the robbers lay in wait for the Good Samaritan of the New Testament story. This irrational fear left me as I grew older and later we gathered many beautiful, juicy blackberries to eat and make delicious jam.

The eastern edge was marked by the driveway which went into Merton Park, a lovely place, landscaped with beautiful old oaks, beeches and numerous exotic fir trees. There were massive horse-chestnut trees which provided the village children with their yearly supply of conkers. During the summer, Merton Hall gardens were opened up for visitors to view the colourful rhododenrons, flower beds, and the 'Shell House', a proper miniature building made entirely of sea shells. One could walk all the way to the Hall and up to Merton Church, and then past the lodge with its white, wooden gates onto the Watton road. Another path went northwards alongside Peddars Way up to Home Farm close to the large house called "The Hassocks", the home of Lord Walsingham. Sometimes we walked the driveway which ran south from Merton Park to Keymer's Corner, before going on to Tottington village proper.

A rough lane ran by Eastmere Farm on its way into Merton Park. In fine weather we used this road to go to the nearest town, Watton, four miles away, but during the early 1920s this track was in bad repair and often muddy. We could go through Merton Home Farm or walk through a wood and come out by Merton School on the Green. In the opposite direction the lane went alongside the thorn hedge of *Long Meadow* to the Cressingham road and into Westmere Farm, towards

Keymer's Lodge

Church Meadows where horses were taken for grazing. Sometimes the horses were taken to the other side of Merton Park for ploughing and threshing on Broadflash, another little farm which Mr. Wace rented. It had lovely lush meadows and ponds where I spent many happy hours with the children of Rev. Thomas when I worked at Merton Rectory in 1929-1931.

Immediately around the farmhouse there were three meadows separated by thorn hedges: the one-and-a-half acre *Little Meadow* where our cottage and the farm buildings were; the nine acre *Long Meadow* which ran beside the lane; and *The Hills* by the side of the farm. During the First World War, when I was about four, a military aeroplane came down on Clayacre Field and made a bee-line for our cottage. Luckily it ran into a pit when it crossed the Lane and ploughed through the hedge of the Little Meadow. The pilot wasn't badly hurt and Mrs Sculfer took care of him until help arrived. She had a walking stick made out of a piece of wood from the wreckage which caught fire and left me with the memory of a peculiar smell. Many years later whilst my family was visiting Wells on the north Norfolk coast, a motor-bike gave off a similar smell which instantly reminded me of that childhood event. The Hills was a large chalk pit covered in grass and little fir bushes, blackberry bushes and one huge oak tree. The farm cow, and Kruger the trap horse, were put here to graze. The pit had a thorn hedge on three sides and Mr. Sculfer's garden and the farm buildings were on the other side. The door of the cowsheds opened onto the Hills as did the large shed used for housing implements such as drills, etc.

At the front of Eastmere Farm, across the Lane, was a footpath which led through fields southwards. Weather permitting, we used this route to save us going along the Lane and Cressingham road to Tottington. I remember cycling along this footpath, thinking I would be clever and letting go of the handle-bars only to find myself on the ground with a buckled wheel; that taught me a lesson! To our left was a small area called the *Footpath Field* followed by *The Pot* and *The Wong* field, both of which joined the Merton Park driveway crossing Peddars Way into Merton Park up to the Hall. Going towards the village, *Clayacre Field* lay on the right sloping upwards to Clayacre hill on the top of which was a plantation and nearby a pit which was supposed to be haunted. From Clayacre the land ran down a slope of sand heaps and rough grass, past *Middle field* with its numerous rabbit holes down which bunnies scampered flashing their white tails as we approached. This warren was never cultivated but there was a deep well and some ruins on the far side. As children we were told never to go near the well as it was deep and dangerous but that didn't stop us. We threw stones down and it took ages before we heard a splash. Lastly came *Big End Field*, which was normally left fallow although Mr. Wace did try to grow oats once or twice but wasn't very successful. To its left, separated by a hedge, was *Chilver's Field* stretching back up to the Merton Park Drive and down towards Keymer's Plantation, which we called Tuddenham's after the people who lived in the fine, thatched cottage opposite Corner Plantation. After 1936 several of these fields were used for the cattle brought in by Mr. Thornber. This limited our use of the short-cut route to the village as we had to be wary of the seventy heifers and that large ferocious bull.

All the Westmere Fields were on the other side of Cressingham Road so it was easy in Mr. Wace's time for the two farms to be run as one unit. In Tuddenham's Plantation there was a small sandpit where we played instead of going straight home from school. Most of the fields had chalk pits which had been dug out to manure the fields in the early nineteenth century. They were dry pits covered with grass and small bushes, ideal for bird nesting and spring flowers. There was one pit on *The Pot* which was always full of cowslips. Children knew where to find things at certain times of the year, hazel nuts in Shepherds Plantation, chestnuts in Cut-throat and Tuddenham's plantation and at *Butter Hole* up the Thetford Road, plus conkers from three enormous horse-chestnut trees just inside Merton Park.

EASTMERE DUCK FARMING: In 1936 a Yorkshire firm called Thornber's Bros. of Mytholmroyd became interested in Eastmere for the rearing of ducks. They could sell any number of fat ducks but suitable land wasn't available up north. The dry, sandy soil of the Breckland was ideal. Mr. R.J. Childerhouse used to invite the heads of the Yorkshire firm to stay with him, and he brought them along to see Eastmere. The snag was that water had to be found. There was an artesian well in the backyard of the farmhouse but no large pit like Westmere. Fattening ducks require huge amounts of water, which has to be given to them; they are not the sort to wallow around in boggy fields.

In her book, *Farming on a Battleground,* Miss Lucilla Reeve, the Estate Manager, relates how she came to find water at Eastmere. She fancied herself as a Dowser, having found water in several other places, and knew that two wells, which were no longer used, existed to the east and west of the farm. They looked at the West well with its sixty feet long, rusty chain which wouldn't reach the water. The Yorkshiremen were sceptical but Lucilla cut a cleft stick off a nearby thorn hedge and began to walk across the field. *"Over and over went the twig and finally I traced two strong springs leading to the well, and one carrying on towards the farm buildings where it was joined by another one; and two more nearer the house".* She convinced the men from Thornber's by getting a professional water-finder to confirm her dowsing and give them estimates for the bores, pumps, etc. *"Everything went according to plan, gallons of water came from the trial bores, and I let a farm."*

Miss Reeve tried to interest the "Duck Kings of Yorkshire" in Bagmore Farm near Stanford and sent them the following verses as a Valentine:

Ten little Yorkshire ducks came to Norfolk — fine!
One pined for Mytholmroyd: leaving only nine.
Nine little Yorkshire ducks, sitting up too late;
Norfolk rat caught one, then there were eight.
Eight little Yorkshire ducks, dreamin' of their heav'n;
One just went there and left the other seven.
Seven little Yorkshire ducks, getting in a fix,
One necked the netting, then there were six.
Six little Yorkshire ducks, sang happy and alive,
The foreman heard a weak voice, and that left only five.
Five little Yorkshire ducks, said "Norfolk food is poor!"
One refused to eat it, and left the other four.
Four little Yorkshire ducks, near wood called "Jubilee";
Gale blew one to Merton, leaving only three.
Three little Yorkshire ducks, wond'ring what to do;
Stoat came and took one, and left the other two.
Two little lonely ducks, began to weep and wail;
One drowned in his tears, left one to tell the tale.
To tell the tale the like of which,
Has ne'er been told before:
For every Thornber duck that dies,
They rear a thousand more!

However, they resisted her suggestion because Thornber's didn't do too well during the first few months. They had thought small arks on the open fields would be sufficient but our east winds proved too much for small ducklings. As a result ten long heated huts were brick-built on Shepherd's Plantation Field, with running water piped in, and a large wooden hut was put on the meadow so we could no longer see the stackyard. This was a plucking hut and an office. The enterprise should have created construction work for the villagers but Mr. Thornber brought in several men including four bricklayers and a carpenter, as well as all the materials from Yorkshire. One of these, a carpenter named Jim Feathers stayed with us at the cottage and helped construct the huts. When I came home on holiday I went everywhere on the back of his motorbike, which was quite an exciting experience in those days when transport was limited and cars few and far between. At that time we travelled miles on bicycles or simply walked and thought nothing about it.

Several changes were made at Eastmere. Captain Moore and his family and Mr. Madoc had to leave the Farmhouse. They went to live at Crab Tree Corner near Wayland Wood where Mr. Madoc had some buildings erected to continue his work as a beekeeper. My Father was given the post of Foreman on the agricultural side and a Mr. Albert Bishop, his wife Alice and sons, Joseph, and Albert, came to live in Eastmere Farm house to be in charge of the ducks. Mother made a firm friend of Mrs Bishop who was a Yorkshire woman like herself. The long huts were filled with newly hatched ducklings which were reared until they were large enough for the table, and then killed, plucked and sent to London every night. This did create a lot of work for people from Tottington and other villages, both in looking after the ducks and in the plucking. It was a smelly business and I remember the swarms of flies in the summer. The words duck and muck go together . The tractors ploughed it into the soil and this enabled the farm to grow increased yields of wheat, oats, barley and rye, sugar-beet, plus the hay, mangolds and swedes for the cattle which were introduced. Miss. Reeve wrote,

I had been in my job for years and all that time had seen little or no money spent on the land. I had had the spending of ten thousand pounds a year on a luxury shoot, the actual sport of which was sometimes only twenty-eight days in a year, and which did no benefit to the land or villages. Now the money spent on this new way of farming was good for land and people. Labour was wanted all the year round and plenty of it, and the ducks needed lots of food. I began to see we might yet be once again a great agricultural estate.

Carpenter Jim Feathers at Eastmere

Albert and Alice Bishop with sons Joseph and Albert, 1940

My Father had an important responsibility in looking after the seventy heifers which were in calf (Shorthorn, Red Poll and Ayrshire), a dozen bullocks in the yards for fattening, and the calves on the meadow, but no pigs or sheep were kept. There was a very fierce pedigree Ayshire bull, called *Dyneley Straight Away*, kept with the heifers on the meadows. When the cattle were brought up to the farm, my Father was the only one who would feed him. We could hear this bull roaring and stamping its feet; it really was a ferocious beast. It wore a mask and had a ring through its nose by which it was controlled and led around in the yard by a pole. Father managed the farm side very well and expanded the production; when the Second World War broke out, several new fields which had lain fallow for years, were put under cultivation. A Mr. Childerhouse, who had come to Tottington to live, was friendly with Mr. Thornber (who remained in Yorkshire) and acted as his Overseer. He often came up to Eastmere to check to see all was well. If anything goes wrong with cattle it has to be a quick decision about what to do. The farm had three tractors, one of which my Father drove, leaving Ted Williams to see after the horses, which had decreased in number to five. Mr Bishop had a car; these were more common although few people could afford to own one.

One wonders what Eastmere could have become had it survived. There were those who saw the Breckland as something akin to a desert where the soil was unsuitable for agriculture, where crop returns were low and grassland so sparce it wasn't worth trying to keep stock except for grazing sheep. Such a view was incorrect and insulting to those farmers and their workers who had striven over many decades to increase the fertility of the land and improve yields of the crops as well as husband dairy cattle and poultry along with the sheep. One only has to peruse the list of stock and equipment from Messrs. Thornber Bros. Ltd. sold by Auction at Eastmere Farm on Thursday 9th July 1942, to realise how much had been invested to make Eastmere so successful.

The Catalogue included:
9 horses; 73 head of cattle; 1150 laying and rearing poultry as well a large quantity of dead stock.

Stock Prices were as follows:
a bay gelding (aged) 37 guineas; a bay gelding (9 years) 41 gs; a chestnust gelding (aged) 87 gs; a black gelding (aged) 45 gs; a piebald gelding 29 gs. A pedigree Ayshire bull; 3 Red Poll in calf heffers £38 each; 7 Shorthorn steers £19 each; 9 Ayrshire in calf heffers £30. 10s each; Shorthorn in calf heffers made up to £52 and from £39 to £26; 4 Red Poll steers (2 years) £16. 10s each.

The machinery consisted of many interesting items, some of which would be very valuable today even if museum pieces:
3 cylinder one horse roll £18 10s; a Fordson tractor £170; a double horse hoe by Hunton £17; a Massey Harris grass cutter £18; 3 furrow Cockshutt tractor plough £35; a gang of 3 tractor rib rolls £44; 2 furrow Oliver tractor plough £47; a 50 gallon water cart £26; 2 tumbrills on pneumatic tyres £62 each; Avery's steelyard £11; 4 wheeled trolly on patent axles with shaft and draw bar £25; 4 ton tractor triler on pneumatic tyres £21; a Massey Harris tractor manure spreader £76; 2 x 200 gallon water carts on pneumatic tyres £42 and £22; a Ransome's 54 inch tractor thresher £560; Clayton and Son's 8 ft vertical boiler £20; 3 h.p. Ruston Hornsby petrol engine £31; Albion power chaff cutter £32; Albion horse rake £23. 5s

WESTMERE FARM: Westmere Hall, to the north of the village on the left of the Little Cressingham road is clearly marked on the old maps of the village. In the Walsingham Papers there is a lengthy and detailed lease of this farm to William Farrer dated 14th november 1774; let for 26 years from Michaelmas for a sum of £385 paid half-yearly. Census records show it was farmed by a Mr. John Lincoln from Watton in the 1840s up to the 1860s: on 590 acres, he employed fourteen men and five boys. During the 1870s and 1880s, a Mr John Marten lived at Westmere and ran the farm as the farm bailiff to Lord Walsingham. In the 1890s, John de Grey took over Westmere Farm but later it was rented by a Mr Alfred Edwards and then Mr John Rayner before Mr. Wace took over. Before and during the First World War, Westmere Farmhouse was lived in by several different families the last being named Worlidge. They had six children, Arthur, Susan, Albert, Mary. Teddy and another little boy, most of whom went to school. Mrs Worlidge had a baby girl but caught scarlet fever and died so the child was brought up for a while by a woman called Macrow who lived in the village. About 1922 Mr. Wace, who was quite old by then, gave up Westmere and Sturston farms but kept on Eastmere. Lt. Col. George de Grey, the son of Lord Walsingham, left the army, married and took over Westmere Farm. The Worlidge family went to live at Gressinghall, and they were missed by all of us.

Westmere Farmhouse

The large Farmhouse was situated up a long driveway known as *the Drove* which had a hedge either side with cultivated fields. It was very tiring to walk along since the deep sand sank over ones shoe tops. The farm could be approached across a meadow where there was a pit. By the entrance to the driveway there were two tied cottages side by side. They were lived in by my Father's Uncle George Williams, and by George Leeder who married my Father's cousin Alice Williams. Both farm workers were Teamsmen who looked after the horses on the farm. Other workers lived in the village itself. The farm consisted of the usual huge barn, stables, sheds, cow and horse yards, which were situated on *Church Meadows*, part of Westmere used for the horses to graze on at weekends. They were soft and marshy with lots of wild flowers in the springtime, but in the winter too wet to walk over. A path was used by people to attend Church: on one side was a large pond, Westmere Pit, where a golden cradle was supposed to be buried and on the other side were the derelict remains of a sizeable building said to have been a priory where a service was held once a year. By bearing to the right of this ruin, the path led to Westmere lake, a fair-sized waterhole fenced off, with a plantation one side and hedges all round the meadow. The soil was just like sand, dreadful to walk on and very dusty so our feet always became filthy. There was a little island in this lake where yellow lillies and black pokers grew, and around the edges were lots of wild

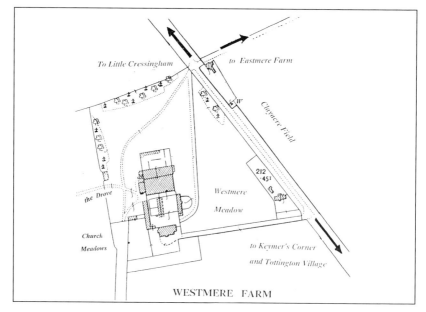

WESTMERE FARM

flowers. The mere was a favourite beauty spot where people picnicked, swam and fished. My Great-Uncle, Henry Macro, died through catching cold whilst swimming there.

Numerous birds gathered in the pit and wildfowl ran everywhere, water-hens, wild geese and sometimes a heron was seen. Water, for the animals on both farms, was carted up in an oblong metal tank on four wheels with two lids on top. It held 150 gallons and was drawn by two horses because the driveway at the back of Westmeree house was full of deep. dirty-looking sand, like a sea-shore, and it was terrible to walk on let alone drag a heavy load over. The pit had eels and small fish in it so sometimes when the tank arrived at Eastmere, Mrs. Sculfer used to catch the eels and cook them.

Lt. Col. de Grey made lots of alterations to Westmere Farm. The house was modernised and added to with running water and electricity laid on (they generated their own), Flower gardens were laid out by the driveway with fruit and vegetable gardens at the side and the back. Two wooden bungalows were built near the entrance to a meadow; one where Mr Newstead the gardener lived, and another on the meadow where the Steward lived. The Colonel and his wife Hyacinth soon had children, three girls and a boy. This created work for the local girls because rooms were made into night and day nurseries; three nannies and several maids were employed. The children even had their own school built at the back of the house. In 1922 a Mr. Dunnell came to be the Steward or Foreman and his daughter and son-in-law, Mr. Thompson, lived with him. Later on when Mr. Dunnell died in 1925, Jock Thompson became the Foreman but he didn't know half as much about farming as my Father did. Col. de Grey brought in a herd of cows and a huge Dairy was built in the cellar of the house, This was run by Mrs. Thompson. It meant that people were able to buy milk, cream and butter from the farm. They fetched the milk everyday in large metal cans with handles, and the workers brought their jugs and containers.

When Mr. Newstead came as gardener he worked with another man from the village called Leslie Macro. Mrs Newstead was the cook for quite a time but unfortunately became ill and eventually died leaving one son called Reggie. My Father's Uncle George died on the sugar beet field in July 1926. Reggie Bone was on holiday and talking to the men when George turned to him and said "I don't 'alf feel funny bor" and then fell down dead from a heart attack. His wife, Aunt Bessie, went to live in the village leaving their house vacant. A Mr. Victor Leader, brother of George Leeder who lived next door, became the cowman and took over the tenancy.

The old Lord Walsingham, the Hon. John Augustus de Grey, was a small man but his wife, was a tall, gracious lady and Col. George de Grey took after her in being a tall, broad man. He wore a moustache and, like my Father, called a spade a spade with no nonsense. He was a true blue Conservative and didn't like any of his workers voting Liberal. He owned a 'Tin Lizzie' Ford van, one of the first motors in Tottington, and he always gave people lifts especially to church where his family went every Sunday and occupied the front pew. In those days it was "Sir" and "Madam" and the Walsinghams were greeted with a salute from the boys and a curtsey from the girls; a polite fawning which seems strangely out of place in today's era of equality. We just did it, copying our parents without questioning our 'betters'.

Mrs Hyacinth de Grey invited all the young girls of the village up to the house every Saturday afternoon for sewing lessons taught by her lady's maid, a Miss Muffet. No one refused her 'request', it was more of an order! Dolly Macro and Dolly Fisher, Eleanor and Esther Thompson, Phylis and Lena Leeder, Ethel Bone, Hilda Fisher, Dolly and Doris Spragg - all the young girls of the village went. We arrived about 2 p.m. and had to wait outside before being let in. Often it was terribly cold and on one occasion I felt so frozen that I couldn't do any sewing. Once inside we were taken upstairs where we sat learning different methods of sewing. This was a skill which all young ladies learned, and were meant to be proficient in. We were grateful for the tuition although we did do sewing at school, and it was good of Mrs de Grey to give us the opportunity, as well as provide tea. All I ever remember making was a brown dress with red stitching down the side. It was round-necked with no collar and did up down the left side with a row of fasteners. Strange how I can recollect that dark brown dress after nearly seventy years. Afterwards we were ushered into the dining room at the front of the house and given tea. We were waited on by a maid being served scones and cakes, bread and jam. During Winter when it was dark we would leave soon after four because most of the girls had to walk back to the village, whereas I had to go across a meadow and then down a lane to get back to Eastmere.

In the Summer children would pick blackberries for jam at 1d a lb and adults were employed on the farm and in the gardens to pick fruit. All the farm workers would have a party at Christmas and were given two rabbits; the more important people would receive a brace of pheasants. Every year there was a Grand Fete at Westmere Farm. People came from miles around as it was held on a Saturday. The children would gather wild flowers and arrange them in jars; I remember on the Friday nights before the Fetes walking miles and miles to collect those flowers. All sorts of competitions took place especially in garden produce. People worked hard to get everything looking nice and the judges came round a day or two before the Fete. There were prizes for the best kept garden, the best flower and the best vegetable garden, in the village. There were many other interesting activities and all sorts of exhibitions in tents plus a marquee for tea and refreshments. A band arrived from Yorkshire and one year the 'Girl Pipers' came. It was like a miniature Norfolk Show and continued late into the evening with people dancing to the band. Unfortunately these Fetes only lasted about five years as everything became so expensive.

In 1927 the old Lord Walsingham died in the house called the "Hassocks" at Merton, the village next to Tottington. The family home was a large mansion called Merton Hall which they could not afford to live in so it was let to shooting parties, etc. The Merton Estate had established itself as one of the most important 'shoots' in England. At one time a man called Sir Edgar Mackay lived there; he had all the children from the Estate at parties, etc, and gave formal Balls. Unfortunately his son was killed on his way home from London, crashing into a telegraph post with his little racing car on the Newmarket Road and died aged only twenty-one. After that the Mackay's didn't stay long and part of the Hall was turned into flats which still exist today. There was a boarding school at the Hall for a while but this section got burnt down. The Hall, much reduced in size, still stands in Merton just below the church in Merton Park.

The youngest son, Richard de Grey, continued to live in the "Hassocks" but Col. George de Grey became the new Lord and decided to stay at Westmere Farm. When I left school at Christmas 1926, like most other children, all I wanted to do was earn enough money to keep myself and help my parents. Domestic service was the main employment for village girls who often left home to work and live in the houses of the Gentry or in urban districts. As an occupation it was in decline but even the1891 Census commented on how few girls there were over the age of ten in country areas. I took a 'petty place' at the Farm as 'between-maid' for Lady Walsingham, which meant I helped upstairs and downstairs, at the beck and call of everyone. Before me, Dolly Macro was a nursery maid at Westmere. In those days when young girls went into service the parents had to find suitable clothes for them to work in. A kitchen-maid would have a long-sleeved, grey or blue print dress and a huge white apron buttoned or tied up behind with shoulder straps which crossed at the back and fastened by buttons onto the waist-band. She had to wear black shoes and stockings and a white cap. Between-maids dressed the same although they also had a black dress for afternoon wear, as sometimes they had to go into the front of the house (kitchen maids didn't do this). Nannies and nursemaids (who waited on the children), all wore the same uniform as 'tweenies' except for the black dresses. Cooks wore large white overalls and caps. Some well-off families did provide the uniform for their servants and so they should considering it was for their benefit. All this clothing went to the laundry (if a laundress wasn't employed) and came back beautifully ironed and starched; everyone looked smart and clean.

The parlourmaids and housemaids changed from their dresses at lunch-time into black dresses with either a more elaborate, large white apron having strings at the back, or a smaller one with a top which pinned on the front of the dress. Caps were usually a white lace head-band with black velvet threaded through which tied at the back. White collars and cuffs were always worn (or the equivalent in a different colour). Sometimes celluloid cuffs, fastened on by pearl studs, were worn enabling them to be easily removed for doing the washing up. Parlourmaids waited at table and saw to the silver, glasses, etc, whilst housemaids cleaned the bedrooms and took over waiting at table when the parlourmaid had a day off work. Westmere Farm had a large staff; it was a very ordered 'upstairs-downstairs' system, with lots of rules and regulations, in which everyone knew their place and behaved accordingly. Later on, at posts with other families there were only two maids and it was more like family life. At that time 'service' seemed a good thing for young girls as it taught us about household etiquette and prepared us for married life; as they say, one never forgets what one learns as a child or in one's youth. Nevertheless, servants were 'skivvies' and often badly treated. They didn't receive a reference until after completing a year's service so young girls from poor backgrounds had to put up with lots of contempt and abuse. It wasn't unknown for young girls to run away from such servitude. Today children spend so long at school and are often spoilt, and want so much more for themselves without having to work for it; maybe certain aspects of the old way were better.

It always seemed to be work and more work, no time for being bored or sulking even if you were unhappy. To do this one had to be 'strong' or 'active' as all the Wanted adverts mentioned. The hours were long and arduous, the wages very low, leisure time was limited to an afternoon off each week plus every other Sunday afternoon and then you didn't go out until after lunch. On the other Sunday we were allowed time to go attend the Church service. My job was awfully hard; I rose at 5.30 a.m. and scrubbed the kitchen floor covered in green oil cloth (linoleum) before cleaning the huge black cooking stove and lighting the fire. A postman came at 7 o'clock and sat in the kitchen with the foreman of the farm, drinking cups of tea. I often looked out of my bedroom window to see my Father bringing home the horses at 4.30 on a Monday morning. One of my jobs was to pluck the turkeys. These were bred on the farm and could be enormous. Often they were as big as me and I couldn't lift them being only fourteen years old.

Lady Walsingham Grey , the Hon. Mrs. de Grey, could be a bit of a tartar. She was always on about girls letting their hair grow long. Bobbed hair was the fashion at the time and she couldn't stand it! She was a finely built woman and had a mass of brown hair which she wore in a roll around her head. When she let it out the hair hung down nearly to her knees. Lady Walsingham dressed well but she wore funny hats. Her husband would say, "You're not going out in that hat are you Cinter?". Everyone was a bit in awe of her. The parlour maid kept her informed of all that happened in the house. There was a cupboard between the kitchen and the study where she used to stand and listen to what went on in the kitchen. One day I left a brush in the drawing room and she called me down and just pointed to the brush and said, "Is that yours?". It made me feel like a worm! At least I wasn't ever beaten as happened to young girls during the late Victorian and early Edwardian period; but then servants were as liable to personal chastisement as the children of the house - we were at the mercy of our employer.

I had never seen a telephone before and one day while dusting the study, I accidently put a book underneath the hearing piece. This caused it to ring sixteen miles away at the telephone exchange in East Dereham so a man came out from there to see. Lord Walsingham just said, "Be careful", and wasn't angry with me. The children's prams were always a silver-grey colour and they had two dogs - a collie which was constantly running off and received a good belting when it returned, and a little black pug which snorted all over the place. Once the Walsinghams brought me a stick of rock from a due they had been to at Watton. I received about 2/6 a week and good food which was a big advantage. However I didn't enjoy the experience and never felt happy there. I stayed six months, February to October, before going to London to live with Aunt Emmeline whose husband Herbert managed to get me a job in an office at Lyons in Kensington High Street opposite Cadby Hall. What a change from being a 'between maid'!

*HALL FARM:*To the south of Tuddenham's Corner at the northern end of the village on the way to Watton was a medium sized farm. It's house faced the main Watton Road and was an attractive looking building situated across a meadow about a quarter of a mile from the shop which was on the other side of the road. There were two ways to get to this farm. One was a driveway through the meadow to the front and the other entrance was from the Thompson road at the back. Traditionally this had been the home of the Salter family, whose ancestors did so much for the church and are commemorated in engravings on the back of several pews taken from Tottington and now residing in Rockland St. Peters. On the old maps it is shown as a large dwelling called Tottington Hall.

Several different families lived there after the turn of the century. When I was young, the tenant, Mr. Rayner had a carriage and horses and an MP named Mr. Taylor lived there. Later on it was let to Mr. George Thomas Nicholson ('a former breeder of hackneys, hunters and shires') and in 1935 to Mr. Robert James Childerhouse, who kept a herd of cows and sold milk, as well as acting as Overseer of Eastmere Farm for Mr. Thornber and Mr. Saunders. When his son Joe got married Bob Childerhouse went to live at Mortimer Farm. Joe and his in-laws, the Fishers, took over Hall Farm and both Father and son were still there when the Army took over in 1942.

The meadow in front of the house was used for nearly all social occasions and for cricket and football. The village always had its Fetes there. The very first tea I remember was in celebration of the ending of the Great War 1914-18. Long wooden tables with white cloths were laid out for people to sit at and a tent erected where tea was brewed, etc. On village Sports Day, Lord and Lady Walsingham attended and presented the prizes. Sometimes auctions were held there; I remember being at one as a little girl and unfortunately wetting my knickers. Mother took me over to Father's Aunt Rebecca who was a very small, old, white-haired lady - goodness knows what she found for me to wear! When these village auctions ceased, a man called Sam Spinks, who was also the Pearl Insurance agent, collected the items to be sold in the Watton Sale Rooms normally on a Wednesday the Market Day. Years later this business passed down to Mr. Noel Abel who developed a very large removal company along with the auctions at Watton.

Most of the meadows in Tottington were boggy in the wintertime, but beautiful wild flowers grew abundantly and we got many a soaking trying to gather them. There were yellow water lillies and pokers, cuckoo flowers, king cups and wild orchids, little white flowers and butter cups. Children soon got to know where certain flowers grew and one pit was full of cowslips, some woods had daffodils and bluebells and snowdrops and in certain lanes there were violets and primroses.

PEARSON'S or CHURCH FARM: This was a small area of land, about fifty acres which was next to Hall Farm both sides of the Watton Road. It was the first farm coming into the village from the north. On the way home from school. the children often helped themselves to the swedes or turnips which grew near Tuddenham's (Keymer's) Corner; they were lovely and sweet but we lived in fear of one day being caught by the 'Bobby'! On the right hand side the fields ran up to the Church and Church meadows; on the left side they joined Thompson road and Hall Farm. The house and farm buildings were set a liitle way back from the main road in a meadow where often the farmer's horse grazed. The Farm house had two families living there, Mr Pearson and his brother-in-law's family by the name of High with four children, two daughters named Winnifred (Winnie) Pearson and Lily High, who became school teachers, plus Robert and Percy High. After Mr Pearson left, the Farm was let to a Mr. Page from Carbrooke who had three children, Betty, Bridget and John. In the same meadow was another house lived in by Mr. Wilfred Herring who was at one time the village postman and also the shoe maker and cobbler, continuing a family

tradition. When Wilfred died his nephew, a Mr. Joe Balls, came there to live; he took over the blacksmith's yard. His wife, Ethel Perkins, died leaving him with three sons to bring up, Donald, Allen and Joseph. They were still in the village in 1942.

Mr. Pearson also had some meadows at the back of the blacksmiths beside Church Lane where men played quoits. On the other side of the Lane were eight semi-detached, council houses, two facing the main road and six beside the lane, built in the 1930s. Further up stood two thatched cottages, occupied by Mr. Arthur Thompson and Mr. Jack Williams, and then the grand old Vicarage. Another thatched cottage was at the end of the lane on the other side, opposite the Church, where first the Quantrells then the Spragg family lived until 1936, followed by Tom Jessup and Daisy (Hunt). Church meadows behind the church were not let to Mr. Pearson, as they belonged to Eastmere Farm.

GRANGE FARM: lay at the end of a little lane of houses running from the main Watton to Thetford road on the left side. In the late nineteenth century my Great- Grandfather, Henry Macro (1821 - 1896) lived there with his wife Mary Buckle (1826 - 1903) who came from a large family many of whom still lived in the village in the 1890s. Her parents were Robert Buckle and Marie Dalton; her brother William (1832 -1911) married Mary Macro - Henry's cousin - and had eleven children. In 1891 William was an agricultural labourer working on Eastmere Farm and living in the cottage on Cressingham Road. His son Walter married Emma Bunnett in 1878 and lived at the Old Workhouse; they had thirteen children. Another son, Herbert, married Mary A. Chaston in 1884 and was living and working on Eastmere farm. Yet by the time of the First World War there were no Buckles in Tottington except for

Uncle Fred Macro in front of Grange Farm, 1900

William's widow, affectionately known as "Polly" who lived next door to my Grandparents, John and Frances Warby, and died in 1928.

When Great-Grandmother Mary (Buckle) died, her son Frederick Macro married Rosie Smith in December 1903 and went to live at Mortimer Farm. Thereafter several people farmed this land including a Mr. Woolsey, Mr. George Oldfield, and in 1933 a Mr. Claude Reuben Quadling, followed by a Mr. Green who was renting it when the Military took over in 1942. Before 1936 nearly all the village bought their milk from this farm, but it was two miles for us to fetch it; a very bad journey in the Winter on the slippery roads, especially on a bicycle. It was a very picturesque place; a large farmhouse with a thatched roof and a pretty flower garden. It stood in a meadow which faced Top lane running from the Crossways through other meadows, across heath land and into woods down to Thompson Watering - a favourite beauty spot. The River Wissey began there and flowed through Tottington village under the main Thetford-Watton road to Stanford Watering. The river separated the fields of Hall Farm from those of Grange Farm. All the land around the New School belonged to this farm and stretched to Wretham Corner, then there was a heathland called 'America'.

MORTIMER FARM: stood about a quarter of a mile along the Stanford road which ran west from the Thetford-Watton road. It was about two hundred acres in size with a sizeable farmhouse built beside the road; at the back were large meadows through which ran the River Wissey. At the side of the farm was a track which went to the church passing a fairly large thatched house; a pretty place by the river where the Estate Agent, Miss. Lucilla Reeve, lived with her GrandMother. On the other side of the river were three cottages built as one structure. My parents lived there when they first married and also a family named Bone ; Edward who worked on Eastmere and Westmere farms, and Mabel (Park) who was the school caretaker. They were my God-parents, and had several children, Elizabeth (Betty), Reggie, Bob, and Ethel who became my good friend plus Alan and Fred who were born in the 1920s after the Bone's had moved to the Crossroads at the beginning of Top Lane. Cyril and Winnie Spragg moved here before they went to lived in one of the New Council Houses built in Church Lane in 1934. Mrs. Ashley, a midwife, lived in the third cottage which later on was occupied by Mr. Macro who used to be the scissor grinder and sold litle oddments like drinks and chocolate. He rode a trade bike with a box on the front and children liked him to call on a Saturday. These dwellings changed hands many times. The pathway eventually

linked up with Church Lane so that Mortimer and St. Andrew's Church faced each other across the meadows, about three-quarters of a mile apart. In 1901 Mortimer Farm consisted of 120 acres of arable land and fifty of pasture with shelter fences of Scotch firs to keep the light soil from blowing away: *That season 138 coomb of white oats, not including the dress corn, had been sold off eleven acres; and although thin and rather piny the barley, . . . was of good colour. The cows, of which many used to be kept here, had been given up owing to the lack of milkers. Steers were grazed, and at two years old sold out as stores, the best of the heifers being bred for dairy purposes. Here the clover lay, grown after barley on a chalky subsoil, . . . and nine acres of lucerne also drilled with barley that Spring was an excellent plant.*

Rural England by H. Rider Haggard

In the years 1906 - 1912, my Mother's Uncle Frederick William Macro was the tenant for Mortimer when it was rented by a Mr. James Whalebelly. I was told that Fred's stepson was nearly killed by a horse and rake as he was sleeping in the hay field on the farm. After Fred emigrated to Australia, Mr. Whalebelly, who lived at Watton, farmed it for many years with a Mr. Childerhouse as Foreman. The latter had three children, Ethel, Marjorie and a boy. The girls were very pretty and I remember them coming to school in a pony and trap. The Childerhouses also had a fierce dog which bit the arm of a girl called

Joan Fisher who worked for them. When Mr. Whalebelly gave up Mortimer about 1923, Mr. Childerhouse had to leave. We were all sorry to see them go.

Mortimer was then operated directly by Lord Walsingham with his sister, Mrs. Blaithwaite living there. Another Mr. Childerhouse, Robert James known as Bob, came from Caston to Tottington and lived at Hall Farm. His son Joseph Arthur Childerhouse married Hilda Rose Fisher in March 1938 and they lived for a while in Sturston farmhouse but when Bob hired Mortimer, Joe, along with his in-laws the Fishers, went to Hall Farm. Mortimer became a large dairy farm from which a lot of milk was sold. We cycled two miles every day to collect free milk since Father worked on Eastmere Farm. One very slippery day I fell off my bicycle, broke the bottles and lost all Mother's milk. Bob Childerhouse had a lot to do with Eastmere after it was taken over by Thornber's Bros. Ltd.

STURSTON FARM: The Farm next to Mortimer on the Stanford Road was named after the village there. In the early days this small farm was connected to Westmere and Eastmere even though it was some distance away, and all three were farmed together by Mr. Wace. Westmere farmland ran along Sturston at the back of the village. To reach it by road was about four miles from Eastmere. At one time the village and the farm must have been important as there were lots of ruins around including the remnants of a moated manor house and old church but by 1920 there were only four cottages on the side of the road between the two farms and this was known as Sturston village.

During the eighteenth century a new Hall was built and large flocks of sheep were kept. The farmland changed hands many times until Thomas 5th Lord Walsingham took it over and built Waterloo farmhouse as well as cottages and planted trees. However, the cottages crumbled away and the land became derelict, so little use of it was made for food production even during the First World War. It may not have been the best of farmland but Sturston Heath running from near Mortimers farm past Pole Plantation to the Eagle Tower Hill, was an attractive place. Miss Reeve wrote , *"it seemed like another world"* with its *"Bracken and ling with rabbits, plover, curlew and pheasants, the scent of wild thyme and the pine woods."*

Sturston Hall was sold in 1912 to an American and taken down to be entirely rebuilt in the United States under the same name. Sturston Farmhouse was lived in by a Mr. Fred Spinks (1872-1931) who married Hannah Oldfield, and worked for Mr. Wace. When Lord

Walsingham took over Westmere in 1922 this included Sturston so Fred left and became a roadman living in one of the Sturston Cottages.

They had six children, Walter Frederick and, Amy Florence (who married Ella and Victor Rose respectively in 1928), William, Mary Elizabeth, Arthur George (who married Ethel Downes), and lastly Harold James Spinks (1914-1988) who married my friend Ethel Maud Bone in 1941. A family called Mansfield were living at the Farm in 1942.

WATERLOO FARM: This lay further south-west of Sturston towards West Tofts. According to Rider-Haggard it was so-called *"because in a single netting the same number of rabbits were taken as men were killled at Waterloo."* Originally it was a warren but the 5th Lord Walsingham reclaimed the land in 1845, broke up the soil, coated it with 70 to 120 loads of marl per acre and manured it with sheep droppings. It remained poor soil and didn't stand the drought so never grew good barley but by 1862, 125 acres planted with corn produced 667 coomb which sold for £885 19s plus another £103 0s 6d consumed on the farm. A year later the 740 acres farm fetched a rent of £600 but by 1870 this fell to £500 a year with rent arrears on it amounting to £283! The cultivated land shrank to about 500 acres, farmed by a Mr Clark in the 1890s at a rent reduced from £150 to £100 a year. Evidently he only just made a living practising a four-course shift of roots, barley, wheat and oats, plus fattening lambs, and selling £30 of rabbits taken from the derelict land which increased in acreage year after year.

Hay Wagon and Farm Workers on Grange Farm early 1900s. Father Albert Worby second from left

Tottington villagers had very little to do with this farm and I never went there but my good friend Ethel Spinks and her husband, Harold, worked there after they married during the Second World War. Its main interest was the house which looked more like a Hall with its pointed tower. It was a lovely old place with numerous out-buildings, similar to the farmhouses of Mortimer and Mousehall, built three storeys high with blue glazed tiles on the roof, impressive chimney stacks and a high stone tower with a spire somewhat like those found on top of a church. The Waterloo spire was topped by a weather-vane with the Iron Duke mounted on a horse. These three superb houses stood in a line and were meant to commemmorate the soldiers who lost their lives fighting Napoleon and the French at the Battle of Waterloo (being copied from the famous farmhouse there). By now they would be Listed buildings so it is a great shame that neglect and the military training activities led to their destruction; all that remains are a few old photographs.

Working on the Farms: Wages were very low on the farms and changed little during the nineteenth century. Norfolk agricultural labourers were among the lowest paid in money income of all farm workers: in 1838 Dr Kay, the Assistant Poor Law Commissioner for Norfolk and Suffolk, estimated that a labourer's family spent a weekly income of 10s on the following:

2½ stone of flour at 6s 10½d
yeast   3d
rent 1s 7½d
coal   10 d
candles 3½d
leaving1½d over for clothing, beer tobacco and all other items.

During the 1850s a farm labourer earned only about 8 shillings per week, and in the 1870s it was a little above 13s. This created widespread poverty, malnutrition and illness which at the time was taken for granted. Of the Norfolk agricultural labourer it can truly be said he 'worked to live and lived to work'. When my Father married in 1909 he received only 12/6 per week in wages whilst working on Mortimer Farm for my Mother's Uncle, Fred Macro who later emigrated to Australia in 1912. By going to live and work on Eastmere Farm as Teamsman (working with the horses) Father earned a little more but was unable to supplement his income by hoeing out beet like

Haystacks and horses on Grange Farm early 1900s

other farm labouers. Just before the First World War many labourers joined the union and there were strikes to obtain higher wages and shorter hours. In this they were very successful. However, the economic recession between 1920 and 1922 reduced farmworkers' wages from 42s to 25s for fifty hours' work. In March 1923 thousands of men came out on strike not to improve conditions but to stop the reduction in wages. Norfolk farmers offered £1 rather than 25s and sought to raise the working week from 50 to 55 hours. There were lots of local incidents but little violence and on 21st april 1925, after five weeks, the workers won a wage rate of 6d an hour. When I left school in 1926, an agricultural labourer's wages were only 28/6 for long hours and hard work.

Haysel (sael = time or season) or the hay-harvest in June-July was different as Father could earn a few shillings overtime, the horses being used to pull the grass cutter and cart the hay. Labourers could be stood off work in bad weather whereas the teamsmen always had a job to do. A large amount of hay (clover, sandfine and fetches) had to be grown for the Eastmere and Westmere horses, although they ate the grass in the meadows during summer time, and from 1922 onwards it was essential for the cattle. Before haysel the cutters and reapers would be taken out of the cart sheds and given a good oiling and their knives sharpened. These were about five feet long almost like a long saw fixed to the side of the machine. The ordinary hay-cutter or sail-reaper (called a 'sailer') could be used by one man with two horses, and had its own built in platform to collect the hay or corn. The driver sat on the left of the machine as the sails went round by the side swooping down onto the platform to push the loose bundles off the back of the machine. It was then left to dry for two or three days being turned over by men with pitch-forks. On Eastmere the hay was gathered up by a horse rake (a toppler) into ricks which were then put into hay cocks by the farm workers and young boys. The cocks were allowed to stand in the fields for about ten days then turned over to allow the air to circulate and take out any remaining dampness before the hay was carted off to to the stackyard where it was piled high and sometimes covered by a large tarpaulin to keep out the rain. Wet hay or corn could never be stacked because it could turn mildew, heat up and catch fire. Often boys would ride the horse to guide it and the wagon between the hay cocks and shout "Whoa" to stop it, and "Hold-gee" to walk forward so as to indicate to the men on the load to stick their pitch fork into the hay and be careful not to fall off. Loading a wagon properly was an art in itself especially as these were often piled over twelve feet above the ground.

Harvest binder with Albert Worby extreme left; Williams and Leeder families centre

Harvest time was a great boon to the workers if the weather was fine. The quicker the harvest was gathered in the more money the farmer would pay although a fixed price was generally negotiated. This money was used by families for paying rent, winter clothing, extra food, presents, etc. In our case, every other year my Mother, brother Eddie and I went by train from Watton to visit Mother's relatives in Sheffield and on alternate years they came down to see us. Her sister was Harriet Moore who married Frank Williamson but we always knew her as 'Aunt Annie'. Then there was the other sister Hilda and a sister-in-law, Rose, plus three boys, Frank, Clifford and Charlie, so it took nearly all the extra money which Father earned.

Harvest arrived when the corn (usually wheat, barley or oats) was nearly ripe (if the corn was fully ripe, the grain would scatter when being cut, carted and stacked, and this would lead to considerable wastage and loss). Several men worked together using their old fashioned scythes to cut a swathe round the sides of the field. The corners were cut to reduce the corn to a round area so that the following day the horses nd binder could have easy access and work in a circle. The scythes reminded me of how back-breaking harvest time must have been during the nineteenth century. Of course where the corn was flattened by wind and rain it still had to be cut by hand as the binder couldn't lift these patches. There were two binders used on all three farms, and these had to be taken out of the sheds and made ready; the sails had to be looked over and often mended, and the mechanical parts oiled. Once the harvest started a tressle was put at the gate of the field to be cut and there the blades were sharpened. The reaper binder, was driven by one man sitting on an iron seat covered with sacks, and controlling three to six horses. Wooden 'sails', like a windmill on its side, went round and pushed the cut corn into the binder where the sheaves were tied with string and thrown out the other side to be picked up by workers, (men, women and children), to be placed in shocks for further ripening. Shocks stood in groups of eight, four each side leaving a passageway between the bottoms to let the wind dry them out. If the weather was bad the corn would have to stand several weeks and if the shocks were not moved they grew again into the ground and were difficult to pick up and cart. Before the First World War barley was not cut by mechanical reapers; gangs of men with scythes fitted with curved 'bails' of hazel or bramble branch acting as a bow to cause the cut barley to fall tidily for gathering. The men moved across the field in a long line and the barley was raked into rows and then carted away stll loose.

We all had lots of fun at that time and as harvest came with the school holidays we were able to spend long hot days in the fields. It was surprising how many people came onto the harvest field to work, catch rabbits or just watch the goings on but no one was allowed to go in the corn or near the binders. As the binder went round the field working its way towards the centre, the circle of standing corn became smaller. The birds flew off but any wildlife which didn't have the sense to flee the field was trapped in the middle. The poor rabbits began to run out and then what a chase. Men, women and children yelling and shouting their heads off, slashing with sticks but in the end it was usually the dogs that caught them. The rabbits were given over to the man in charge and divided up first to the farm hands and then to outsiders. Hares, pheasants and partridges were allowed to escape; the Keeper, who brought his gun and dogs to the field, saw to that - it wouldn't do to spoil the shoot for the gentry in October. After the rabbits were shared out they were 'gutted' and a hole put through one back leg so the other one could be threaded through. They were put on sticks and carried home on men's shoulders. I am glad that today children are taught to preserve wildlife and not to destroy it like the blood-thirsty lot we were.

Harvest time: families in the field before WWI.
Father Albert Worby in foreground holding son Edmund and daughter Hilda

96

As it was school holiday time children often took their Fathers dinner at 12 o'clock and the men had half an hour for their 'elevenses'. When they used three horses on the binders these would have to have a rest. If the men were going to work late so as to finish off a field the horses would be changed for fresh ones brought up from the stables. Mothers sent their children with baskets covered in a white cloth covering a basin suet pudding and hot vegetables. men usually had cold tea to drink. My Father drank his without milk as in the hot weather milk tended to go off; even in winter he still had it the same way. The children would play around, lots of hide and seek, and then take the baskets home again. In the afternoon workers stopped for tea, 'fourses', as it was known. Mothers came with their children and fresh sandwiches, cakes and hot tea and brought it out to the fields. The men often had home-made beer and one day my brother was drinking some of this when a wasp stung his mouth. During Mr Wace's time from 1912 to 1926 families stayed on to play and watch the corn being cut down and the rabbit hunt. Men who were not able to have food brought to them had a sort of packed tea of half-a-loaf of bread with cheese or cornbeef or fat ham and onion eaten with a knife, plus cold tea. After Lord Walsingham took over all the farms he provided the fourses. His maids cut up sandwiches and slabs of cake and made hot tea which was put in huge metal cans and these would be taken to the harvest fields by the men. This was good in one way but it stopped all the families getting together and having chats, and this broke part of the pattern of old village life. In 1936 when Mr. Thornber took over Eastmere my Father, as Foreman, had to ask my Mother to make food ready and someone would collect and take it to the men on the fields. By that time I was away in London and so missed out on a lot of the activities and the local gossip. However Mother wrote to me twice a week about varous activities on the farms and new people in the village particularly the farmers who often changed at Michaelmas time.

When the shocks had dried out they would be carted by wagons to a stack near the farm where it was easy to thrash on a dry straw or brick foundation. These wagons had two large wheels at the back and two smaller ones at the front where two horses were attached to the shafts by chains and traces. They carried two men on top with another two men walking at each side throwing the sheaves on by pitchfork. 'Hold-gee' boys would ride the horses and guide them between the rows of shocks and through the gates. It was a happy time coming off the harvest field, chatting and running around; all the women got together and the men stayed to finish shocking up. Also there was the thrill of bouncing across the fields on the back of a wagon but as children we were never allowed on top of a load. After the corn was unloaded the bottom of the wagon was teeming with hundreds of crawling insects. The binders were left out all night but the men liked to take them to the next field in readiness for the following day's cutting, hoping for a dry morning. It was a long day starting at 5.30 a.m. and finishing very late: after 1942 on Capt. Denny's farm at Hingham, I worked until 11 o'clock at night when the clocks went on double time (they were put back two hours instead of one). After the shocks were carted away, a horse rake went over the fields and if they were not ploughed up, a chicken hut was put out for the poultry to feed, so there wasn't much opportunity to go gleaning for odd ears of corn on Eastmere Farm.

The teamsmen put their coats and dinner bags on the horses' collars and rode them side-saddle. Funny that they never rode those great beasts astride. On reaching the meadow near the farm buildings men would dismount and take their belongings off the horses and loosen the reins so the horses could have a nice long drink of water from the iron tank filled from Westmere Pit. This tank was always kept on the meadow just for the horses. No other animals were allowed to drink from it. My Father was very strict about this but I never understood why the horses had to have this special treatment. What was wrong with the beautiful spring water from the farm pump - unless it was too cold for them and Dad was afraid of the horses getting collic. After the horses had drunk as much as they wanted they made their way into the horseyard and the stables which had ten compartments each with its own manger and cobbled floor covered with straw. The horses were unharnessed and brushed down and given a good meal and later turned out onto the meadow where they would roll over and over in the grass. About 4.30 - 5.00 in the morning the Teamsmen would fetch the horses back to their stables to be groomed, fed and watered until work time. At the weekend the horses were taken to some meadows near the Church and fetched up on a Monday morning coming home across the field footpaths.

In the early days when Mr. Wace rented the farm, mares used to have foals which were reared on the farm. A little man came round with this huge stallion. It made him look like a dwarf but he walked miles with the beast on a rein; I wonder it didn't tread on him. We more or less knew what it came for and were very excited when the foals arrived. Father and Ted Williams would be up all night making sure the mare had a safe delivery; the same as they would if one of the horses caught collic. Both men loved their horses and being cousins they got on well.

Hilda Worby with horses Short & Bunny and dog Floss, 1930

Spragg family on tumbril cart 1930s

A Teamsman's day was long and the work tiring; apart from ploughing, They walked miles and miles with their horses and spent so long with them that a close bond existed between the men and their animals. This was especially true for my Dad with his 'Bunny' and 'Short'. All Teamsmen had their own way of communicating with horses but they shared common words of command like "Gir-up" for forwards, "wish" to go right, "Cub-ear" to go left, "Whoa" to stop, and "hub-back" to move backwards.

Men had to be highly skilled to build a stack of corn, flatten and thatch it so that it could withstand all weathers. My Father was often in charge and with the help of an elevator powered by a horse, a stack could be completed in a day's work. Men took great pride in this activity; the 'stacker' was responsible for everything and he was usually helped by two other men, one pitching from the elevator and one doing the binding. When the stack reached the eaves it was tapered to a point like the roof of a house and then it was thatched. Tom Spragg did the thatching of the stacks and my brother often helped him on a Saturday by placing the wet straw straight into a wooden frame which had be taken up a ladder on the side of the stack. Tom would pull out the straw and fasten it down with brotches made of hazel sticks. Eddie carried on this work after he left school working for the Mindham Brothers thatching or reeding houses and barns.

During the Autumn or Winter these stacks were threshed, i.e. the corn was separated from the straw. At the beginning of the nineteenth century such stacks were hand-processed - a very lengthy and labour-intensive business. Then corn was taken to be laid out in the huge barns and there it was beaten with a flail; basically two sticks joined by a flexible knot which could be used in a circular action like a whip. Groups of men would work together striking the corn in a steady rhythm - a skilled and tricky operation but mainly tedious, hard work. The introduction of threshing machines did away with this age-old practice. A complete tackle consisted of an engine, driven by coal and water, with a wheel connected to a threshing box with its drum and chaff cutter, plus an elevator which was placed near the stack. The farmers couldn't afford such large and expensive machines so they hired them from a contractor. We were all excited when the engine belonging to the brothers Bob and Henry Oldfield, came to thresh the stacks. Henry Oldfield was my Father's Uncle by marriage; his wife was Eliza Williams, my Grandmother's sister, but Bob, being the eldest, always seemed to be the boss. Both were little men with dark hair who wore moustaches. They kept their engine on a piece of land

Threshing corn on Eastmere Farm, 1930

near Mortimer Farm and we often met it puffing away on the road. The coal was kept in a heap by the cart shed on Eastmere Farm but it didn't burn very well on a domestic fire, although it wasn't too bad if we had a huge wooden blaze already.

Unless one has seen such monstrous beasts in action, it is hard to imagine, let alone describe, the thrill, the noise, the dust and the sense of danger of all those moving parts. No wonder so many people go to see these "Iron Ladies" at Burrell's Museum in Thetford or at Bressingham Gardens and that special shows are devoted to them. Usually Bob was the driver who secured the belt from the engine to the drum at the right tension. He stayed on the engine to work it and Henry was the stoker whose skill was to keep the fire hot with enough water for steam to drive the wheels and pulleys. Often cart loads of water and coal were needed during the day to keep the engine going. Into the top of the engine's fire box was screwed a large plug with a hole containing a lead filling. If the engine overheated the lead melted and the water rushed in to put out the fire. Some of the drivers didn't like the fire going out so they ignored this safety device and used a full plug with no hole. However, if the engine became short of water and this safety plug failed then the whole thing was likely to blow up. It seldom happened but in the year after I was born one famous incident occurred at Benniworth near Louth in Lincolnshire; on August 1st 1913 an engine blew itself in half killing the driver.

There is a fascinating clip of threshing as it used to be carried out in the film of Hardy's novel 'Tess of the D'Urbevilles'; it was very dirty work and difficult to avoid small pieces of corn going into clothes and down one's neck. People wore large handkerchiefs and scarves to keep out the dust and the smoke; everyone was blackened by the end of the day. Men stood on the top of a corn stack or a cart and pitch-forked sheaves onto the top of the wooden threshing box where a couple of men or women stood on a platform to cut the string binding the sheaves and push them into the drum. This was dangerous work and required concentration as the whole box vibrated and rocked to the rhythm of the drum's beaters separating the grain from off the straw. The elevator clanked away taking the straw up to the top of another stack where men spread it out evenly. A boy was employed to keep a horse moving in a circle under the elevator to make it work. Most of the weed seeds collected in the drum and the chaff was put into bags to be mixed with mangolds, swedes and cake to feed cattle and horses. The corn came out at the bottom of the box into sacks which were put on a tumbril and taken to the barn where it lay to dry off. It was bagged up again later and the teamsmen took it by horse and wagon ten miles to Thetford where it was put on the train and sent to market. This meant a very long and tiring day because there was a steep hill to climb at Croxton.

As the original corn stack shrank, mice and rats worked their way down to the bottom platform of hedge trimmings. Once all the sheaves had been threshed, the bottom was turned over for the dogs to pounce on the vermin which ran wildly in all directions. As children we gathered round to watch the entertainment; one day my friend Nesta had a mouse run up her leg and hide in her clothes and when she went to bed it jumped out much to her surprise. The men tied binder string round the bottom of their trousers in case rats tried to run up their legs. My brother began working on the farm when he was eleven years old but then he was such a big lad he was able to handle the horses. Children were around at weekends and in the evenings but during the harvest period an average day was 12 hours actual work, usually from 7 a.m. to 9 p.m. five days a week. On a Saturday men finished at 12 noon and since this was pay day they gathered in the cart shed to collect their earnings. I cannot remember there being a harvest supper in the village or at Eastmere and Westmere Farms. Parties were given at Christmas time. Perhaps the 1914-18 War stopped a lot of celebrating and it wasn't taken up again. There was always a Harvest Festival at both the Church and the Chapel.

Unfortunately Henry Oldfield died in 1926 and afterwards Bob didn't continue. His wife was dead and buried in Tottington churchyard so Bob went to live with a Mrs Anderson in Thompson. In any case by the late 1930s the combine harvester appeared and did away with the traditional harvest for most farm workers. These machines not only cut the corn, but threshed and baled as well. Nowadays their modern descendents tear across the huge hedgeless, treeless fields of Norfolk completing the harvest in a matter of days. By 1940 we had three tractors on the farm so all the work was done much quicker; this saved the poor labourers feet and of course the horses - although they still had their uses pulling carts - but the increased mechanisation costs jobs and led to horse-power being made redundant. I wonder what my Father and Grandfather would make of all the farming changes which have occurred in my lifetime. To them harvest was a special event; hard work which lasted a month, as men, women and children laboured in the fields to cut the corn, tie up the sheaves, pile them in shocks before they were carted away and stacked ready for threshing. It could be unremitting, dawn-to-dusk, back-breaking work, but as a child it was great fun; an interesting and enjoyable time when everyone came together to work and play.

After the harvest the fields were ploughed up and Winter wheat was sown by a large drill pulled by three horses. Smaller drills were used for setting root crops During the Winter in the bad weather, men cleaned the yards of manure and this was put in a mound or thrown on the fields. A tumbril was filled and the manure was dumped in heaps for the men to come along and spread it by forks. We did have a muck spreader pulled by a horse and this threw the muck all over the place. Later on a lot of artificial manure was used. After Mr Thornber came to Eastmere the duck muck made the crops really grow. My Father had fields ploughed up which had not been cultivated for years and grew good crops of corn during the war. When we had a big manure mound on the farm, my Father grew huge pumpkins on it and these kept us and other families in food for the winter.

Apart from the arable farming Lord Walsingham kept a large herd of dairy cattle on Westmere Farm and when he took over Eastmere in 1926 he began keeping a herd of pigs and they roamed all over his farms. There was a huge boar which my Father warned me to beware of and never to chase the pigs. His word was always law and we never doubted his common-sense. My brother, mother and I took our old pram out to collect acorns for which we received 6d a bushel; these were fed to the pigs. We were not a pork family but lots of the villagers

The 'Sandringham' class Savage No.474 built in King's Lynn 1889 standing outside the woodstore in Tottington. Henry Oldfield sitting on the engine and Bob Oldfield second from left.

kept pigs and often when we were at school we heard the poor pigs squealing as they were slaughtered.

As well as the hay and straw much of the farming was concerned with producing fodder for the livestock. Everything had to be planned on a farm at least a year ahead for no crop was grown two years running on the same piece of land. The old Norfolk Rotation included root crops like turnips and swedes for the feeding of cattle and sheep. All the straw and manure from the animals was spread back on the land to keep it fertile and produce heavier crops. In my time mangolds and swedes were put in a long mounds and covered with straw and earth to be kept during the Winter when they would be dug out and sliced for the cattle and horses to eat. Sugar-beet was relatively new, being introduced from Holland and did not become widespread in Norfolk until the 1920s. Even then Norfolk farmers needed convincing; they felt the crop would deprive the land of its goodness and reduce the arable fodder. When the plants had grown shoots, gangs of men went around hoeing and thinning them out (a job I hated). The men were paid so much a row and called it piece-work. Sugar-beet was harvested in the Autumn; again men worked in gangs and pulled them up one from each row, banged them together to shake off the soil, cut the tops off and laid them in rows across the field. The beet were carted by tumbril and put in heaps near a convenient gate to be picked up by lorries and taken to the nearest sugar-beet factory in Kings Lynn. The lorries worked quite late at night to try to get them in before the bad weather came. although I've known beet to be lying about in the snow and frost.

In the late Autumn after the Harvest and sugar-beet were safely gathered in, men would set to ditching and cutting hedges. Hedges were cut by 'slashes', a long wooden handled knife and it really was used for slashing; pieces of straggly wood were threaded into the hedge to thicken it all ready for the numerous birds nests in the springtime. Later on electric cutters were used although not on our farms. Today they make an awful mess of the hedgerows not like the old way when men wound and bound the hedges together. Most of the hedges were of thorn and in the spring would be full of what we called bread and cheese, the soft green shoots which were tasty to eat. As soon as the fields were ploughed and cultivated, the Winter corn would be sown. A strict rotation was essential to maintain the fertility of the soil which, after all, was the livelihood of the whole village.

Harold Spinks on tractor, Eastmere 1941

THE GAMEKEEPERS

The Breckland was well known for wildfowl, rabbits and hunting even before the nineteenth century when Merton became a famous shooting Estate, along with Hilborough, Lynford, Clermont and others. In 1759 a famous incident occurred concerning William Tooke, from the nearby village of Thompson, who shot some pheasants on the land of Sir Thomas de Grey the local Knight of the Shire, *"on which the latter dispatched his gamekeeper to Mr Tooke with a message no-one should kill game on his lands without his consent"* ; whereupon Tooke went to a common near the house of de Grey and destroyed all the hares he could find. The antipathy continued and even more antagonism occurred in 1774 when Sir Thomas de Grey asked Sir Edward Astley to present a Bill to the House of Commons *"for enclosing the waste land, commons, and pastures in the parish of Tottington"*. This would deprive villagers of their traditional rights upon the commons and create landless men. Tooke owned forty acres in Tottington and opposed the Bill. On 7th February Astley brought both petitions to the House of Commons. The Enclosure Act won the day. Tooke had been introduced to John Horne, a clerk in Holy Orders reading for the law and hoping to be called to the Bar, who wrote an anonymous letter to the 'Public Adviser' attributing partiality to the Speaker. This scandalised the House which ordered Mr. Woodfall, the publisher, to appear before it, and Horne was arrested whilst in Tooke's house. The matter was cleared up with a public apology but Tooke and other villagers lost their right to use the common lands; Sir Thomas de Grey became Lord Walsingham in 1780.

The Enclosure process went on for another hundred years into the nineteenth century but local people still considered the woods and commons as public lands and the wildlife as extra food and a means to supplement their income. Recognising this the Tottington Enclosure had awarded 60 acres as a fuel allotment for the poor but by 1845 part of the land had been fenced round as a covert for pheasants, and gradually common land disappeared. It might not have mattered had farming prospered. creating more jobs and higher wages, or if there had been industries in Norfolk to offer alternative employment to the farm workers. As is well known, the early part of the nineteenth century was a time of great distress for the agricultural labourer and his family, with unemployment, low wages and high corn prices, leading to poverty and discontent expressed in agrarian riots throughout East Anglia. This situation was made worse by the population growth in Norfolk which nearly doubled in size from 273,479 in 1801 to 442,714 in 1851. The great necessity was food and surprisingly agricultural labourers remained some of the worst fed of all workers in the nineteenth century.

Even in the 1850s agricultural labourers' wages were only about 8s a week whereas cottage annual rents ranged from £2 to £5, so if the landlord took between 1s and 2s a week, there wasn't much left to feed a large family. During the Crimean War in 1854 bread went up to 1s per 4 lb loaf, sugar to 8d. per lb, tea to 6p. per ounce, cheese to 1s. 6p. per lb. Most farm labourers could not afford to buy pork let alone mutton or beef; to them meat meant pheasant, partridge, rabbit and hare. For this reason, what the law called poaching was an essential aspect of peasant life, however hazardous and harshly punished; it saved families from starvation.

The wealthy, who had the right to vote and make laws, prized and

Gamekeepers of Merton Park at the turn of the century

protected their property. Farmers often turned a blind eye to minor incidents but those who owned large estates and made hunting, shooting and fishing, profitable enterprises, saw the poacher as the worst menace; to be fined, sentenced to prison and hard labour, or transported to Australia. From the time of the Black Act in 1723, the Game Laws were repressive and vindictive. For poaching wasn't just the preserve of the poor peasant. It was also a lucrative sideline which gave rise to criminal gangs; in the 1830s partridges and pheasants sold at 3s and 8s a brace respectively, and hares fetched from 2s. 6d. to 3s. each. During the nineteenth century the *Norfolk Chronicle and Norwich Gazette* reported many cases of poaching; amongst those convicted were farmers, blacksmiths, wheelwrights, shoemakers, bakers, carpenters, brickmakers, shepherds and even gamekeepers. Gamekeeping became an important occupation from the eighteenth century onwards. An advertisement of October 1820 said:

WANTED: A good GAMEKEEPER over a large Manor, unmarried or married with no children; he must understand the whole of his business, be complete master the art of rearing and preserving all kinds of Game, and also of killing Vermin, he must be accustomed to all the tricks of Poachers, and must not be afraid of them, he must be strong, active, hardy, sober and honest, and have an undeniable character from his last place.

It was an unenviable job spying on farmers and labourers alike. Wages were not high but the Keeper might gain a free cottage, some coal and firewood, his clothes, tips and hunting fees (in the 1890s this was about 15 shillings a week). The temptation to supplement his wage by illegal killing was always there, and some made arrangments with local poachers for a cut.

Nights, spent lying out in all weathers in pursuit of poachers, tested their nerves and was burdensome but the keepers had to keep poaching down otherwise their jobs were forfeit. Originally all sorts of methods were used to stop the illegal taking of game - man-traps and spring-guns; the latter loaded with shot and set off by trip-wire could be used to scare someone but often they killed or maimed innocent men, women and children. They were widely advertised by notice and public crier to warn people and deter their entering land as trespassers. However public outcry led to an Act of Parliament in 1827 which made spring-guns illegal. As a result the Game Laws were tightened up and by 1831 transportation became common as a punishment for poaching. In most cases, confrontation, threat of the Keeper's dog or just the gamekeeper's physical presence were often enough to deter or scare off poachers. Nevertheless, the taking of game was widespread at all levels, and the Gamekeeper had to keep his wits about him

Usually gamekeepers stood apart from the village and were closely linked to the police. A reward of £100 was offered for the Merton Gang which raided Lord Walsingham's Estate during the early nineteenth century. On December 24th 1819, a man called Gaymer and 14 others went to Merton New Wood to kill game; seven had guns and the rest bludgeons. The Gamekeeper, named Watson, was drawn to the Wood by the sound of gun firing and came with nine helpers. "A dreadful contest ensued" ; Watson was assaulted and robbed, three others were severely beaten. The facts were detailed in court: William Pearman, Robert Bailey, Wlliam Mottam and Charles Howes were given 7 years transportation; Samuel Young and Henry Plain were given two years imprisonment in Swaffham Bridewell; George Jessup and George Mapes were given 1 year each in Aylsham Bridewell, *(from the Norwich Chronicle and Norwich Gazette of Jan 15, 1820 and Feb 26 1820).*

The new police were established in 1839 and by 1841 there were 143 policemen in Norfolk, the ratio being 1 'Bobby' to 2,142 people. By 1846 237 cases of transportation had taken place largely for poaching. Police were used as infiltrators to break up a poaching gang in 1850. The total number of poaching cases in Norfolk from 1857-62 numbered 1,450 of which only 38 were recorded for the Wayland Hundred. A Gamekeeper, James Bush, lived in Tottington from 1841 to 1861, which appears to have been a quiet period; no cases are recorded from the village but there was one serious incident at Merton. On the 10th Dec 1859 George Crowe and Samuel Dickerson both labourers were given 8 years penal servitude for shooting at Lord Walsingham's Keeper Israel Buckle, which was a very harsh penalty considering there were several cases in that year of men night-poaching and shooting at keepers yet given only 5 months or less hard labour. The Buckle family were Gamekeepers from generation to generation for nearly two hundred years. Israel (bn.1818) was the son of Israel Buckle (1769-1873) and his wife Mary Howlett (1796-1831) who are buried at Merton on the left at the back of the churchyard after entering through the wooden gateway. A younger brother, Robert Buckle (1799 - 1874) married Marie Dalton (1802 - 1886) and is recorded in the 1841 Census as living in Tottington; they were my Gt, Gt, Grandparents on my Mother's side.

Whilst the gamekeepers and police were enforcing new laws like the

1862 Poaching Prevention Act, the development of Merton as a Shooting Estate continued apace. During the nineteenth century many coverts, which acted as wind breaks, were planted for pheasant rearing, e.g. Cardogan, Raglan, Prince Albert, Cardigan, as well as Sturston and Cherry Row, and those of Blackbreck and Nettleshill south of Merton village. A unique system of growing hedges of Scots pine was introduced to shelter the fields and oblige the pheasants to fly high. This has resulted in the strange, mis-shaped pine trees which stand in rows and are a major feature of the present landscape. As the sporting value of the land grew, more and more trees were planted and pheasant rearing became an obsession. Good 'shoots' were easy to let whilst the rentals of farms fell by a third. Before the First World War the then Lord Walsingham introduced red grouse but these have long since died out. The Breckland was an excellent environment and tens of thousands of wildfowl were reared annually since it was quite common to shoot a thousand birds or more in one day, including pheasant, partridges, several varieties of duck, pigeons and swans. Many of the local people were involved in one way way or another with this slaughter either as gamekeepers, the Hunts and Buckles, or as beaters driving the birds out of the woods, or as poachers. Reading the records one gains the impression that anything which moved was shot including otters, deer, rabbits and rats!

Whether this sporting activity was worthwhile or not is open to

Using ferrets to catch rabbits, pre-WWI
Foreground: John Williams and John Worby

question. With the late nineteenth century decline in agriculture and the fall in the price of cereals, farming wasn't financially viable and landowners felt that the shoots kept the large estates going. Rider-Haggard wrote that *"profit derived from sporting rents was overrated as the great expense of preserving was not sufficiently considered"*. Lord Walsingham admitted that *"the sale value of game killed . . . about represented the actual cash profit over the cost of its upkeep"* but felt, *"the majority of owners in that district would receive no advantage from their land were it not for its suitability to the purpose of game rearing"*. Yet Merton's Estate Agent, Miss Lucilla Reeve bemoaned the spending of £10,000 a year on 28 days shooting:

> . . . *Shooting has been the curse of the estates and the countryside . . . when you have seen the woods neglected and acres of land used for no other crop than brank or other food for game, thousands of pounds spent each year in order that they might be driven over the coverts one way before luncheon, turn about and driven back to the guns the other way in the afternoon - I neither call this sport or good for the land or the people. Without game and rabbits I could have turned the Merton Estate into one of the finest agricultural estates in the country. . . .The money we got from letting the shooting could have been more than made up by increased rent from the farms. These have been very low because of the damage done each year to the crops by pheasants.*
> (Farming on the Battleground)

From October to February nearly everyone of any consequence joined in these shoots and if there wasn't a lot to do on the farms at that time men went for a day's 'brushing' and so earned a little more money. Children had to keep out of the way when shooting occurred but the young boys liked to go brushing and sometimes they got dreadfully soaked and cold what with the winter weather and wet undergrowth. Keepers would be in charge and organised everything: the gun positions were carefully marked and enough beaters hired so that plenty of birds flew into the path of the guns. Ladies and gentlemen came from different places sometimes even London for a day's shoot. Usually the keeper dogs retrieved the birds and they were put in a game van, like a small wagon with a canvas hood, and taken to a sorting place. For a long time the other Teamsman, Ted Williams, used to drive the game van with two of the Eastmere Farm horses and it would often be dark when he came home through Merton Park with lights on.

Rabbits and hares were also hunted - there were so many of them that their numbers had to be kept down. Nevertheless keepers tried to stop poachers using a noose of twisted brass wire placed about a thumb's height above the ground to 'snare' rabbits, and banned the traditional 'gin-traps' which once trodden on, snapped upwards clamping the paw. Poachers were discouraged from working with greyhounds on parts of the open heath by the barbed wire fastened about a foot from the ground to stakes which were laid out in a zigzag pattern. Keepers considered weasels and stoats to be vermin. Stoats dig into burrows and kill rabbits by biting their necks; men used to say *"There's nawthing wrong with an old rabbit a stoot have kilt"* because the meat could always be used to feed a dog or the ferrets. Some farmers could mimick the cry of a frightened rabbit in order to lure the stoat from its shelter and then shoot the animal when it sat up on its hind legs like a dog begging; or they would burn off the sedge in Autumn and catch stoats in traps.

The Warreners trapped rabbits in large numbers using nets to enclose an area of a burrows, and setting dogs like lurchers on them. Ferrets were unmuzzled but secured by lines to withdraw them from the rabbit holes when the work was done. The frightened rabbit rushed out of its burrow to escape but flew into the net where it was picked up by a dog which brought it to the Warrener or one of his helpers. The animal's neck was wrung and it was 'gutted' and then 'huddled' (the blade of a knife was passed between the bone of the thigh and the great sinew to make a hole through which the other foot was passed). In this way the rabbits could be strung on a pole for convenient packing and carrying. We were never allowed to touch partridges or pheasants and people were pretty honest about this. Occasionally there was news of the odd poacher and of course if a funny shaped rabbit got into the pot no questions were asked. We lived on rabbits and enjoyed the meat; they were lovely cooked in so many different ways, baked or boiled. in a pie or pudding, and could be eaten cold and packed up in a dinner bag. When rabbits are gutted the intestines are taken out leaving the kidneys, heart, and liver, all intact. We were taught quite early in life to skin rabbits; quite easy really almost like taking a romper suit off a child. The skin each side of the body was pulled back after the paws were cut off. The back legs were pushed up through the opening. A sharp knife loosened the flesh near the tail and then the skin was pulled up over the ribs, the neck and head. The eyes were removed and the rabbit dejointed and all the flesh was used, even the brains were a delicacy. A gypsy came round on a Saturday morning to give us about 6d for a rabbit or mole skin which had been hung out to dry. If anyone caught a hare it was never broadcast because we were not suppposed to take them; we ate hares but they they have a different taste to rabbits and were not nearly so popular. Sometimes people would come on the farms and used greyhounds to catch the hares which were kept until nearly rotten and cooked in a jar; this was known as 'jugged hare' and considered a delicacy.

My Grandfather, John Warby, was the last Warrener in Tottington; the disappearance of this old-fashioned occupation was somewhat foolish. All my young life there were so many rabbits that they became a menace, eating up the corn, etc. They were kept under strict control at Eastmere, seldom was a hole seen on cultivated fields but they were found in the hedgerows. Rabbits took over the sandy unused pieces of land adjoining the fields which they invaded to eat the corn. There was quite a long strip in front of Jubilee Plantation where only breaks and cankerweed grew and this was heavily populated with rabbits. Farmers tried gassing them but this wasn't satisfactory so a deadly disease called mexamatosis was introduced. It was terribly cruel to the animals destroying their nervous system; the poor things could be seen dragging themselves along with swollen heads and bodies and nearly always blind. It was a very short-sighted approach as the meat was no longer fit to eat and this removed a major source of protein from the traditional rural diet. The old way was better when the Warrener's ferrets gave the rabbit a quick clean death. So much money was spent on rearing pheasants for the shoots, surely a few men could have been employed to

Warrener: John Worby

keep the rabbits in check? Now that Tottington is in the Battle Area and more like a wild life reserve, the rabbits are plentiful again and look healthy. Keepers are still employed by the War Office to keep the vermin down. As live ammunition has been used so widely in the area it might be difficult to have an organised shoot but these are still held on Merton Park Estate.

Lord Walsingham's former Estate was about 8000 acres much of it reserved for game and shooting. He employed several gamekeepers who had their separate territories including the farms which were let. They had a particular form of dress and looked alike in fawn Norfolk jackets and breeches and buskins with soft cloth hats like deerstalkers. They always carried a gun, usually a 12 bore, and kept the pidgeons and crows in check because they ate the corn shoots especially near a wood. A Mr Fred Woolsey who lived at Merton, was the Head Gamekeeper in all the years I was at Tottington, but one particular keeper lived in the next village of Little Cressingham and his name was Tom Tolman. We didn't like him, being such a burly fellow who always had his double-barrelled gun under his arm. Many a time he accused us of taking birds' eggs (and sometimes he was right, much to my shame now). We were not taught to be kind to wild animals and birds as the children are today. The keepers tried to protect the birds nests but children would take eggs for no particular reason. However, we never touched robin eggs as there was an old superstition that your arm would fall off and we believed it. Sometimes whilst out walking we would accidently tread on a nest of eggs near the hedgerows, and pee-wits, plover, and lapwings often had their nests destroyed by the horses' feet and farm implements.

If we spotted Mr. Tolman coming along a hedgerow near the farm the first thing we did was to get our cats safely in the shed because if they strayed he was likely to shoot them saying they interferred with his game birds. Partridges and pheasants always have their nests on the ground so cats can easily catch the little ones. Of course the same was true of foxes which were shot occasionally but they were considered sport for the 'Hunt' with its hounds and horses. It caused great excitement to see the red coats and the beagles which came from Merton Hall and were kept in the stables there, but the farmers didn't like the Hunt coming over their land treading down the young corn. We seldom saw a fox in the wild but their handy work was only too evident when they raided our chicken houses at night coming out of the woods nearby. Once we had some young pullets and somehow a fox got into the chicken house and killed them all. Not content with catching one

114

Gamekeeper: Arthur Hunt, 1907

and running off with it they bite the necks of as many as they can. In the same way foxes destroy all the pheasant eggs if they get into a hatchery. Mind you all animals can be spiteful to one another. We had a chicken called Joey, the only one left out of a setting and it went to roost on the back of my Father's chair. Eventually when we put it in with the hens they nearly pecked it to death!

When Mr. Tolman left a Mr. Sturman took over and stayed at the lodge on Tuddenham's Corner, He had a motor-bike so got around a bit more but we were not so frightened of our cats being destroyed by him. The children in the village used to go 'nutting' in the Tuddenham's Plantation and up Butterhole along the Thetford road. We, at Eastmere, always went to Cut-throat and Shepherd's Plantation, and my Father wore a big smock coat with large pockets to put the nuts in.

My Uncle *Arthur Leonard Hunt* (1874-1970), son of Walter Hunt (1833-1922) was the Gamekeeper who looked after Tottington village. 'Hunt' was a common name in the area and there were several families in and around Thompson; my own Great Aunt Elizabeth Collin Warby married a Christmas Hunt and lived at Pockthrope in Thompson, resulting in numerous descendents. However, 'Old Watt' came from Shropham where his parents John and Mary lived at the Keeper's Lodge. He had two brothers, William, also a Keeper, and Robert. Watt's first marriage to Susan, resulted in two children before she died; his second, to Emma Roseanna Oldfield (1849-1929) produced nine other children. She was the daughter of Hannah Sturgeon (1815-1852) and James Oldfield (1810-1881) the brother of Hannah Oldfield, who was the Grandmother of Rose Alice Warby (1879-1967) whom Arthur Hunt married in 1900.

Originally they lived in a house in Merton; to reach it we had to cross

Fishing on Thompson Watering, early 1900s

a little bridge over a large ditch beside the road. When Tottingham became vacant as a territory, Uncle Arthur came to our village to live in a large, attractive place called Water House, set in pretty woods near Thompson Watering. This was an artificial lake, surrounded by trees, where people went fishing, which is still its main use today. The 5th Lord Walsingham had a tributary of the river Wissey dammed and the pit was allowed to flood to create a mere in 1847. There was a boathouse there with a large sluice gate surrounded by thick wooden boards about a foot high, where water gushed through to form part of the stream running from Thompson onto Stanford Watering. It was a noisy and exciting place but parents warned their children not to play near it as the narrow passage way of the sluice was very deep and dangerous. We often went to sit on the side of the Watering and watch the wildlife: there were lots of flowers such as king cups, water lillies and bull rushes plus all sorts of birds including swans, ducks, wild geese, and water fowls. It was the perfect place for a gamekeeper's family except for the swarms of gnats flying around which often sent us home covered in itchy bumps. I used to be bitten something dreadful and had really sore legs. If couples went courting there this gave the game away and people would say, "Ah I know where yu wus las' night". Sometimes we used lavender water or eau-de-cologne to keep the gnats away and Auntie Rose wore a piece of elder in her hat.

When Uncle Arthur was a young man he was a close friend of my Father; together with several other young men they used to go bell ringing to the local villages. Everyone enjoyed going to see the Hunts; not only was it a lovely place but we were made so welcome. The house had a huge sitting room which led off to a living room up three steps; it was always full of my other cousins and relatives. Auntie Rose had six children: Alice Mary (1900), Minnie Helen (1901), Sidney Arthur (1904), Reginald (1905), Jack (1906), Frank George (1913); and she brought up a grandson born to Minnie in 1919, christened Joby Nelson Leonard Hunt. When Mother went to visit she played their piano and we would have a great sing-song. I stayed there once or twice and often on a Sunday evening we went for a cycle ride to see them, a journey of nearly four miles from Eastmere. When I was young everyone rode bicycles but later Frank bought a motor-bike as did Joby.

Of the children, Jack carried on the family tradition and went as Keeper to a village called Sporle and married a lady called Dolly. Reggie joined the Army and brought home his pal, Harry Street, whom his sister Minnie started a relationship with. They married in 1929 and lived at Thetford. Frank married Dolly Macro, lived in Tottington village, and had a son named Malcolm Frank who sadly died in August 1932 after seven weeks; but thankfully, their second son, Colin, survived. Frank was called up during the Second World War and enlisted in the Norfolk Regiment which was sent out to Singapore. Practically as soon as it arrived, the Japanese attacked, and he was captured, spending the remainder of the War as a prisoner in Japan.

Arthur had several dogs, mainly Spaniels, which were kept on chains outside although there was always one to be found inside the house. He also had lots of chickens and ducks; rabbits were kept by the children who helped Arthur with his huge garden, full of flowers and vegetables, of which he was rightly proud. He bred huge numbers of birds during the rearing season from May to July. Eggs were collected from nests in the fields and put under a broody hen. Wire cages kept the pheasants in during the Spring and hatching time. As with young chickens, hard boiled eggs had to be given to the newly hatched pheasants so my Aunt had a busy time feeding all the chicks. The hens strutted around with all the little pheasants and lived in hen coops; ducks were often brought up this way too. The pheasants were given a good start in life before they drifted away into the cornfields but only heavy feeding thereafter prevented them flying off to other Estates. It was hard work but essential to produce a good stock of game to reinforce the depleted ranks in preparation for the shooting season.

Arthur Hunt was still Gamekeeper at Tottington when the Army took over in 1942; the family moved to live at Pockthorpe, in a funny, little cottage with small rooms and low ceilings. Joby still lives at Thompson having married a girl called Shirly Syer. Aunt Rose died on 6th November 1967 aged 86 and Uncle Arthur died in 1970 aged 96, having lived with Frank and Dolly on Merton road just outside Merton Park. Dolly died on 14th March 1985 and Frank still lives there with his chickens and ducks selling eggs to local villagers. His son Colin married Annette Dring having two children, Stephen and Jane Sally both of whom are married with their own children, which makes cousin Frank a Great-Grandfather.

As far as I know Keepers are still employed in the Battle Area by the War Office to keep the vermin down. Much of the land has been allowed to return to its wild state as true Breckland with a unique flora and fauna. Last time we visited, the rabbit population had re-established itself with a vengeance and there were plenty of pheasant and pigeon as well as deer.

Arthur Hunt with Rose (Worby) plus sidney, Jack and Frank

118

THE SHEPHERDS

At one time sheep were the main livestock on the old Merton estate run by the De Grey family. During the 1830s and 1840s, the 4th Lord Walsingham harnessed and improved the poor Breckland soil by marling the land and encouraging his tenant farmers to keep large flocks of sheep. These were walked on the heathland pasture and folded on turnips and clover during the winter, continuing a practice established in Norfolk by estate owners such as Thomas Coke of Holkheim during the 18th century.

Place names like *Shepherd's Plantation* and *Shepherd's Field* on Eastmere Farm along the Cressingham Road, often denote long-term usage, and Tottington Census Records testify to the importance of sheep rearing in and around the village. From the 1830s to the 1850s Edward Bennett (born Ovington, 1796) lived in Shepherd's House near Green Lane; William Cook (born Saham Toney, 1803) and his eldest son, James (born 1826), lived by the West Hall; and Joseph Frost (aged 30) was also recorded as a shepherd in 1841. A number of 'sheep-boys' were recorded in the 1851 Census: William Macro (aged 18); Edmund Boughen (11); Samuel Chaston (11); John Macrow (11); Robert Oldfield (10); Robert Stubbing (15); and Thomas Cook (13) son of William Cook. My own Gt. Grandfather's third son, Henry Worby (aged 14) was recorded as a 'shepherd-boy'.

In many rural areas shepherds were among the most skilled and respected members of a village community. They worked long hours alone with the sheep on the heath, making their own decisions. Such solitary work created men of an independent nature with peculiar knowledge such that shepherding was often passed on from Father to son, generation after generation. However this does not appear to have been the case in Tottington. Edward Bennet married Mary Cocks, the daughter of William Cocks (from Thetford) and Elizabeth Mackrow (from Sturston). They had a large family but none of the children became shepherds. The Cook family did for a while but it was a hard life and none of the sheep-boys carried on the role. Farmers had to be certain of such men before entrusting the welfare of a flock of sheep to the ability, common-sense and trust-worthiness of a man and his dog. As the farms changed hands each new tenant employed his own shepherd.

Throughout the 1860s to the 1890s, shepherds came and went from Tottington. The 1861 Census records John Webb (born Bury St. Edmunds, 1800) living in the Shepherd's House; William Brunny (aged

30) from Icklingham in Suffolk, a shepherd lodging with John Flatt; and Alfred Watson (aged 10) as a shepherd boy. In 1871 James Dennis (aged 38) and his son (aged 19) were working as shepherds for the farmer John Lincoln (from Watton) who farmed 590 acres of Westmere and employed 14 men and 5 boys. The disastrous 'Black '79' and the cold Winter of 1880-81, ruined agriculture and caused millions of sheep in England to die, but in Tottington, during the 1880s, George Fuller (born 1841) and John Wilson (born at Bridgham, 1813) were shepherds, as were Isaac Boughen (born at Sturston 1831), and William Hancock (born in Ovington, 1821), from 1871 to 1891. William's son Walter Hancock (born 1854) and John G. Quantrill (born 1867), living at Eastmere Farm Cottage, were shepherds from the 1890s up until the First World War.

When I was young, a man called Mr Belham was a shepherd at Hall Farm. They lived in the village and had five grown up children. Nellie, worked for Lord Walsingham as a sewing maid; Lily who also worked there for a time before she married Arthur Oldfield, my Father's cousin. Jack, the eldest son was wounded in World War I leaving him with a stiff leg; as a result he only ever had one pedal on his bicycle. He hired the little meadow and buildings next to my Grandfather's. The last shepherd in Tottington was my Uncle Thomas Spragg (1876 - 1951) from the nearby village of Thompson, who married Father's eldest sister Florence Warby (1878 - 1962), and had ten children. Thomas came from a long line related to the Lake's and Pooley's, his parents being William Spragg (1835 - 1908) and Sarah Downes (1836 - 1917) the daughter of Isaac Downes (1801 - 1868) and Sarah Wyer (1799 - 1879) from Stow Bedon - two of whose children married Oldfield's. Thomas's own Gt. Grandparents were James Spragge and Elizabeth Archer (md: 10.12.1811); his Gt.Gt.Grandparents were Henry Spragge and Anne Fulsher (md: 8.11.1762).

After they married, 20th September 1900, Thomas and Florrie lived in Thompson but soon moved to a pleasant, thatched cottage opposite St. Andrew's Church in the lane near Church Meadows. He was a small, dark-haired man with a moustache, well-known for telling jokes, and very fond of his baccy; he would cut a piece off his twist and chew it until his mouth and teeth turned quite black. Tom owned a pony and cart, several collie dogs and looked after a flock of about 200 black-faced South Down ewes kept by Mr Wace from Carbrooke who rented Westmere, Eastmere and Sturston Farms from 1912 up until the 1920s.

Spragg's House in front of Tottington Church

For a time he was assisted by his sons, Cyril (born 1909) and the twins, Albert and Frederick (born 1912) who were named after my Father and his brother. When Col. George de Grey took over Eastmere Farm in 1926, his interest was the dairy herd at Westmere so sheep-rearing went into a rapid decline. Tom ceased to be a shepherd; instead, along with his son Tommy, he worked a small-holding just past The Crossways (which was the field where Henry and Bob Oldfield used to keep their threshing machine and engine).

Tom Spragg often wore a brown smock and a large, wide-brimmed hat, as well as breeches and buskins and heavy hob-nail boots. Shepherd's smocks were usually white, made of drab twilled linen, and often had long, hanging 'poacher's' pockets to hide the occasional dead rabbit. Today the shepherd's tools are part of folk-lore and only seen in films or museums. Tom's proverbial crook was iron rather than wood, fashioned by the local blacksmith to a specific design. Since each breed of sheep differed in shape and size a uniform crook would not suffice. They were used like walking sticks but their main purpose was to catch hold of sheep - not around the neck but slid up the hind leg so that the thigh was immovably fixed in the curve. By neatly twisitng the wrist, the shepherd could throw the sheep over on to its back and then examine it with no trouble. It was unusual for the shepherd to shear his own sheep; this was a highly skilled task which required patience and strength in order to cut the fleece off the sheep in one piece, and was carried out by a team of workmen who travelled from farm to farm. The wide-bladed scissors called 'shears' were an ancient tool used for clipping wool (and sometimes for hair-cutting) but over time the basic design has been adapted to alternative uses like hedge and plant clipping, trimming lawn edges, thatching, etc.

During the harvesting of crops, sheep were moved every few days to feed on the leaves of swedes, turnips and mangolds, cut off and left in the fields. All farm workers carried shet knives used for eating food, gutting rabbits and cutting off lambs' tails but sometimes shepherds carried a small hatchet called a beet-chopper. This was used to break up the root crops into small pieces so that the animals could eat them more easily especially since older sheep often lost their teeth and could starve to death without assistance. Iron hurdles, like gates on six small wheels, were taken from field to field and a piece of land was sectioned off. Restricting the area was rather important as the shepherd had to be careful not to allow sheep to gorge themselves as their stomachs would blow up with gas and this could kill them.

In daylight sheep could be identified from colour marks painted on the fleece and through the sound of the sheep bell worn by the leading animal which the rest of the flock followed. Candle lanterns and then hurricane lamps were essential for night duty and finding one's way around the pens especially during the lambing season. During March Tom Spragg built a nice snug lambing yard out of bales of straw near the farm buildings, and lived in a little wooden hut on wheels with a huge roaring fire outside in an iron grating. He used to come over to Eastmere Cottage for a cup of tea or a glass of wine and a chat with Mum. If a sheep lost its lamb, the dead animal's coat could be put on a substitute lamb and in this way orphans could be cared for. Sometimes, when a lamb was weak or its mother died, Mrs Sculfer would take it into the Farmhouse and fed it using a teated milk bottle. It was very important not to lose any of the lambs as Tom received a bonus for them. Most of the lambs had dark faces but we always looked for the white-faced ones. It all depended on the 'tup' which is what we called the male breeding sheep; we never used the word ram.

I remember, as a child, seeing Uncle Tom Spragg at the sheep dipping. A team of men came and brought their own equipment; a large tub, deep enough to submerge even the largest sheep, was filled with water taken from a clean pit (pump water was considered too cold and could chill the sheep) and a packet of yellow dipping powder was added. Fixed to the tub was a slatted drying rack where the dipped sheep lay whilst excess water was squeezed out back into the tub. A board allowed the sheep to slide down and run back to join the flock. Each sheep was caught, lifted and lowered feet upwards and held there for a specified time for the dip to be effective. As with the shearing, it was difficult and thirsty work so beer was brought in large stone bottles and drunk from mugs during the morning and afternoon breaks. It was also a social occasion which many villagers turned out to watch and the local 'Bobby', P.C. Legge, was there to ensure it conformed to the local by-laws.

Thomas and Florence Spragg had a large family:

May Daisy	14. 10. 1905-	married Francis Reynlds
Thomas (Tommy)	24. 10. 1907	unmarried
Cyril Frank	10. 4. 1909	married Winnifred Perkins
Eva	4. 10. 1910	married Frank Duke
Albert Edward	31. 3. 1912	married Rene Blanche Morris
Frederick Ernest	31. 3. 1912	married Muriel Golding
Dorothy Blanche	18. 1. 1914	unmarried
Doris Louise	18. 1. 1914	married Joe Sullivan
Kathleen Frances	23. 6. 1917	married Arthur Edward Bourner
Clifford Carles	2. 7. 1923	married Helen Ring

Tommy, Cyril, Fred, Albert, Eva, Doris, Dolly, May,
Tom and Florence Spragg, Clifford and Kathleen

Somehow or other Aunt Florrie had hurt her foot whilst in service (it was always wrapped up) and she could not walk properly; indeed I never remember her walking! She was like my mother, a little on the stout side. When bobbed-hair came in fashion she kept her hair short. Money was a perpetual problem for them, what with a large family they were always in need of things. Their house often needed repairs but then many of the dwellings in Tottington were not maintained well and were usually cold and damp. Naturally families were close and tried to help one another. Uncle Tom had lots of sheep dogs and one of these became my favourite pet.

Like other young children I always wanted a puppy and plagued my Father to get me one. My Mother used to tell us stories of their dog Nell, which only encouraged me. When I was aged twelve I sat on the sofa with my Father and begged him to let us have a dog. He sang a song to me, "Daddy wouldn't buy me a bow-wow. I've got a little cat and I'm very fond of that but I'd rather have a bow-wow-wow". In the end he relented and Uncle Tom gave us a cross Collie, he had bought to train as a sheep dog but she was too young. We named her Floss, a lovely little puppy black with four white feet, a white collar and front, and a white tip on her tail. The cats didn't like her at first but soon settled down. Floss was a bundle of mischief and we all fell in love with her. Everywhere we went so went Floss. She chased the low flying pee-wits across the fields making herself sick but later developed more sense. Playing hide and seek was a favourite pastime; one off us kept her whilst the others hid around the farm but Floss always found everyone. Ball games were her special passion;

Hilda Worby with Floss

124

football, cricket, and tennis, Floss would be there to trap or catch the ball. My brother used to throw a ball high into the air, nearly out of sight, but she would still run and catch it. We allowed her to live with us indoors, sleeping in her own wicker basket by the wall oven. and never put her on a chain. One night, accidentally, I left her outside and Father gave me a right telling off; he became as fond of Floss as anyone. She never grew very big but eventually the time came for her to be taken for training. When we saw her tied behind Uncle Tom's cart and frantic to get away, we cried, it nearly broke our hearts. He taught her a lot including obedience but in the end Tom said we had spoilt her and she wasn't any good as a sheep dog. It was with great joy that we received her back. In exchange my Father gave Uncle two navy blue boys suits for his twin sons. Money was scarce and these did him more than a good turn.

When Floss was quite young she followed my Dad around and one Sunday morning he was cutting down nettles with a reef hook and, not aware that Floss was behind him, swung the hook and cut her nose in half just along the line of her mouth. We were all so upset but she recovered and it taught her a valuablke lesson never to get too close in future to someone who was working. We were taught to take good care of her at all times. There was a mongrel collie called Jerry which had belonged to one of Lord Walsingham's gardeners. He was a terrible wanderer, and on one occasion managed to get into our garden. My Father was ploughing across the fields in sight of the house and when he saw what happened, left his horses and ran all the way home. He was afraid that Floss would have puppies so Mother and I didn't half get a telling off. Jerry often got a good beating for his efforts but it never deterred him. Actually I would have liked Floss to have had some pups as she was such a lovely dog and I'm sure her offspring would have been the same.

After my brother and I left home Floss became my Mother's pal, but whenever we returned on holiday, she was ready for a ball game. She sat for hours on our sofa watching for my Mother to return from playing piano at the socials in the village. Her barking told us precisely when Mother's bicycle was coming down the lane. The chickens never had to be rounded up, Floss brought them all home safely. Without adequate exercise she put on a lot of weight as she grew older but she lived to be fourteen dying in 1938. It was like losing one of the family; she was a great friend: her loss nearly broke my Mother's heart, and I have never forgotten her.

Tommy Spragg's Ford Car

My Father tried to replace Floss with another dog called Mick but we only kept him for a short while as he suffered from fits and had to be put down. Next came Nellie, a mongrel and not a patch on Floss; we never took to her as she was anybody's dog, although we always treated her kindly. She had some puppies by a pedigree collie, and Father kept two, a black and a brown one. The latter grew up to be a lovely dog marked exactly like a collie, white collar and front and a beautiful thick coat. We called him Jumbo and since Nellie ran off every so often, Father gave her away to a man from Thompson village. We loved Jumbo as much as Floss but occasionlly he was put on a chain and slept outside. He didn't appear to mind and was the most obedient and knowing animal I ever knew although not a player of games like Floss. Mother took him for long walks and he even went to London with them for a holiday and wasn't a bit of trouble. All of which makes one realise how important and valuable well-trained dogs were.

The Spragg children, my cousins, went to school in the village, up to the leaving age of fourteen. The boys helped Tom with the sheep and later worked on the farms but the girls went into domestic service in London. May and Eva left first, followed by Doris (Ducky) and then Kathleen (Babs); Dolly stayed at home to look after the family and never married. The eldest son, Tommy, was a real character and would try his hand at anything. He bought an old Ford whilst in his late teens. It had no windows and a canvas roof and was one of the first cars in the village. One night when Tommy first had the car he decided to go to

Watton four miles away so he took his young brother and two of the village girls, one being myself, and we spent the evening walking around the town. On the return journey, in the dark, the car ran out of petrol. Luckily we were near Merton Hall stables where a car was kept for the Estate. Fred went across and borowed enough petrol for us to drive home. Now my Father was very strict about me being out late as I was only fourteen. After we arrived back in the village I still had two miles to cycle, so Dad was very angry and waiting at the top of the meadow for me. I was terrified about getting into trouble but after he had a go at me, and I explained, the matter was over and done with. In that respect Dad was always a fair man.

Tommy did quite a bit of taxi-hire work since people wanted to ride in a car and paid him to drive them various places. That vehicle ended up pulling a plough on the allotment which he worked with his Father. Tommy also had a little crystal wireless set. I can remember one night when we came out of Church and went into Aunt Florrie's and Tommy had this set on the table After much probing with the 'cat's whisker' we heard Big Ben strike eight o'clock - what excitement! Tommy was Church Warden for years and still maintained that responsibility when the War Office took over in 1942. He was very kind to his mother and drove her around a lot in the car. all the family were good children and often pushed Aunt Florrie on a bicycle so as to take her with them when they went out.

By 1942 several of the children had married and moved away from Tottington: Daisy May and Eva went to London as soon as they left school to work in service; Albert ('Arno') and Clifford were away in the Army; Freddie ('Trip') was a tractor driver and Cyril was working with the ducks on Eastmere Farm whereas Dolly was still at home looking after her parents. Tom and Florrie, together with Tommy and Dolly, moved to Thompson Village when the Army took over. Tom never ailed a day in his life but fell down dead aged 74 in 1951 whilst digging his garden. Aunt Florrie lived to be 84 dying in 1962. By 1999 all their children had died (Doris and her husband passed away in 1998) except for Dolly who was still living in Thompson and Clifford living in Maidstone, Kent. There were twelve grandchildren who are now married with children of their own.

THE COTTAGES

Their weekly wage is a pittance and yet their cottages are well-furnished, neat and spotless; their gardens well kept, and their children well dressed. how they can do it on from twelve to fourteen shillings a week is a marvel! It is an hereditary gift from their Danish ancestry. . . . .they are busy, kindly souls, whose one thought is for their homes.
The Land of the "Babes in the Wood" by Rev. Kent (1910)

At the back of my Grand-parents house near Aunt Field's, before one came to Alma Watson's place, was an old derelict cottage. We used to play there as children after the First World War but were warned not to on account of its falling down. The roof was off and the walls were cracked and crumbling, revealing strips of thin, inch wide, wood onto which white, chalky material was plastered. Bit by bit the building collapsed but the workmen on the Estate never pulled it down to make eveything safe and tidy. Now I know that these were the ruins of a clay lump cottage, so typical of Tottington dwellings. The older 'wattle and daub' construction used a skeleton of timber with staves of ash or oak inserted which were then interlaced with hazel wands. A mixture of clay and dung was plastered onto this base and sometimes stones or flint added to the outside whilst the inside walls were smoothed off and whitewashed. Later on, weather-boarding (similar to modern plaster board except it was more like a large fence of hazel strips covered with clay lump) was attached by wooden pegs or nails.

The chalky boulder clay was plentiful in pockets amidst the sand and the great chalk-pits of Thetford, Northwold, Hockwold and Methwold and East Harling testify to the long exploitation. In Tottington there was a place called Chalk Pit and along the road to Watton there were no end of these small depressions. The chalk could be mixed with straw and horse or cow dung and moulded into blocks of various sizes. These were sun-baked and used in building the outer walls of cottages. It was surprisingly durable material particularly when treated with lime wash to keep out the wet, but a crack would let in the rain, and the whole structure was liable to disintegrate or collapse under the weight of the thatched roof. The creation of blocks required no great skill and it was fairly cheap although time consuming. A pond or depression was cleaned out and a clay-bed spread, then coarse sedge was mixed in by a horse walking round on a lead tethered to a central pole. The resulting mixture was packed into wooden moulds which were about twenty inches by twelve by nine. Some parts of the Breckland possessed long kilns, making thousands of bricks and pantiles a day from the clay material, and Merton Estate had its own brickworks. In an area where well-grown timber was scarce and expensive, it was easier to build with these bricks and tiles, and a few of the houses in Tottington were of this nature.

The Census return shows that in 1801 there were only 21 dwellings in Tottington. If they were anything like the thatched, clay-lump cottages found elsewhere in Norfolk their general condition must have been very poor. In 1842 Chadwick's Report on the *Sanitary Condition of the Labouring Population* embodied a report by a Mr Tunsleton in which he described cottages in East Anglia as *"deficient in drainage and sanitary arrangements, imperfectly supplied with water. . . such conveniences as they have are often so situated as to become nuisances full enough of draughts to generate any amount of rheumatism and in many cases are lamentably dilapidated and out of repair"*. New ones were built from brick but the 'Norfolk News' (1863) included one article entitled *'The Cottage Houses of England'* by a Mr Clarke, which speaks of leaking roofs, sagging walls, broken windows, no gutters or drains, poor sanitation, cold damp conditions, overcrowding, and the danger of cholera and typhus. The Royal Commission on the Employment of Children, Young Persons and Women in Agriculture (1867-1869) included a section by the Reverend James Fraser, an assistant Commissioner, He noted that out of the three hundred villages he had visited in Norfolk, Essex, Sussex, Gloucester and parts of Suffolk, only two had a cottage provision ' *both admirable in quality and sufficient in quantity'*. In his opinion *'the majority of the cottages that exist in rural areas are deficient in almost every requisite that should constitute a home for a Christian family in a civilized community'*. Such conditions had a terrible effect on rural labouring families especially illness and death from periodic diseases like bronchitus, diptheria, tuberculosis, scarlet fever, as well as consumption and malnutrition.

Overcrowding also became a serious problem: in 1867 the nearby village of Hilborough had a population of 252 accommodated in 53 cottages, 22 comprised of one bedroom and one living room only. Tottington was even worse with 300 people from 61 families living in 30 dwellings. Yet by 1900 there were about forty dwellings of better quality mostly built under the direction of Lord Walsingham and belonging to him as farms and tied cottages which were rented out or went with the job of agricultural labourer. As far as I remember no one owned their home in Tottington during this century. There were some large properties in and around the village like the Rectory and the Farmhouses but a description of my Grandparent's house and my parent's cottage should serve to illustrate the ordinary villager's abode.

My Grandparent's House: My Father's parents, John and Frances Worby, lived in a rented house at the top end of Tottington village, on the road going towards Thetford, after it had crossed the River Wissey, and then passed several houses including the Reading Room where meetings took place. Originally their house was a village inn, brick-built walls covered in white-washed mortar, above which was a thickly thatched roof with a central square chimney of brick and another one at the northern end. There was a single-storey addition with a tiled roof built onto the back of the house to form the kitchen. This was a room added at a later date to increase the living space of the house; so there was a big step down from the kitchen to the sitting room floor.

The front of the house facing the road had five bedroom windows; square sash frames each divided into two glass panels, the bottom half with lace curtains. Below these were three long windows between which two doors existed each having little wooden porches with tiled roofs. A fence of brotches, held together by wire separated small flower gardens and a grass verge from the road. At either end gates opened onto paths. One went down the right hand side of the house where a linen line stretched to the right, through a vegetable garden with fruit trees, towards brick built sheds with tiled roofs. There Grandfather kept his horse and cart in a stable, his Spaniel dogs and the ferrets (he was the last Warrener in Tottington) plus all his garden tools.

The house wasn't that large by modern standards, but was divided into two sections. The northern end facing towards Watton was occupied by my Mother's Great Aunt, 'Polly' Buckle - formerly Mary Macrow who had married William Buckle, the brother of Mary Buckle, who had married Henry Macrow, my Mother's Grandfather. 'Polly' was a little old lady who often wore a black shawl. She had two rooms downstairs (a small sitting room with a corner window facing the road, and a kitchen at the back), plus two bedrooms upstairs. By the side of the house was a gate which opened into the back garden where there was a well next to the door she used as an entrance. At about the age of twelve, Dolly Macro and I used to go and sit with Polly on dark winter nights when Mum went to see Aunt Field or Dad went to Grandmother's next door. Polly was a nice, friendly woman and it was unkind of the children in the village who used to knock on her door and then run away.

130

Opposite her back kitchen door, down a little path between currant bushes, was a brick shed with two doors into separate toilets. These were old fashioned bucket privies, each with a wooden box covered by a double seat - a large hole for adults and a smaller hole for children to use - with newspaper squares for toilet paper. The human 'poop' was buried in the garden, or a horse and cart came to collect the muck once a week. These outside toilets were quite common in Norfolk houses even in the 1960s until mains drainage was laid on. Tottington villagers didn't have the luxury of running hot and cold water let alone flush toilets!

A central path divided the back garden in half. All sorts of vegetables were grown as well as black and red currents and gooseberries with numerous fruit trees including apples, plums, damsons, and pears. Most of the villagers had large, well kept gardens which were essential to their welfare. Of course they had flowers but gardens weren't just a hobby or a show-piece for the neighbours, although Tottington people were as proud as anyone to show off their handy-work. They were a necessary self-provision without which the larger families could not have survived. Wages were low and food could be expensive; garden produce supplemented a meagre income. There wasn't a lot of meat around nor the variety of processed food which families buy in such abundance nowadays from the supermarkets. Fresh fruit and vegetables

The house where John and Frances Worby lived, with Frances and daughter Blanch in front. The house was once a village Inn.

131

came from the garden and, along with the chickens and rabbits (both wild, which were eaten, and tame which were sold at Watton Market) it saved my Grandparents hundreds of pounds during their lifetime.

At the front, the left-hand door (panels on two cross pieces of wood) was the main entrance for the Worby household. It led into a small square hallway and off to the right was a door which opened inwards to the living room, where, on the left against the passage wall, was a large set of drawers on top of which were two china dogs sitting either side of a box of stuffed birds. The room had a large oak-beam running across the ceiling which was white-washed all over. Immediately on the right, facing out onto the main road, was a tall window divided into four glass panels, beginning about a foot off the floor, and hung with heavy curtains from a large pelmet. Resting in front of it was an old-fashioned chaise-longe (a red sofa without a back but with a curved, rolled end and cushions, on four rounded wooden legs). I can still see my Grandma sitting on that sofa looking through the window, watching people going up and down the Thetford to Watton road. As the house was on a bend she could see everyone who came into the village. I am afraid everyone thought Grannie was a 'nosey-polly' spying on what everyone was doing! Perhaps she was but in a small, close-knit community the comings and goings of villagers were the stuff of local gossip; no sooner did anything happen then it was all round the village.

In the far right corner of the front room was a door going out into the other passageway. To its left was a large open fireplace inset with an attractive green and white tile surround showing Bible parable scenes - something which now people pay the earth for. In the middle of the fireplace was a grate with parallel bars holding the wood fire. An iron plate either side of this grate was used for boiling pans and on the front of the fire was a trivot (a small metal plate with two hooks to fix on the bars) on which could be placed an extra cast-iron pan or kettle. Above this was a ten inch wide mantle place with its row of ornaments. Sometimes a board was placed beneath this in the chimney to stop the smoke coming out into the room! Although the house could be cold especially during the Winter, once that fire was lit and roaring away the front room became quite warm. The ash from the wood (seldom coal) dropped through the grate either straight onto the bricks or into a small metal container which was emptied onto what we called 'the muck heap' or spread on the unused part of the garden. Along with 'human soil' these ashes added to the soil's fertility.

Two high, round-backed, wooden arm chairs with turned legs were positioned either side of the fireplace. Grandfather's was on the right.

Grandma's was opposite where she could sit, again looking out of the window but she also had a round easy chair between it and the fire. Behind her chairs, the wall contained another door going out into the kitchen whilst the corner nearest the set of drawers had quite a large, brick-floored pantry with shelves all round for the food and crockery. The centre of the living room was occupied by a large table with chairs. The brick floor was covered with 'rag' mats made out of cut-up pieces of old clothes; often these became filthy with the accumulated dirt and dust and had to be shaken and cleaned constantly, (at one time coconut matting was laid underneath but later this was replaced with linoleum).

The other front door, at the south end of the house, was not used but it opened into a long passage with the best room (the parlour) on its right. This sitting room was seldom occupied perhaps because of the heating required. It was opened up at Christmas and for parties and when one of the family died, so that the body could be placed in a coffin on view; families kept their loved ones then. Nowadays, hardly before it is cold, the body is off to the undertaker! To my mind this is dreadful but more people die in hospital or in homes today rather than in their own houses which in any case are not made with extra rooms; and death has become a taboo subject making those living feel uncomfortable and embarassed. That room had a long window with four glass panes, a pelmet and heavy curtains. It's fireplace was back-to-back with the one in the living room. A panelled door at the far end of the sitting room led out into a little porch similar to those at the front entrance but with a half-glass door opening out into the garden.

The large bedroom above held at least four single beds which were used by the children, although where such a large family managed to sleep requires some imagination! The other bedrooms were smaller and my Grandparents slept in the room above the main front door. Once when I was eight years old, Uncle Field died, so my brother, Edmund, and I stayed over. I remember my Auntie Emmeline, from London, being there at the time - she seemed to like bossing us children around and I got into trouble for not taking care of my new black hat. On another occasion, the youngest son, Uncle John, a policeman in Islington, and his wife, Aunt Doll, were staying there, but he had to go back to London on a case. Aunt Doll was always a little nervous of my Grandmother so I went to sleep with her, even though I was about twenty at the time.

The other back door near Polly Buckle's residence, led into a large brick-floored room which was used as a kitchen. There was a sink but no taps for running water as this had to be fetched from the well outside. An oven stood in the wall with a fire underneath and there was a copper in the corner with a raised fireplace. It took the menfolk a lot of their spare time to chop and saw the wood required for heating. Of course there was no electricity in the house and no gas lighting either. Candlesticks were carried from room to room and taken to bedrooms at night. Oil lamps were placed in the middle of the tables; some of these lamps had lovely globes (in the middle, covering the wick, would be a tall glass chimney and over this was placed a round decorated globe). Some families had hanging oil lamps which were safer as children couldn't knock them over. Later on people had aladdin lamps which worked by a mantle under the globe. These broke easily but only the better off owned them. It was quite a business in the larger houses filling the lamps with oil and cleaning the candle-sticks, always placing a box of matches with them. Lamps could be dangerous but surprisingly there were few accidents. Once, Polly Buckle, who couldn't see very well, was filling her lamp and poured oil all over her table. Of course this could have set the house on fire but luckily Eva and Dolly Spragg popped in and set about cleaning up the mess. Eventually people had torches but my Grandfather became quite upset with his grandson Percy Worby who was playing with one; he thought Percy would burn himself or set the house on fire! When we went outside in the dark we either used a hurricane lamp which burnt oil or a lantern with a candle inside. Bicycle had oil lamps or gas lamps which used carbide. This had a strange smell and looked like small rock pieces.

EASTMERE COTTAGES: The two clay lump cottages on Eastmere Farm were covered in creamy coloured mortar. My parents lived in one next to the farm from 1912 until 1942, and the other one was occupied by Mr and Mrs Ted Williams; it was the same size as ours and stood on Cressingham road at the entrance of the lane which ran to Merton Park and through the Lodge Gates onto Watton four miles away. Their cottage had a living room, a tiny pantry and three bedroms, plus a kitchen cum wash-house on the side, a toilet and shed. I never knew how his wife, Violet (Harriot Mace) managed as she had five children who were much younger than me. She was terrified of going to the well to draw water; if she ran out she would ask someone to fetch a pail and when I was older I often did this for her. Wells were very deep and pails were let down on a chain fastened to a roller which was wound by turning a handle. My Father's Uncle George Williams had lived in this cottage but moved to a semi-detached house on Westmere Farm. His

son Ted worked with my Father as second Teamman until the military took over in 1942.

Our cottage stood in the corner of a meadow with a huge garden netted all round, where Father had fruit trees and grew the vegetables. Mother had all the odd little places for her flowers as well as each side of the garden path; she had a passion for buying different types of seed and seeing what she could grow. The cottage had four windows facing the meadow and farm lane so we could always see anyone coming to visit us before they reached the house. I could only have been about two years old but I have a faint recollection of my Father's brother, Fred Worby, coming to say goodbye before he went off to the First World War; and I remember my old Grandfather walking along the footpath across the fields.

At the side of the cottage was a door which opened into a little place we called the porch. Behind this door was a large cupboard where we washed up, etc, as well as washing ourselves except when the weather was too cold; we had no bathroom or sink! Bathing was on a Saturday night in front of the sitting-room fire during winter but in the kitchen during summer. We used the old-fashioned tin baths and shared each other's water as it had to be heated by the copper or in a large saucepan or kettle on the sitting-room fire. My Father made himself scarce at these times. The kitchen next door contained a fire-place and the copper plus a window where our pails of water were kept on a wooden stool.

Washing up was often done on the sitting room table which was scrubbed white wood and covered with an oil cloth which could be wiped down easily. Without running water we had to fetch it from the

Uncle Jack, Eddie and Albert Worby with Hilda hiding behind hedge

pump on Eastmere Farm or use rainwater from the butts outside. After a meal was cooked Mother cleaned out the big iron saucepan and filled it with water to wash up. Nor were there any drains (except in large houses) so all the water had to be thrown onto the garden, or into the 'gutter hole' where all the rubbish was put (no black plastic bags in those days and no 'refuse collectors' either). The far end of the kitchen had a large pantry with shelves all round and a small window. This held the crockery, safes for food, big brick pots for bread, pots for wine and wine bottles, plus occasionally a rabbit hung up.

The ceilings were fairly high; it wasn't one of those places where you had to duck so as to avoid banging your head on the doors or ceilings. A door on the right hand side of the porch went into the sitting room which had quite a nice, large window on one side and the fireplace and oven in the wall on the other. My parents didn't have a lot in the way of possessions; there was a 'scrubbed' table in the middle and a very heavy polished table beside it. The latter had to be got rid of when Aunt Field died because we inherited her piano, to replace our smal harmonium. We had a red sofa similar to the one in Grandparents' house; my dog Floss used to stand with her back legs on this and her front paws on the window-sill waiting for Mother to come home.

The only easy arm-chair standing next to the oven, was used as a bed for Floss. My parents had upright wooden arm-chairs but Dad's had the left arm removed as it kept faling out. Charlie Wright, the carpenter, made a small high chair for my brother and I, which later had the arms taken off. It was placed close to the fire so I could sit next to Mum. She kept it even after leaving the Battle Area and it was sold at auction by Abel's of Watton when my Father died in 1963. Also a lovely old clock hung on the wall along with lots of pictures. To make the rooms more homely, the floors were covered with coconut matting on top of which were coloured rag, 'pegged' rugs made by people on dark winter nights. My Aunt Field had much better rugs made out of wool and after the 1914-18 War, a firm called "Readicut" started advertising net matting and wool already cut into strands. Rag rugs were made mostly on a good clean sack. The needles were like wooden screw-drivers with a sharp point which opened up by pressing a lever and pulling the cloth through the sacking. Wool ones were a bit different as the lengths of wool could be tied in a knot through the holes of the net matting.

In the far corner of the sitting room a door led into a small bedroom which in the early days was too damp to sleep in. Until the house was repaired and we were able to use it, my brother had to sleep in the other small bedroom with my Father and I slept with my Mother in the big bedroom; at least we were warmer. The bedrooms had wood floors which were covered in coconut matting with rag mats before we had lino. The bedsteads were made of iron and we slept on feather beds on top of the hard mattresses. We had stone hot water bottles yet often put coats on the bed to keep us warm. The big bedroom had a fireplace but it was only lit in times of illness. Everyone used chamber-pots (practically unheard of today) as we couldn't go outside across the dark, cold yard, to the toilet during the night. We had what we called a 'slop pail' - a white enamel bucket with a lid in which to empty the 'slops' as we called them. Some people today remark, "However did you manage?", and yet if it was necessary I think most people would still manage, they would have to!

The fire places made a lot of work. Bars and sides, the hobs and fenders had to be black-leaded. This came in a tin like black boot polish which had to be put on with one brush and polished with another, (but you couldn't use it on your shoes as there was no shine to it on leather). People used to take a real pride in the state of their fire-places, and of course cleaning them was a major job for maids in the large farm houses. One of Mother's steel fender had to be emery papered to bring it up shiny. This stood off the ground about eight inches, so was handy to put the kettle and saucepans on; sometimes we put our feet on it. The brick surrounds of the fireplace was also black-leaded. Built alongside the fireplace in the wall was the oven which had a brass knob to open it and above this were two brass handled dampers which were pulled to and fro to clear the soot from the flue. Higher up was a little iron door that was used to clear all the soot from the oven -but only when one was cleaning the main chimney. Between the oven and the ceiling was a space which could have been made into a little airing cupboard but wood for carpentry was very scarce.

The oven was covered by a cretonne curtain when not in use but I pulled it aside and chalked on the black door, using it like a school blackboard. Mother used to get so cross with me and said Mr. Wace, the Farmer would be angry. This didn't deter me and I can well recall her saying to my older brother, "Go on hit her. Stop her!" I always thought Mum loved my brother more than me and of course was naughty because of it. I was so fond of playing school; Aunt Field gave me a little desk which I kept in the end bedroom, and used all Mother's old 'Home Companions' for childrens books. During the First World War paper was very scarce and afterwards we only had the inside of paper bags to write on; we couldn't afford to buy writing paper when I was young in the 1920s.

Mother would let us stay in bed on a Saturday morning until she finished cleaning the fireplace. In front of it was a large cloth rug which had to be shook outside but it was heavy and hard to lift. I was always glad when that rug was put down again as it looked so bare and cold without it. A very heavy steel stand hid the bottom of the fireplace and behind it the ash was caught in a metal tray and emptied into 'the gutter hole'. Nothing was wasted, everything was put in this dump opposite the lavatory door and then used for compost on the garden. The fire itself was in a grate about twenty inches from the floor, with hobs either side for saucepans to rest on and a trivot in the front. The oven was only used once a week on baking day so everything else was cooked in pans on the fire. Later on Mother had an oil stove which could be used for cooking or boiling the kettle. The kitchen wasn't used very much in winter, it was far too cold. Only as the days grew warmer did we change over and clean out the sitting room fireplace and dress it with fancy paper and flowers. Then we would use the kitchen fire until the cold Autumn days returned.

Our toilet and Dad's shed were made of brick, built away from the back of the cottage. We gave various names to the toilet, 'Petty' or 'Closet', 'poop house' or 'House of Parliament' were as commonly used as lavatory, and of course many people said "the loo". Our little house was a nice size with brick floor and white-washed walls. It had a small open window of striped wooden pieces going across. There were two wooden seats, and I was afraid I would fall down the big hole. In the early days it was an earth toilet and was emptied at the side by my Father about every six months, but later we had a bucket installed with only one seat. This I hated as somehow it was always full up and horrible; not in the least hygienic even though the seat was scrubbed white, and the wooden lids kept out the smell. Nor did we have toilet paper - just squares of newspaper on a piece of string- and we had to be careful how much we used! In the towns and villages a cart would come round once a week at night time and men would empty the buckets but as Eastmere was some way from Tottington we had to deal with it ourselves; at least those burials in the garden were good for the soil. Mum hung her baths on the wall of the toilet shed; we kept our bicycles there and children often played inside out of the rain. It was a place to go if one wanted a break or to get out of doing the washing up. etc. At night one had to take a lantern to see with. This had a glass door which opened so that a candle could be placed inside and the wind couldn't blow it out. Later torches were much more convenient.

Next to the toilet was a long shed, about 12 ft by 14 ft, where we kept coal and the dry wood, as well as potatoes in the winter in frost-proof

Hancock's Cottage in Green Lane

wooden boxes. Often a hole was dug in the garden and lined with straw; potatoes, swedes, carrots or beetroot, were put in and well covered with straw and then earth. There was a rack at the top of the shed for all the garden tools and sacks hung on a huge beam running across the top. Bicycles were kept there and it was home for the cats. Unfortunately they would do their business in the coal pit even though they had the whole garden to go in. Next to the shed was a thorn hedge and a wire fence which Mother often grew her flowers up, such as nasturtians and sweet peas. The fence which went right round the garden, had one gate at the back opening into Shepherds Plantation field and another small iron gate going into the Little Meadow. Beside this was a larger five-barred gate for vehicles like carts and lorries to reach the cottage from the farm. There was barbed wire on this gate and when I was about four years old I cut my right hand on it, so badly that the scar remains to this day. The gate was seldom used except for something large to be delivered or as on that fateful day in July 1942 when we had to move away from our home.

Since the cottages were 'tied', if we wanted any repairs done we had to contact the Estate Agent and eventually someone would come. The Estate didn't employ many men and there were four villages to be kept in order. Sometimes an outside firm would be hired especially if it was a big job. When Mr. Thornber took over Eastmere in 1936, he did have a tap put in our yard to save us going over to the farm pump with pails. We were promised running water inside the bungalow but the military takeover put paid to this. I often wondered what would have happened if we could have stayed there.

WASHDAY: Women did their main wash on a Monday. There was no running hot and cold water from sink taps and no such thing as a washing-machine. On the Sunday before, Father filled the copper in the kitchen with soft water from the tanks outside or fetched it from the farm pump across the meadow near the farmhouse wall. Above that well was a huge wheel with a heavy wooden handle each side. It was turned to bring up the water which poured through a tap on the wall. The copper was quite large, holding about six pails of water, and encased in brick with a door beneath. This covered a small box-like fire which heated the water. Father had to chop lots of small sticks and wood for it on a Saturday. Firelighters were generally used; paper was scarce as we only had one newspaper a week called the 'Thetford and Watton Times' containing all the local news. Sometimes Dad lit the fire for Mum but one day when she was doing it, a large rat jumped into her lap which was an unusual event although mice were occasionally seen.

I hated washday as everywhere was wet and cold and miserable and I think everyone else did, unless they were too involved to notice. When I grew older I helped Mother so it wasn't as bad. She never seemed to mind - indeed she would hunt up everything she could find to wash - she even had her Aunt's washing to do which made it rather a heavy work-load. The clothes at that time were made of strong material: men wore long-sleaved vests and long pants with thick khaki or check-flannelette shirts, corduroy trousers and long woollen socks for work. A white cotton shirt was kept clean for Sunday, waistcoats worn beneath jackets were fashionable or else long-sleeved jerseys, plus the obligatory cap for work. Denim and jeans were unheard of, synthetic fibres like nylon didn't exist. More underclothes were worn by women: stays, corsets and vests, plus knee-length knickers and sometimes underskirts. Long cotton dresses, twill skirts, white blouses and flannelette nighties were the norm. Fashions did change dramatically between the Wars: shorter dresses often with no sleeves, flimsy nighties, pyjamas, short panties, thinner vests, a brassiere and no corsets, ankle socks instead of stockings, shorts in place of long tousers. All these and different materials gradually made wash day much easier.

In the Summer, Mum would do the washing on what we called the door way, an expanse of bricks by the back door. Next to the wall was a long bench on four legs on which Mum put her tin baths. If the weather was bad or cold she had to do the washing in the kitchen. When the first lot of water had heated this was emptied into a bath for washing the 'whites' (consisting of table-cloths, sheets and pillowcases, my white pinnafores, etc). These she washed by hand, rubbing them with a hard lump of soap on a scrubbing board which had a thin piece of metal covering the wooden slats. Meanwhile another load of water was heating up in the copper for these whites to be boiled in for twenty minutes. They were put into the copper along with soda (no soap powder was used until Persil and Oxydol came on the market in the 1930s).

The clothes were taken out with a two-foot piece of wood like a broom handle known as 'a copper stick' - this could be dangerous and Dad often used to say, "You mind wha' ya doing' gal". Next all the colours would go into the copper but not the woollens and socks which were washed by hand. It was more like a Turkish bath and Mother would be lost in the steam! More fresh water was required for rinsing - a tablet of blue (called a 'Penny Blue') was partly dissolved by pulling it through the cold water to give the clothes a good white colour. All the tablecloths, pillowcases, pinnafores and white shirts were starched. White lumps of rice starch were mixed with cold water, and perhaps a little powdered borax was added with boiling water, stirring vigorously all the time, until the starch formed a thin creamy paste; the thicker we made it the stiffer the clothes. The latter were given a quick dip in this before being put through a mangle, into a linen basket and carried up the garden to be pegged on the wire lines for drying. It was a hard day's work; often Mum would still be washing when we arrived home from school at 4.30 p.m.

Then there was the tidying up; the doorway had to be scrubbed and the baths hung up in the toilet outside, etc, let alone collecting all the washing in before it was dark - unless it was a good day when we would fetch them in by moonlight. Sometimes the frost would leave clothes stiff like cardboard and the shirts nearly walked in by themselves! Drying could be long and diffricult; there were no airing cupboards, usually a line round the fireplace or on a guard sufficed, while the men were out of work. All the linen was folded and damped down before ironing. Tuesday was ironing day; awkward, time-consuming and something of a nightmare. We had to have a roaring fire in the sitting room to put the irons in. These were the type which required a shield to be put on. Often they became so dirty that the 'smuts' or specks off them made the clothes look dirtier than before they were washed! Matters weren't helped if the soft water left little specks and tiny insects on the clothes. Some people used box irons where a block of iron was heated in the open fire and placed inside the box.

There wasn't any electricity or gas but an iron could be heated on an oil stove although not very satisfactorily. No wonder the women of the village didn't go out to work; being in the home was a full time job. Only the richer families in the larger houses could afford a washer woman to do their clothes for them. Yet every week the washing and ironing was done and people wore clean clothes, without the advantage of modern technology. Nowadays we put everything into an automatic machine, press a button for a program and after about an hour all the clothes come out ready to put on the line. Most people have tumble driers and airing cupboards plus steam irons. No more blue or starch or boiling and plenty of 'biological' washing powders to choose from as well as synthetic materials which are light and easy to iron. Thus 'women's work' is made much easier.

BAKING DAY : Before the days of ready-made, cut-loaf bread, many country people made their own, usually once a week depending on how many mouths there were to feed. However, Mother didn't often make ours. The baker called twice a week in a horse and cart and would sell white 'tin' loaves, flour, yeast and food for chickens. Mother would do her week's bake on a Saturday morning or early afternoon and as I became older I learnt to help. Children also had cookery classes at Thompson school; we had to walk three miles to attend. My Father would see that Mother had plenty of firing wood for the oven which was heated by an enclosed fire underneath the oven in a brick wall beside the fireplace in the sitting room. We constantly had to keep putting small wood pieces on the fire because if it went down the food would be ruined. In the early days all we had was wood but later we used a little coal as well. The oven was quite large and held two shelves. Mum did everything on the sitting room table using a proper pastry board. She always did the pastry first for rabbit pie, apple pies, jam tarts or mince pies, and then finish up with short cakes and buns.

After the baking was finished Mother would put the joint of meat in the oven and sometimes baked rabbit, or rabbit pie. We were not allowed to kill any pheasants so if the joints looked a funny shape it was still rabbit. Not being allowed to keep chickens in the early days we seldom had them to eat either. Hens ran all over the farm but we took only the eggs which were laid in the horses' stables. Much later when Eastmere Farm changed hands we were allowed to have our own chickens and eggs which was a real blessing.

It was surprising how much even a small family of four could eat. Dad, my brother Eddie and I, all had packed food for lunch, but in the evening and at weekends we ate a proper cooked meal. On a Sunday we had roast potatoes and some vegetables but in general Mother made meat basin puddings with scraps of meat or rabbit; they were delicious. Sometimes she filled them with streaky bacon, pumpkin and onion (I hated the pumpkin). Village folk were fond of their 'Norfolk' dumplings made of plain flour, baking powder, a pinch of salt and water, and generally eaten with gravy, exceptionally tasty when cooked in a stew. They were really nice cooked in the oven on top of a casserole.

Sometimes they were eaten as a sweet with jam or custard and resembled fluffy balls. They were mixed with a knife to a stiff paste and rolled in floured hands to be dipped in boiling liquid and cooked for about 20 to 25 minutes. When you probed with a knife and it came out clean the dumplings were ready. We ate a lot of suet dumplings which were more substantial made with self-raising flour, salt, suet and water. These were taken onto the fields for the men's dinners, as were the big suet puddings cooked in a cloth or basin, containing some sort of meat and onion, pumpkin and bacon, or just eaten plain with gravy. Mother often made the latter with a knob of butter, seasoning and maybe an Oxo cube with vegetable water. If the saucepan was large enough these puddings were put in boiling water and cooked for two hours then potatoes, carrots, parsnips, swedes or turnips were added and boiled for an extra half-an-hour. I always had the top off the pudding much to my brother's annoyance. He used to say, "Why should she always have the crust?". Usually we had a substantial pudding, if not for the first course then for the afters, which would be either a spotted dick (currants and sugar added), or ginger pudding, or jam roly-poly (a suet crust with jam in the middle and tied up at each end like a huge sausage), all boiled in a cloth. These sweet puddings were favourites with children. However, by the time we had had two pieces of suet pudding with gravy and then a plate of vegetables and maybe some meat, we didn't need any second course. The older generation still make suet puddings but the younger ones tend to make sponge puddings using margarine and eggs instead. Later on we were able to purchase milk from Westmere Farm and Mum always made milk puddings but before then they were a rarity. Often we had boiled rice and treacle or Nestles milk. Considering Mother could only afford one tin of Nestles a week we managed very well.

Mrs Ethel Moore's house in Green Lane

Cottage where Jack
and Maud Williams
and Mr Thompson
lived in Church
Lane

Our food was plain but wholesome and we never went hungry. Not many of the farm workers had bacon and eggs for breakfast except on a Sunday. Having to get to work so early, the wives wouldn't have time to cook. For years my father had two oxo cubes disolved in hot water with seasoning and bread. Often we had the same before going to school, whilst some people had bread and milk. Admittedly not a lot of nourishment but at least it was warm and energising. When the men had their break in the morning, they ate thick slices of bread and cheese or meat and an onion, but cold tea was their mainstay. Every drop of dripping (animal fat) was saved and eaten on slices of bread or toast, beef being exceptionally tasty. Lard was eaten on bread with a pinch of salt added. On a saturday morning, children from the village walked three miles through the Park to Merton Hall to fetch dripping for their Mothers to bake a batch of short cakes. These were made from rolled out pastry with currants or sultanas and sugar; they were cut up into squares and taken into the harvest fields as 'fourses' with bottles of tea and sandwiches. If visitors called they were offered cake (with mincepies and sausage rolls at Christmas) along with a cup of tea or a glass of home-made wine. Most families made their own wine from fruit or vegetables and sometimes this was very potent; a tumbler full would knock you for six. Lemonade was made from yellow crystals in glass bottles, by adding hot water and sugar, and then diluted for the children. We drank cocoa and camp coffee but nothing was instant and there were no such thing as tea bags.

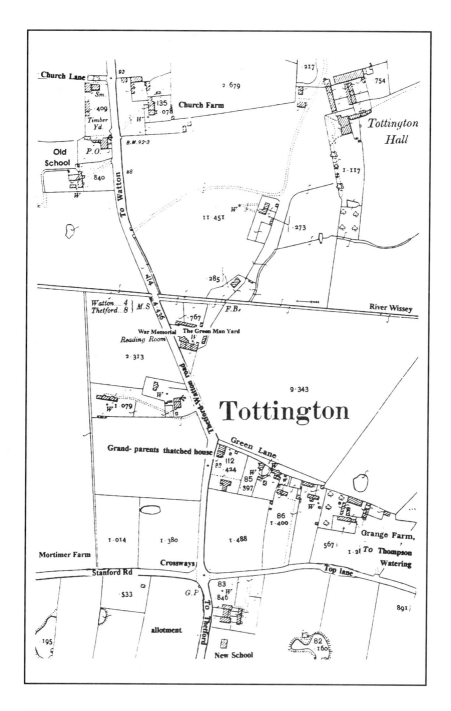

Church Lane
Sm.
.409
Timber Yd.
Old School
P.O.
840
W
93
135
.078
Church Farm
B.M. 92·3
88
217
754
Tottington Hall
2 679
1·117
II 451
W
·273
·285
Watton ... 4
Thetford ... 8 } M.S.
.767
F.B.
River Wissey
War Memorial
Reading Room
2·313
The Green Man Yard
9·343
W
W¹ .079
Grand- parents thatched house
Green Lane
112
.424
85
397
86
1·400
Grange Farm,
567
1·2¹ To Thompson Watering
Tottington
Mortimer Farm
1·014
1·380
1·488
Crossways
Stanford Rd
Top lane
·533
G.P
83
846
W
891
allotment
82
·160
New School

146

A 'LITTLE LARNIN'

THE OLD SCHOOL AND ITS TEACHERS: Tottington's own National School ('for Promoting the Education of the Poor in the Principles of the Established Church') was built in 1849 for the parishes of Merton, Sturston, Tottington and Thompson, financed by the 5th Lord Walsingham. It stood near the village shop along the main Watton-Thetford road and had a large white gate for access, and separate entrances to the building for boys and girls. A nice wide path with grass lawns either side led to the school building which had a flower garden at the front. The whole structure had a cobbled-together appearance. The main frontage had the typical facade of any average nineteenth century house, with a central wood-slatted door beneath its own little porch resting on two wooden posts. On each side was a five-panelled window in its dressed stone frame, and below the trough level of the pantile roof there were two small, three panelled, dormer-like windows, set into the front wall. This was the living quarters of the Governess and the teacher.

To the right there was a smaller structure which jutted outwards - a large, open wooden porch with four front posts and waist height wooden panels, above which was an upstairs room with its own window beneath the gable. The porch had seats inside and the woodwork acted as a frame for ivy and other climbing plants, although these tended to come and go depending on the time of year and whether

they were cut back or not. Tacked on at the right side were a couple of sheds with wooden slatted windows in which were kept the pony and trap. Children went through a large wooden door in the outside porch into the cloakroom and then through another door leading into the large classroom which had two fireplaces and long windows all round. Unlike the new school it didn't have a high roof. There were some other buildings and several tall trees which made it an attractive place; indeed it didn't look like a school except for the large bell which hung high upon a post in the playground, although later this was taken down.

The 1851 Tottington Census records a widow, Mrs Mary Munnings (aged 60), as the school-mistress. From then until the mid 1870s the school was run by Mr. John West Taylor (aged 37) from Frome in Somerset, as the Headmaster, and his wife, Mrs. Mary Ann Taylor as the Headmistress; in 1879 a Miss Emmeline Wakely was in charge. Unfortunately many mid-19th century 'teachers' were barely educated themselves; even illiterate villagers could eke out a few pence from part-time work in the schools. Such unqualified persons were hardly professional and varied from the dedicated to the uncaring and wholly incompetent. Payment, accomodation and security of position were usually poor depending upon the endowment and the generosity of the villagers.

During the last quarter of the nineteenth century about seventy children were registered at Tottington School but the average attendance varied between fifty and sixty. Forster's Education Act of 1870 tried to publicly control schools but not until 1876 were children compelled to attend school. In a village community there were always other gainful pursuits like gleaning, hoeing, picking up stones, scaring crows, or beating; children worked with or without permission during and out of school hours at the first opportunity. Attempts to regulate the employment of children in agriculture were piecemeal, prohibiting it below the age of 8 years but allowing it afterwards as long as a certain number of school attendances were verified. Legislation didn't apply to children over 12 years and 'exemptions' meant the Certificate of Attendance was waived during the hay and corn harvest, and suspended if a written application was made by farmers to local petty sessions and approved by the magistrates.The 1880 Education Act compelled school attendance up to age 14, but in less accessible areas this proved unenforceable and widespread absenteeism occurred; indeed the children of some families hardly attended school at all.

One gains such an impression from reading the Tottington School log-book; numerous entries show that half the pupils absconded if there was a Fete or a major funeral, or a call for pickers, weeders, or beaters for the shoot. The Labour Certificate Legislation 1881 did allow children 'permanent exemption' if they could pass an exam to show they had reached the fourth standard of education as prescribed by the Education Department. My Father told me that he left school in 1894 at the age of 11 when Miss Amelia Margaret Crawford was School Governess and a good teacher by all accounts. She came originally from Herne Bay in Kent, and was established as School-mistress in 1881 aged thirty-nine. A well-educated 'outsider', Miss Crawford brought a different persepctive to the school and to the village itself. Mrs Elizabeth Watson, a widow aged forty-three, was the Attendant. The latter's daughter, Alma Watson (aged 25) became maid at the Old School house. The very young Polly Reeve (aged thirteen) was listed in the Census as 'teacher' although she was more likely one of the National Monitors who helped to teach the youngest children, keeping them in order and preparing the classroom materials. Many years later, her daughter, Lucilla Reeve was to write about the Watsons in her book The Earth No Longer Bare: *I remember one woman whose husband had been killed in a marl pit. She had been left with several small chldren to bring up and took in washing. She was very old . . . . one daughter lived with her and one son. They were not strong and the daughter was almost blind - from having done much fine sewing by candlelight . . . . How kind they were to the small children who had tramped to school in winter and got wet feet. Mother would leave her wash-tub, or the turning of the heavy mangle . . . . . and daughter her sewing, in order to see to the children. They earned a few pence too by cleaning the school and seeing after the head-mistress who lodged there.*

At that time my Mother's Aunt, Alice Elizabeth Macro (1861-1940) was the uncertificated Assistant teacher living at the school with Miss Amelia Crawford. Alice was one of the children born to my Gt. Grandparents. Henry Macro and Mary Buckle, but always known to me as Aunt Field. Miss Lucilla Reeve relates another story which refers to the two teachers: *Our village boasted two music teachers and it was for me unfortunate that mine was to be the schoolmistress. She did not like me and I was terrified of her, and staying behind to have a music lesson seemed almost as bad . . . .as when I was kept after school to re-do a puckered seam. If she and her assistant were having a cooked meal it would mean the piano in the schoolroom for me, and much the worse lesson - probably hunger made her more "touchy." If they had afternoon tea I would perform on the American organ in the parlour whilst they partook of tea and cakes. This instrument had ornaments with dried grasses and metal framed photographs of the family who all seemed to eye me with contempt - they were no doubt musical. It was a small room, and the rattle of the impedimenta on the organ, rattle of teacups and talk of the teachers, coupled with my attempts to use my feet to get wind for my hands to get sounds from either "Now the day is over" or "The Blue Bells of Scotland," nearly burst the walls apart. There was one occasion when I was blundering through a march called, I think, 'Funebre', when I pulled out two stops by mistake and the resultant loud blast so shook the instrument a bearded framed gent, as well as a vase of grasses, crashed to the carpet. Two shillings for the vase went on the next lesson bill and soon after I was considered sufficiently proficient not to need any more lessons.*

As in many villages, Tottington's school often responded to the needs of the local landowner, the church, the tenant farmers and village activities. at the expense of education and learning. Indeed, whilst parsons and squires campaigned against village drunkenness and during the 1870s, effectively put an end to the old 'largesse' of the organised Harvest Festivals, farmers discouraged education preferring their boys to be young and their men ignorant : *"an educated man was discontented, independent and more fond of reading newspapers than of work"* (Springall). Farmers were fearful of the *"over-education of the labourer's children"*; in their view *"A little Learning is a dangerous thing"* (Alexander Pope) but to those who could become numerate and literate, knowledge was a passport to a better future. The common opinion was that education aided the exodus of the young from villages and reduced the number of lads willing to work on the farms: *Education has certainly done much to depopulate the rural districts . . for if a lad cannot read and write or do a sum he is of no use in a town, and what he learns at school has no reference and no value to country life or farm labour.*   *Rural England (1902) by R. H. Haggard*

By 1899 there were only 45 children on the Tottington School Register; *"Average was very low owing to so many families leaving Tottington"*. Nevertheless, Miss Crawford had tried to improve the 'learning' but as so often, the local vicar was the village School's inspector, checking that its teaching, equipment and standards were in order. The Rev. E. H. Swann visited quite regularly and the H. M. Inspectors' Report, 13th November 1899 reads; *The school is well conducted snd very carefully taught but writing and spelling are rather weak in the 3rd and 4th Standards and History was not well known. The*

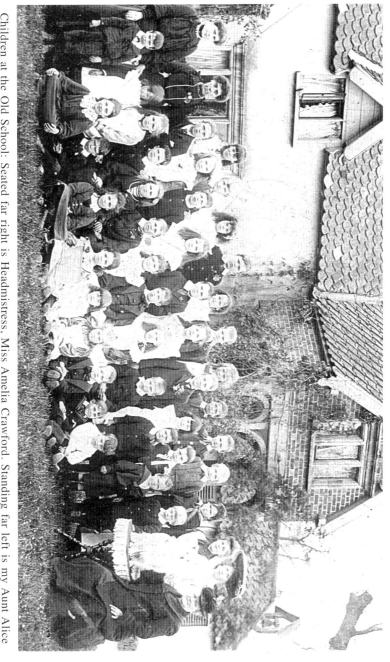

Children at the Old School: Seated far right is Headmistress, Miss Amelia Crawford. Standing far left is my Aunt Alice Macro (later Mrs. Field) and my Mother Miss Alice Moore (later Mrs. A. Worby) May 11th 1901

151

Infants are efficiently taught and care should be taken to keep the room tidy.

For a long time school holidays were arbitrarily decided by the Vicar or by Lord Walsingham, taking account of the harvest, haymaking, hoeing, gleaning or the shoot. The Education Act of 1902 tried to take control of local schools and regulate their operation which was often haphazard. A standardized timetable was devised on a national basis, and the use of the local Norfolk dialect was frowned upon. Apart from a daily scripture class, lessons consisted of the 'three Rs' with a heavy emphasis on strict discipline and rote learning by chanting. Maths consisted of arithmatic and multiplication tables up to 12 times; English emphasised copybook writing on slate boards and spelling aloud; reading was restricted to the Bible and a small library of about one hundred Victorian books, many of them of a religious nature; there was a little History, Geography, basic Science, with some Music, as well as excellent crochet and needlework. I still possess many of the intricate tablecloths and mats produced by the teachers and pupils of the old school.

One tangible effect of having a good village school and a strict teacher like Miss Crawford, was that it altered speech and dialect. Children were not encouraged to speak broad Norfolk, and my Father never did. People who spoke the dialect were thought to be a bit rough and common. Between the Wars only the older generation were heard using words and expressions with the familiar Norfolk 'twang'. Of course some villagers neglected to pronounce letters like 't' and 'd' as well as endings, and altered the sound of vowels such as 'a' to 'u', or lengthened them to an 'ar' or 'er' sound. It is difficult to print the distinctive Norfolk dialect, one has to listen to the intonation, but a sentence might go like this: *"Co, them thar old ducks wer'n't arf-a-kickin' up a din las' night. Whate'er wer yew a doin' on. Bet yu wus laert hum. Didn't yew git a tellin'-orf ?"* Typical sound alterations occur in the following words: *wus* (was), *hed* (had), *git* (got), *orf* (off), *ter* (to), *ser* (so), *dun* (done), *ain't* or *int* (isn't), plus split words like *'but-er'* and *'bet-er'*, as well as using *'of'* for 'have'. A dictionary of peculiar usages and phrases would include: *'Bor'* for a man, *'Maw* or *Mawther'* for a woman, with *'old'* being a common adjective; *'Huh'* as an expression of disapproval; *'doss'* (waste time sitting down); *'dudder'* (shake / tremble) and *'dingle'* (like dawdle); *'soffen the matta?'* ; *'Where yew-a-gorn?'* ; *'Don't tawk ser bloomin sorft; 'Praps tha'll larn yu ter think wot yer-a-doin'; 'tha's a rummin tha' is' ; 'tha's plenny gud enuff fer yu'*. Also the occasional archaic usage could be

Old School Pupils: Miss Alice Macro on the left and Miss Amelia Crawford in the middle at the back

heard as with *'vexed'* meaning grieved or sorry rather than angry. The favourite swear word was *'Blast'* and nearly every sentence included *'that there'*. Naturally enough our teachers at Tottington School tried to discourage such language but it was hard to erradicate. When I went to work in London as a teenager, people used to ask me to tell them things so as to hear my Norfolk twang!

Just after the turn of the century, Miss Crawford went to live in a lovely little cottage in Green Lane near Grange Farm, with Alice Macro. By 1904 my Mother, who had moved from Sheffield some years earlier, was living with her Aunt Alice and acting as a Supplementary teacher. My Uncle, John Wright, the blacksmith, was made a Parish Manager of the school, a post which he retained for the next twenty-five years, attending to all the repairs and renovations. Alice married William Field in 1905, a nice little man with greyish hair and a moustache which made him appear old to me; I think he was a little in awe of 'Mrs Field'.

In 1906 one of my Father's sisters, Gertrude Worby, was appointed caretaker of the school. Sadly, Miss Crawford died of dropsy 11th June 1907 and was buried in Tottington Church with the whole school given a day's holiday; she was a grand old lady (as can be seen from the

Wedding photo of Miss Alice Macro to Mr. Field, 1905.

school photographs) who was part of my childhood memories even though she died before I was born.

A Mrs Hall took charge of the Old School on 24th September 1907 along with a Miss M.N. Hildegard, sent from Thetford on supply to work with the infants. On 4th December 1908 the Rev. E. Swann followed Mr. H. Wilmot as Chairman of the School Managers and a Miss Perkins was appointed a Supplementary Teacher, followed by a Miss Balls. There was an epidemic of scarlet fever in 1909 requiring the school buildings to be vigorously cleaned: the School Minute Book, 5th February 1909, records *'Head Teacher, Miss Alice Macro, away ill'*.

It is strange how some people leave a lasting impression on one's life. Aunt Field became a very well known and respected person in the village, having her own special seat in the church two rows behind lord Walsingham's family. She was a tall, slim, person who wore long skirts and high-necked, light-bodiced dresses, rather like the old Queen Alexandra. She wore button boots and dark clothes except for a white blouse. Her dark hair was arranged up off the face in a little pad at the front and one either side. This caused her face to appear even longer and a little stern, not a bit like my Mother's which was round and merry. They shared the same brown eye colour but Aunt's were soft and deep set - the deepest I've ever seen. Upon going out or attending

Miss Alice Mary Moore with
Miss Amelia Crawford

church she wore a big hat and a veil and if it was very hot she took a parasol; Mrs Field always looked very dignified. Until recently, when I sold off lots of oddments, I kept a monacle she wore on a long black cord, which was one of the items I inherited from my Mother, including many ornaments, some of which belonged to Miss Crawford; and the Old School hand bell which I gave to the West Tofts Camp in 1995 for their display about the villages of the Battle Area.

Sometimes Aunt and Uncle Field came out the two miles to visit us at Eastmere. There would be great excitement as we could see them coming across the fields. One night I was sitting on Uncle's knee before getting ready for bed when I let off wind making a rude noise. and scampered off to the bedroom; the embarassment remained in my mind for a long time. When I was eight years old Uncle became ill, he had a lump appear under his arm. People didn't talk about cancer then and said he had a tumour, but he died leaving Aunt Field on her own. By then her brother Fred Macro had married the schoolteacher, Mrs Elizabeth M. M. Hall, a widow with two children and in 1912 they and Fred set sail for Australia leaving our family as Aunt Field's only relatives in the village.

Mother did her washing and generally helped out, and I was allowed to stay over since Aunt was very nervous living on her own. Aunt Field's bungalow was in Green Lane at the southern end of the village. When we visited we were afraid to move let alone touch anything, although we longed to have a tinkle on her piano. She kept a tidy, pleasant place, much posher than ours; most of her rugs were made from wool and she had a nice carpet in the parlour with some oil paintings on the walls. It had a sitting room which we seldom went in and three bedrooms with a little hall inside the front door which was entered into by a porch, There was a trap door in this hall which frightened the life out of me; we didn't have one at home and I always thought there was some one up there. One of her bedspreads, knitted by the schoolchildren in diamond shape pieces sown together, was very heavy and lasted for years. It ended up in the basket for our collie dog, Floss, to lie on.

I was never taught in school by Aunt Field and yet I learned a great deal from her especially about the Bible, and Jesus who was very real to her. I sat at her knee and she explained things to me until late in the evening when we put on our long white nighties and lit the candles to go to bed where prayers were always said. I slept with her in this high feather bed which was like getting into a cloud, so soft and warm having been heated by a stone, hot water bottle. I helped Aunt field in the garden but one day I ended up with a poisoned finger through weeding. After that Dad wouldn't let me sleep there anymore but other girls from the village, like Dorothy Macro, Dorothy Fisher and Esther Thompson, used to stay, and a new school teacher, Miss Bowman, lodged with her quite a long time, until they built the school-house in 1928.

Aunt Field's Cottage in Green Lane with Grange Farm in the background

Aunt Field's house had about half an acre of land on which she grew all her own fruit and vegetables. Whoever designed the garden certainly knew about fruit trees - blue and yellow plums, greengages, and amazing Victorias - set in a square of four and they were absolutely laden with fruit. Every year she sold these along with other fruit and vegetables to people on their way to Grange Farm to buy milk, and she had lots of customers. There wasn't a pension then for widows so no doubt she was glad of the money but she was a bit mean with the produce - we never had any, only the windfall apples and damaged plums. On one of the lawns was a huge 'Dr. Harvey' which were late apples, very tasty at Chrismas time. Another big tree had summer red apples lovely to look at although they didn't keep. I took a really nice one home on a Saturday and placed it on my dressing table in my childish belief of leaving it for Jesus. After spending the week at Aunt Field's I went home the next Saturday and couldn't understand why it was still there.

Aunt Field kept everything really pretty with flowers and lawns. Opposite her front door, on the other side of the lane, she had a high rockery and there were flower borders along each side of the thatched bungalow. At the end of the building was a large chicken house, probably a cart-shed in the past, and a little gate at the side of the bungalow led into the back gardens where there were other buildings and sheds, separating her garden from that of the Hunt family. The first was a brick built kitchen besides which was a beautiful orange blossom tree. Aunt didn't cook there as she had a three burner oil stove with an oven on top, inside the bungalow. Next to the kitchen was a closet with a bucket toilet which men emptied once a week, and several sheds where wood and tools were kept. In front of the back door were two lawns divided by a path which which went up to the top garden gate leading into another lane. A derelict building at the end of one lawn joined another house occupied by Oscar and Alma Watson, both short thick-set people. The Watson family had lived in Tottington a long time: Simon Watson (b. 1795) was a shopkeeper and letter-receiver, the Father of Edward, a blacksmith (b. 1827) and Arthur, a wheelwright (b. 1829) who married Elizabeth Richards. Arthur died young as a result of an accident in a clay pit and so Elizabeth was left to bring up their five children on her own: Alma Roberta (b. 1855), Thirza Agnes (b. 1857), Oscar (b. 1859), Milly Beatrice (b. 1861) and Wallace (b. 1862). Elizabeth took in washing and cleaned the Old School; Alma became a seamstress but developed cataracts and had very poor eyesight. She wore these tiny, old-fashioned spectacles but looked anywhere except through them. Everyone loved Alma: she was a dear old lady well-known for giving children lemonade and ginger biscuits; she suffered from a huge goitred neck, kept her grey hair swept straight back from her round face and always wore a straw hat, even when indoors, as well as a pinafore. I often fetched water from the well just outside her back door which was usually open for a chat. Oscar died before the last World War but Alma was still alive in 1942 when Lord Walsingham had her placed in a home.

I don't remember Aunt Field or any of her generation riding a bicycle but when I was about ten one of her nephews came down from Yorkshire in a Morris Cowley. It was the first car I had ridden in and you can imagine my joy when he took her to visit another aunt in Watton. The Cowley had a canvas hood which could be drawn up over the front seat, plus what was called a 'dicky seat' at the back where I was put. I felt like a queen sitting there passing through the village and all the other children staring with their mouths open.

Aunt Field became friendly with a cousin Tom Buckle who came originally from Thompson but lived at Hopton. Eventually they married but they didn't get on too well and she came back to her own place in Tottington. Soon afterwards she adopted two boys, Albert and Basil Pawsey from a home in Thetford. She had a worrying time with them especially when they were older and had young ladies. Albert did marry but Basil, who later married Joan Buttle, was still with Aunt field

The New School opened 1910

when she caught pneumonia and died in 1940. Tom Buckle claimed her little bit of savings and an attractive green dragon tea set, and said Mum could have all the other things which included the piano. Tom died soon afterwards; he had wanted my parents to look after him but Dad wouldn't do that. Why he needed Aunt's money I've no idea since he had quite a bit of his own which he left to a cat's home.

THE NEW SCHOOL: On March 15th 1910, Aunt Alice requested a Testimonial *"severing her connections with the School as Head Teacher"* (Minute Book). On 4th April 1910 a New School was opened at the end of the village on the Thetford-Watton road next door to a small green tin hut which was used as a Methodist Chapel. By the time I was born the Old School building had become an important meeting place for the villagers as a Working Men's Club being used for most social gatherings and for Sunday School as previously. The New School was a one-storey building with white mortar walls except at the bottom eighteen inches which was exposed brick. The tiled roofs came down low over the entrance and at the gable ends there were three tall windows each consisting of three frames; the top one swung open but the two beneath were sash-windows and all were divided into glass panels. It was a very solid looking building with tall chimney stacks, and the village was very proud of the New School.

It took in 45 children from Stanford which pushed the number on roll up to 85. The Headmistress was a Miss Twite. My Mother had tendered her resignation as Assistant Teacher in Oct 1909 only to withdraw it, but eventually resigned 16th August 1910. Miss E. Balls resigned in December 1911 and went as a Supplementary Teacher at Heacham. She was followed by a Miss E. Gladwell who left to go to Lowestoft in 1913; a Miss Pearson (1914 - 1916) and then a Miss Gertrude Ellen Becket who left in 1918. I first went to school during the Great War in 1916 aged four years. My Mother took me the long journey in a large pram. I can remember coming home one day and seeing overhead a 'Pulham Pig' (so named because it resembled a fat pig but in reality a small airship about fifty feet long stationed at Pulham in Norfolk and used by the Royal Naval Air Force to spot German Submarines in the North Sea).

At home there were no fires or oil lamps to dress by although my Father always rose about 5 a.m. to light a fire before he went to see his horses. My brother and I had to rise early as it took an hour to walk to school. I had long auburn hair which was plaited the night before to sleep in but brushed loose by Mother in the morning - an experience I did not enjoy. Even now I can see Mum standing by the door waving us goodbye and then often as not she would call us back and give us a little paper wrapping with currants and sugar to eat on the journey. Sweets were scarce and chocolate a luxury. Sometimes Mother made us treacle toffee out of treacle and brown sugar with a nob of butter and honey and a teaspoonful of vinegar to set it. This was boiled for quarter of an hour, then put in a greased tin and allowed to cool. Lines were drawn across the surface so it could be broken up into squares. Knowing mother the toffee never came out the same twice!

It was a long walk to school, about one and three-quarter miles across the fields, and even further if the weather was bad as we had to go up the lane onto the Cressingham Road. In Springtime the wild flowers were lovely and lots of waterlillies, cuckoo flowers and wild orchids grew on the meadows which were often wet and inclined to be boggy during the winter months. In those days no one wore rubber boots. We had strong leather, lace-up, black boots with studs and staples on heels and toes. They were a little unsightly though not uncomfortable but the girls hated them. A man called Mr. Herring (nicknamed 'Tippy') made most of the shoes for the children. They used to tease him and tap on the window of his shop near the village Post Office run by Mrs. Balls and her daughter Gladys.

When the weather was fine we walked from Eastmere Farm along the footpath and through two fields before coming to the hard road at the corner called Keymer's (or later Tuddenham's) after the people who lived there in the thatched lodge house with a veranda all around it. Sometimes we met up with other children who lived at Westmere Farm and walked into the village along the Thetford Rd. After we passed the Blacksmith's yard, the shop and the Old School, we came to a small stream. Children would get under The Arch, which ran flat across the road unlike the usual hump-backed bridges, and look for tiddlers and 'Tom Thumb' fish in the narrow stream, the River Wissey.

It was a favourite playing area. When we were older and cycled to and from school, many silly scraps occurred at Keymer's Corner particularly on the way home. If the weather was fine, those who lived at Eastmere used to go home across the fields about one and a half miles. When the time came for us to part from the Westmere children, somehow we would start squabbling, throwing stones and calling each other names across the fields and the road! As adults we wondered why we ever did such things instead of enjoying good friendship.

Usually the two school rooms were warm as the huge open coal fires were lit by the caretaker, Mrs. Pryke. The firm of Julnes & Son, at

May Day Celebration at Tottington New School, about 1914.

Top row: Willy Reeve, Cyril Spragg, Harrold Moore, ..., Roger Perkins, ..., ..., Kathleen Sculfer, ...,
Scarfe Moore, Charles Murrell, Vivien Hunt, Vic Leeder, Percy Macro, ..., Arthur & Will Spinks.

Middle row: Eileen Sculfer, Elsie Thompson, ..., Lily High, ..., May Spragg, Wally Moore, Bobby Reeve,
Winnie Perkins, ..., ..., Nora Sculfer.

Bottom row: Ivy Fisher, Mary Spinks, Joan Fisher, ..., Ida Tuddenham, Eva Spragg, Lily Thompson.

161

Watton, usually supplied the fuel. Somehow I never managed to warm up until dinner time. How nice it would have been to have had central heating. For the dark winter afternoons the rooms had paraffin oil lamps suspended from the ceilings on long chains, but they were seldom lit as we used to come out of school at quarter past three, (many of the children had a long way to walk home). We never had electricity in the village so I didn't know what a light switch was, until I went up to do sewing lessons at the Walsingham's Westmere Farm. The walls were painted with light green distemper and the tall windows let in plenty of light. There were no curtains just long black blinds on rollers which were pulled up and down by string.

The desks were old and dirty looking, long and narrow, each seating about five pupils (although there were some for two). The hard wooden seats were permanently fixed to the desks by heavy cast-iron fittings, which scratched or cut our skin. Entry required us having our knees bent and it was impossible to stand up straight once in. They were most uncomfortable causing dead-legs and bruising our knees. The lids, decorated with decades of marks and 'engravings' from past pupils, had their own ink-wells at the top with little china pots filled up by the class monitor. Into this dark blue ink we dipped our wooden 'pens' with their long sharp tin nibs and scribbled away in our exercise books. The teacher, Miss. Baker, used to compliment me on the content of my compositions but I often got carried away as my brain raced faster than my pen. As a result my hand-writing wasn't the tidiest and my index finger often turned blue. How messy compared to the modern biros which children use today.

There wasn't a school uniform but everyone was expected to be clean and tidy. The boys dressed in whatever they could get hold of but they wore little white collars which hung over their jackets. The girls always dressed wearing a starched white pinnafore, made from calico, over our dresses to keep them clean. They were fashioned from a yoke which fastened at the back with buttonholes and had large frills on the shoulders. I remember a favourite black and white, checked dress made by my Mother, a white calico dress trimmed with small scallops of lace from top to bottom, plus a cream crochet dress made by my Aunt Annie in Sheffield. I wore a black 'tammy shanter' hat and we had thick woolly scarves which were tied at the back of our waists.

The girls and infants hung their coats in the porch at the front of the school whilst the boys hung theirs in another porch at the back. We had to line up before entering the rooms; a little one for those up to eight years old, and a larger long room for the older children who were seated in three age groups, 8-11, 11-12, and 12-14, each doing different work. School began at 9 a.m. The infant door was left open until the register was taken then we all sang hymns and said a prayer - the traditional assembly which has all but disappeared in most schools seventy years later. Then the dividing door was closed and the toddlers taught separately. I remember using slate pencils and large slates to write on, cleaned with spit and a duster. We played with coloured beads and shells plus clay and plasticine for modelling. The older children began a typical day with scriptures for an hour and then went on to arithmatic. A fifteen minute break in the playground was followed by other lessons, and much of the teaching was by rote-learning, watching a pointer held by the teacher, repeating words and sentences collectively. At least it worked as we all learned our alphabet, spelling and our 'tables', which is more than can be said for some of the youngsters today judging by what one reads in the newspapers and sees on television. Breaks and lessons were signalled by a bell at the top of a tower being rung. Lunch was from 12 to 1 p.m. Some who could do so went home but those of us who brought food were allowed to sit in the infant room by the fire. There were no meals or hot milk provided and indeed nowhere to wash or drink except for the old-fashioned hand pump in the school yard. In the far corner of the playground, at the end of a long wall which separated the playgrounds, were toilets, placed back to back; these were smelly bucket toilets emptied by a man who received more pay for this fowl task than the school caretaker for looking after the whole building. In the School Minute Book there is an interesting criticism before the First World War about my Uncle Frederick Macro, removing the 'nightsoil' and leaving it spread out on his fields!

We played all sorts of games on the grass and gravel during the breaks. Boys and girls had separate playgrounds but some of the governesses were more lenient and would let us be together. There would be a sudden madness for tops and whips. When we had time we even spun these on the hard roads as we went to and from school. I never managed this very well, but my brother was good at it. Hoops and marbles would appear as if by magic but glass albis were considered more valuable. We pierced a tin lid, tied a string through the whole and rolled it on the ground. Conker time was great fun unless you were hit by one in the face when someone became vicious and swiped at the conker too hard. The boys had their favourite methods for strengthening conkers, like pickling in vinegar, and gave them numbers according to the contests won. The girls skipped and hop-scotched a lot

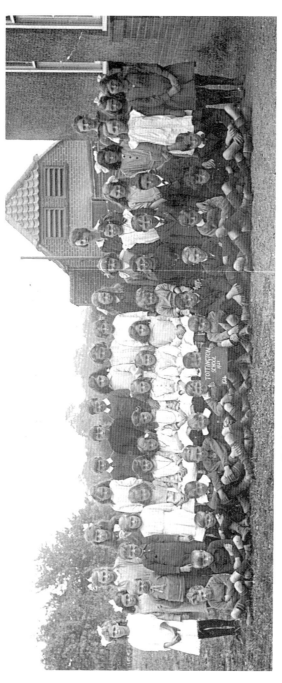

Teachers and Pupils at the New School 1921
Governess: Miss Baker and Teacher: Miss Lily High

Back row: Evelyn Robinson, Dorothy Macro, Mary Spinks, Ivy Fisher, Hilda Worby, Fred Spragg, George Moore, Albert Spragg, Girlie Childerhouse, Eleanor and Esther Thompson, Connie Tuddenham, Lily Thompson, Eva Spragg, Betty Bone, Oldfield, Ida Tuddenham, Dorothy Fisher, Joan Fisher.

Middle row: Harold Spinks, Percy Worby, Susan Worlidge, Nesta Sculfer, Doris Spragg, Hilda Fisher, Dorothy Spragg, Phylis and Lena Leeder, Marjorie Childerhouse, Ethel Bone, Roger Perkins, Edmund Worby, Percy Macro.

Front row: Maurice Wright, Albert and Teddy Worlidge, Frank Hunt, Bobby Reeve, Gordon Hancock, Cyril Leeder, Fred Harris, Bobby Bone, Arthur Spinks, Reggie Bone, Wally Moore, George Harris, Arthur Worlidge.

and there were numerous songs and rhymes to be chanted. All sorts of ball games took place but the boys tended to play football and cricket. Children can be really cruel and spiteful to one another and there were the catty ones who said *"Oh, you can't play!"*; it was nearly always the ones who did well and tried hard in class who were hurt by nastiness.

When I was much older and the infant teacher was away, the governess asked me to go into the class and teach the little ones. I enjoyed doing this and always wanted to be a teacher, as my youngest son now is. However, there were times when some of the older girls were a bit spiteful and jeered, calling me 'teacher' as an insult, and this spoilt it all. One boy started to call me *"snipe!"* and this name stuck to me for years. How I hated it. I never liked that boy and even when we were grown up it rankled. My Father used to say, *"Why do you get so upset? A snipe is a sharp pretty bird"*. In general my brother Eddie, a tall, stern straight-laced chap, never allowed me to be bullied and always stuck up for me at school. Yet when we quarrelled he too would call me *"snipe"* and I would call him *"Fat Skull"*. Mother being deaf couldn't always hear us rowing but when Father came in his cap would fly across the room. That soon shut us up!

In my time, Miss Baker was our favourite Governess and stayed at Tottington school the longest. She taught us to garden and we created a flower bed stretching from the front gates to the door of the school; and the boys had a large patch for the vegetables. In 1921 she helped us put on a production, a play called "What Shall We Name the Baby? which was a great success. I played the maid and my brother Eddie was the Father; it also included my cousins, Albert, Eva and Fred Spragg, Nesta Sculfer, Dolly Macro, Reggie and Betty Bone, Dolly and Joan Fisher, Wally Moore, Phyllis Leeder, Eileen Jessup, James Dunham, Arthur Spinks and Girlie Childerhouse.

Being at a small school, children did their best to sing, recite, or act in plays, not only to please and gain success but also to raise money for a Christmas Party or a seaside outing. A girl called Esther Thompson had a sweet voice and often sang duets with Gordon Hancock. One song in particular had Esther dressed up as a little girl singing,

I am my papa's little girl,
I am his treasure and his pearl.
then Gordon as a little boy would reply,
I am my papa's little boy,
I am his treasure and his joy.

Tottington School Play about 1921 'What Shall We Name The Baby?'

Back row: Uncle: - Albert Spragg & Reggie Bone; Aunt: Betty Bone.
Middle row: Mother: Eileen Jessup; Father: Edmund Worby; Maid: Hilda Worby
Aunts: - Eva Spragg, Wally Moore, Dolly Fisher, Arthur Spinks, Joan Fisher.
Front row: Nurse with baby: Dolly Macro; Other relations: Fred Spragg,
                 Nesta Sculfer, James Dunham; Girlie Childershouse; Grannie:
                 Phyllis Leeder

I don't remember the rest of the words but their voices blended well together. We also had a Folk Dancing team; four girls and four boys of the same height were picked and I was lucky enough to be one of those chosen. Our Governess would go with us and we danced in several villages at the Fetes, etc. As we grew up everyone learned to do ballroom dancing.

Miss Baker lodged with Mrs Pryke who lived at 'The Crossroads' in the middle house of three. A young man named Barrett, a Prudential Insurance Agent, also lodged there. Romance blossomed and Miss Baker became Mrs Barrett; in the Summer of 1925 they went to live at East Harling and stayed for many years. When Mrs Pryke's husband died she gave up the caretaker's post and Mabel Bone (nee Parkes) took over but it was a long way to walk from her cramped cottage across the meadows to the school, especially when the weather was bad and during the dark winter nights. After Mrs Pryke left the village the Bone family moved into her house at The Crossroads which was better accommodation and much easier access to the school.

School House built in 1928 in the school playground.
The teacher Miss. Bowman and her Mother

Every year the Norfolk Education Committee ran a competition where pupils had to write an 'Essay on Birds and Trees'. I entered three times and won twice; a Book Prize and a medal in both February 1925 and July 1926. The books are still in my possession: 'The Natural History of the Garden' by W. Percival Wewstell, and 'The Book of a Naturalist' by W. H. Hudson. Sometimes the School Inspectors came and we would have to recite and read aloud or do mental arithmatic or be questioned on Geography and History. On the whole we dreaded them coming and I think the teachers did also. If we were away for any length of time Inspectors came round to find out the reason. Very little truancy occurred since everyone knew where everybody was and what they were doing. Doctors and dentists arrived in a van and a nurse came regularly to inspect our heads for lice; our eyes were tested and on the whole the children were well looked after. I was seldom reprimanded although the cane was administered as a punishment in the school; the Governess kept a stick and teachers used a ruler. If a child was punished parents sometimes came to the school and told the Governess off saying, *"I aint-a-havin' yew a-hittin' my kids"*, whereas most people said, *"Serve yew right. Yew musta deserved it. That'll larn ya"*. I've read in other books about teachers being 'thrashers' and Fathers ordered to school to hold their sons whilst the mistress caned them, but Tottington school wasn't like that. Nevertheless, certain moments stick in the mind and often these are the worst memories of childhood.

Three houses at the Crossroads where Mrs Oldfield lived for years until 1942. Mrs Pryke and then Mrs Bone lived in the middle one with a Miss Lefley at the end.

One, which I haven't mentioned all my life happened when I was five years old. My Aunt Annie in Sheffield sent me some beads which I took with me to school. That morning we were given beads to play with in class. During break-time a girl called Eleanor Thompson heard my beads rattling in the little check dress I was wearing and accused me of stealing them. She reported me to the infant teacher, Kathy Sculfer, who told the Governess. I was made to stand in the doorway between the two classrooms, and in front of the whole school Mrs. Becket gave me a good dressing down. My Father was furious and went to see her and received an apology for the mistake. However, the Governess never apologised to me nor did she explain the incident to the other children. I was deeply hurt and have never forgotten the insult. Things like that affect children for the rest of their lives, and I was the type of child who was easily hurt and offended. Mother told me that when I was young and became upset, I would cry so much that it made me ill. Years later when I was twelve a teacher gave me a smack in the face for talking in class. On another occasion, in 1926, a young new teacher called Miss Dennis, came to Tottington School. I smiled to reassure her but she took it the wrong way, thought I was being cheeky and shouted, "Take that silly grin off your face". When we became better acquainted she was ever so apologetic for telling me off. Such

Teachers and Pupils at New School about 1922

Back row: Governess Miss Baker, Percy Macro, Will Spinks, Harold Moore, Roger Perkins, Charlie Belham, ... , Charles Murrell, Billy Fisher, Albert Spragg, Teacher Miss Lily High.

Fourth row: Elsie Thompson, Wally Moore, Edmund Worby, Scarf Moore, Vivien Hunt, Teacher . . . ., Nora Sculfer, Ivy Fisher, Mary Spinks, Bobby Reeve, Teacher Miss Bell.

Third row: George Harris, Girlie Childerhouse, Dorothy Macro, Dorothy Fisher, Hilda Worby, Ida Tuddenham, Betty Bone, Fred Harris, Eleanor Thompson.

Second row: Arthur Spinks, Esther Thompson, Phylis Leeder, Doris Spragg, Dorothy Spragg (twins), Nesta Sculfer, James Dunham.

First row: Cyril Leeder, Eva Spragg, Gordon Hancock, Reggie Bone, Lily Thompson, Joan Fisher, George Moore, Percy Worby, Percy High.

incidents were unusual as normally I got on well with lessons and with the teachers, and when it came to my fourteenth birthday in December 1926, I was sorry to leave.

As with any institution, Tottington School continued its own life long after I had left the village and gone to London. Because I was away during the 1930s it was difficult to keep in touch with the changes which occurred. There was always a Governess and an infact teacher: I remember Mrs. Baker and a Miss. Baker, Miss Bowman who arrived in 1926, Miss. Johnson, and the young Miss Carman, an infant teacher who came from Hockham village and with whom we used to go for lunch-time walks. After I left teachers came

Teachers and Pupils at the New School 1935

Back row: Miss. Bell, Roy and Courtney Jessup, Peter Thompson, Sidney Drake, Ray Pitcher, Freddie Rands,
              Geoffrey Jessup, Cliff Spragg, Miss. Bowman.
Third row: Gladys Williams, Gladys Oldfield, Olive Hancock, Betty Wyatt, Lily Williams, Ruby and Grace Buttle,
              Gladys Thompson, Iris Leeder, Peggy Wyatt, Linda Leeder.
Second row: Vera Rands, Doris and Phyllis Oldfield, Hilda Nash, Marjorie Lester, Audry Jessup, Sylvia Williams,
              Audry Smith, Joan Buttle.
Front row: William Hancock, Betty Leader, Reggie Lester, John Leeder, Ted Lester, Joe Balls, John Lester,
              Reggie Newstead, George Williams, Joey Jessup, Freddie Bone, Douglas Bell, Derek Rands.

170

and went frequently but I know there was a Miss Hodgson, a Miss Bell, and a Miss White. Miss Bowman and Miss Bell stayed throughout the 1930s. They went back home to Stalham at weekends but Miss Bowman had a bad car accident which left a visible scar on her right cheek; thereafter, Tommy Spragg often drove them. In the School Minute Book, on the 15th June 1940, Miss Lucilla Reeve recorded a Presentation, *"of Fish knives and Forks with servers to Miss Bowmann and a tea service to Miss Bell"*, where people *"spoke of the excellent work that the teachers had done in their ten years of duty at the school"* . . . *"how sorry we were that they were compelled by circumstances to leave but wished them both good luck and Good Speed"*.

Edmund and Hilda Worby as schoolchildren.

171

Girl Guides and Brownies - 1925
Back: Miss. Lucilla Reeve, Lt. to Lady Walsingham
Dorothy Hunt, Hilda Worby, Esther Thompson, Gladys Griffin, Mabel Hensley. . . . . . . , Ethel Downes,
Phylis Leeder, EleanorThompson, ... Cissy Carter.
Front: Ethel Bone, Lena Leeder, Hilda Fisher.

SUNDAY SCHOOL: This continued to be held in the Old School building and was taught by the Day School teacherss. Nearly all the village children would attend at 2.30 or 3.00 p.m. We learnt all sorts of hymns and prayers and texts were taught from the Bible. This was an accepted part of village life. Nearly everyone belonged nominally to the Anglican Church and young people were expected to attend Sunday School, up to a certain age. The same was true for most children right up until the 1960s but nowadays it seems there are so many alternatives and few parents practice any religious beliefs let alone go to church or send their children to Sunday School. We enjoyed going, and The British Bible Society ran a competition every year where children had to find certain verses in the Bible and fill in a form with their answers. If we were correct then the prize was a Bible or a copy of the New Testament. My brother Eddie and I won both and I still have my copies after all these years.

Sometimes the Vicar, a Rev Robb, attended and once he became so annoyed that he threw his spectacle case at Albert Spragg. Each Christmas we had a lovely party and the old Lord and Lady Walsingham would come in their carriage from Merton. He sang his 'pretty pear tree' song and pulled faces to make us laugh. The Rector and the Vicar used to attend as well and we had all sorts of games including musical chairs. After tea the parents joined in and the Caretaker of the Club provided the food. One clergyman, a Mr. Trownsell would bring a huge bag of dolly mixtures. The children stood in a circle and then he threw the sweets in the air and shouted "scramble". We rushed to grab then and stuff them in our greedy mouths. Surprisingly we were never ill even though the sweets were not wrapped and fell on the dusty wood floor. Sometimes the Rev. Trownsell also did this at the Day school. He kept ten white Highland terriers which trundled behind him wherever he went, and several people who called at the Vicarage unannounced received a fright.

By about 1928 the Sunday School venue had moved to the Church. A Mrs Kidd from Wretham, a Miss Lily High, Eileen, Nora and Kathy Sculfer, Gladys Balls, and Dolly Spragg, all helped with the activities at one time or another. After Choir practice at night in Winter children left Church Sunday School and went sliding on the frozen ponds on the meadows. Sometimes they entered Tuddenham's Plantation and took chestnuts or hazel nuts and were frightened that Mr. Sturman the Gamekeeper would catch them.

THE WORKING MEN'S CLUB: After 1910 the Old School was used as a place for social gatherings and activities. The Rector and the Vicar regularly attended and there were all sorts of games including musical chairs. After tea the parents would join in and the Caretaker of the Club would provide the food. Men and youths went to the Club for indoor sport, etc, and nearly every week a Social or a Whist Drive was held and afterwards a Dance until 2 a.m. The Boxing Day 'Party' was one of the most important events. Nearly all the families in the village attended no matter what the weather was like, although we had a mile and a half to walk. Later on we cycled but during my early teens in the 1920s very few people had bicycles and even then they were the fixed-wheel variety. The Socials were mostly free more like a party where different people entertained. Several people would either sing or recite or do a short play.

Usually my Mother played the piano for most social occasions from 7.30 p.m. to late after midnight almost non-stop, and she sang, often with someone else. I remember one of the songs was 'Rise, Rise, Beautiful Sun' which Mother sang with Agnes Parkes wife of George Oldfield, a farmer at Grange Farm. It couldn't have been easy for Mum as she was deaf. Later on Thomas Spragg senior played on the drums and this helped with the rythm, and a boy from the nearby village of East Wretham played on the spoons to accompany them. It was exciting and enjoyable to be on the road outside and hear the old jo-anna going. If people didn't get up to dance Mother would stop playing and tell them to start dancing. She came from Yorkshire and wasn't afraid to speak her mind. She wasn't going to sit there playing with no one else doing their bit! Mother did this service for 2s/6d. After sitting from 7.30 'till gone midnight, and sometimes 2 a.m. if it was a Whist Drive, she had nearly two miles to walk home in all weathers, on lonely roads and fields. She wasn't afraid; at least in those days there was no danger for a woman to walk alone in the countryside. After my brother Eddie and I had left home, Mother had to go by herself as my Father seldom attended in later years. Of course when we came home on holiday we cycled with Mother. By the 1930s everyone was riding bicycles. (When the war came we had to black out the lights. Only a glimmer was allowed and the rear light was covered with a dark piece of glass or paper). Usually we had oil or gas lamps but later on torches were used. Sometimes the Bishop family from Eastmere Farm went as well so there was company for Mother. After I left home in 1931 and was in London, I used to buy two sheets of music from Woolworths every week and send them to her. This kept her up-to-date with all the

Flashlight Photograph 1926 Social at the School where Mrs. A. Worby played the piano.

Top Row: Billy Fisher, Albert Oldfield, ... , Albert Spragg, Scarf Moore, Roger Perkins, ... , Wally Moore, ... , Edmund Worby

Third row: Irene Starling, Cyril Spragg, Winnie Perkins, George Oldfield, John A. Kohler, Mr. Fisher, Mrs. Alice Worby (pianist) Leslie Macro, Miss Bowman (Governess).

Second row: Mabel Carmen (teacher), Mrs Pryke, Florence May Kohler, Hilda Fisher, Mrs. Bone, Dorothy Robinson, Ethel Bone, Ivy Oldfield, Ivy Fisher, Ida Tuddenham, Dorothy Fisher, Mrs. F. Spinks, Laura Wright.

Bottom row: George Moore, Gordon Hancock, Maurice Wright, Fred Spragg, Esther Thompson, Hilda Worby, George Harris, Percy Worby.

175

new songs; I still have most of the song sheets in my possession.

We had a variety of dances; the Waltz, Polka, Foxtrot, Velita, St. Bernard's Waltz, the Barn Dance, the Military Two Step, and what was very popular, 'The Lancers'. We liked to get asked for that as we could have a good swing round off our feet, especially if a girl was small. There would be four male and four female dancers and at one point during the dance we would all join arms and swing round. Usually there were three sets of eight dancers. One of my cousins always asked me to do the Boston Two Step or Veleta with him. Later lots of these old dances faded away as newer ones took their place. When I was quite young my brother and I learnt to dance by going with Mother to the Dances and sometimes through dancing lessons. I often taught people, assuming the man's part and this rather hindered me later in life as I was accused of taking the lead instead of following - as a lady partner should do. Mother was a good dancer so when someone else took over the piano to give her a break for a cup of tea, I would take the opportunity to waltz her round the floor.

The Socials were held in the Old School Room with two roaring fires lit by hanging oil lamps. In later years I went in a nice long green dress but forgot to take the sales ticket off the back. That put paid to my youthful pride! There was a cloakroom in which to hang all the coats and jackets. The Caretaker's sitting room was used for refreshments and there were lots of lovely home-made buns, cakes and sausage rolls, mince pies, etc. The room didn't hold many people so there were always queues waiting to get food. If we wanted to go to the toilet we had to go through the Caretaker's house into the back yard with a candle. This situation didn't alter right up until the time when we left the village in 1942; there never were any flush toilets in Tottington. By the time of the war, Dance Bands were being hired, usually from Watton. There were lots of soldiers around and also the Czech Air Force had come to East Wretham, so there were no lack of partners for the girls. Unlike some places in Norfolk we never heard of any trouble between the soldiers and the local boys. In any case many of the young men of the village had been called up and were away at the War.

Even at a Reunion in 1993, surviving evacuees of the village talked of these past events and how much they enjoyed the music and the dancing, when Mrs. Worby played the piano. Often there was a parade of Fancy Dress and we all marched round the room to be judged. The Rev. Kent would come as did, Lord and Lady Walsingham in their horse and carriage from the village of Merton; there was a hushed silence greated their arrival. The old Lord was a smallish man with white hair and a moustache, and his stance was a little bent, whereas his wife was tall and elegant. He would sing to us and one song was 'All in a beautiful field there stands a pretty pear tree,' with lots of verses. He would ask all the children to join in the chorus . It ended 'with leaves' but he sang "learves" which made us all laugh, as did the funny faces he pulled. They were a dear old couple and very much respected. When he passed away in 1927 a lot died with him. George de Grey, the new Lord Walsingham, didn't mix in the same way although he had his good points and joined parades and church celebrations.

There was a social for New Year's night at the Club Room and sometimes one at Merton Hall, three miles away. These were grand affairs with bands playing in two ball rooms. Mother didn't go to these but when we were older, a group of us walked across the Park to the Hall, coming home at 3 a.m. in the morning, often in the snow during Winter. The Park was supposed to be haunted by 'the grey lady' who was seen or heard usually in December. Of course we imagined we heard footsteps and frightened ourselves silly.

There was another brick and flint building, called the Reading Room, higher up in the village, in 'The Green Man' yard. It was used for meetings and for the Girl guides and Brownies. The Old Lady Walsingham was head of the Girl Guides and the Eastate Agent, Miss. Lucilla Reeve was her Lieutenant. A man named Mr. Tuddenham became the Caretaker of the Working Men's Club and lived in the Old School house. He was there several years before a Mr. Wyett, the village postman, took over. Mr. Wyett had a motor-bike and side-car and would fetch people from the stations either Thetford, Watton, Brandon, Stow Bedon or East Wretham. A local train ran from Thetford to Swaffham about three times a day. Later on he acquired a little car.. He also sold petrol in cans and Smiths crisps and bottled drinks for the school children. As postman he delivered twice a day on his bicycle early in the morning around 7 a.m.and again at 2 p.m. in the afternoon. The post was only 1/2 d for a postcard, 1d for an open letter, and 1 1/2d for an ordinary letter. The post took a day from anywhere. At the time of writing this, the First Class Post is 25p (about 60d in old money) and second class is 19p, and you never know when a letter is going to arrive. Such is progress!

GOD'S HOUSE - THE CHURCH OF ST. ANDREW'S

Nothing symbolises more powerfully the continuity of the community. . . . . The church provides a continuous link with the earliest days of the village's settlement . it is part of its contemporary role to be a guardian of the village's history and a reminder of its past.

The Country Parish by Anthony Russell

I think it right to say that Tottington villagers were religious not just in the sense of being God-fearing, Church-going people but also in that wider pantheistic sense of seeing God's presence writ large on Nature's face. Whether they were great believers, in terms of Faith is another matter. Most were christened, married and buried but few men attended Church regularly; women went often as did their children before Sunday School. We were brought up to be 'good Christians' in word and deed, to read the Bible, say our prayers, and behave 'correctly' - the old-fashioned virtues of honesty and decency.

For most people, 'a Christian' meant being baptised, confirmed, reading the Bible, keeping the Commandments, and trying to do good to our neighbours. We accepted the Bible as the true 'Word of God'; the Devil and Hell did exist; there was 'evil' in this world. Religious observance seemed compulsory, and much of the yearly ritual of rural activity centred around the Christian calender and its festivals. A number of the families were of a Non-Confomist background and attended the Methodist Chapel, but most people were of the Anglican persuasion and attended our Church of St. Andrew's - whether for a social occasion, to meet, talk, show off their clothes, or to hear their voices singing familiar hymns. The C. of E. was still strong and influential in rural areas, owning land, collecting rents and tithes; its Vicars were important men who were listened to with respect, and often obeyed. For that reason the church, 'God's House', was a vital and regular feature of our existence; spiritually and physically a focal point of village life. To generations of villagers, God was rightly entitled to a large and imposing house. It was a fine example of the Mediaevil churches found all over East Anglia, most of which were built under pressure from priests, religious houses and landowners to accommodate the whole population of the village or area.

St. Andrew's could be seen from all directions since its tower dominates the surrounding countryside. It still stands, hauntingly, above the surrounding fields left fallow because of the dampness of the ground. Situated at the top of a narrow road called Church Lane, which

St. Andrew's Church with its white wooden fence in 1910

St. Andrew's Church as it is today

179

was on one's left going out towards Watton before reaching Tuddenham's Corner (formerly known as Keymer's Corner) just after the Smithy. During the 1930s the Council built eight semi-detached houses here (six still remain on the right-hand side although empty and patched up for use by the army), after which were two cottages and then the large Georgian Vicarage surrounded by a brick wall and standing amidst beech and fir trees, (now all demolished). Opposite the church, in a corner of church meadows, stood a small, thatched house where my Father's sister, Florence Worby and her husband Thomas Spragg lived until 1936. Their son, my cousin Tommy Spragg, was the Church Clerk or Warden in the 1920s up until 1942.

The site itself was a place for worship long before the Norman invasion but there are no Saxon remains. In 1196 John le Strange with the consent of Robert de Mortimer, gave the care of St. Andrew's to the Priory of St Mary and the Nuns at Campesse in Suffolk. It was appropriated to that house in 1302, the rectory being valued at 30 marks and the vicarage at 6 marks. After that the Church must have been rebuilt since the tower, the nave and the aisles, show the decorative style of achitecture which dates from the 14th century. It remains an imposing edifice although long in a state of disuse and disrepair. The typical square tower is in four stages which diminish as they rise up to the parapet level, but this is camouflaged by elegant buttresses strengthening the structure at each corner. We know from records that this tower was topped by a traditional lead spire taken down in 1802. There was a fine west doorway and the windows were attractive examples of Decorative architecture but this was difficult to appreciate when everything was blocked up with rusty sheets of corrugated iron; thankfully, during the 1990s these were removed and replaced with plastic sheeting which gives the building a much tidier appearance. However. only the old photographs can conjure up images of what it was like; those of us who attended the services every Sunday, year after year, are left with our memories.

My family lived one and a half miles away to the north on the Cressingham road but could reach the church by walking across fields and meadows. If it was wet weather the field tracks would be too muddy or it would mean walking in water and messing up our clothes, so then we went along the road as we did when cycling. Sturston people who had no church of their own, could do the same coming to St. Andrew's across Mortimer Meadows to the south. There were two services on Sunday: one at 11 a.m. and the other at 6.00 or 6.30 p.m. Sunday School had been in operation since 5th October 1817 when it

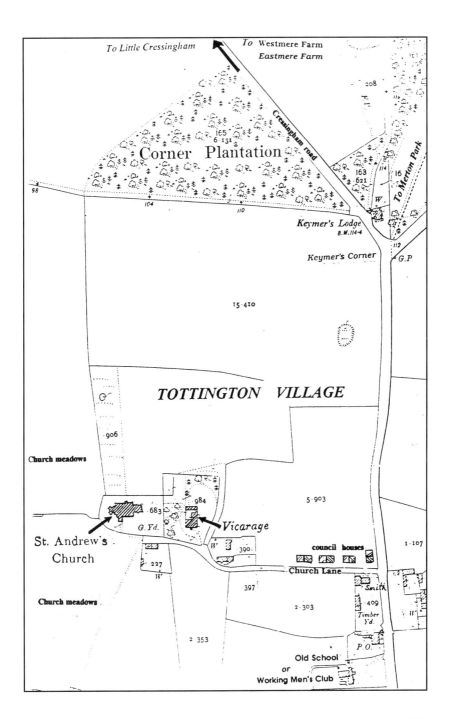

To Little Cressingham

To Westmere Farm
Eastmere Farm

208

Corner Plantation

165
6 131

Cressingham road

163
621

114

16

To Merton Park

98

104

110

Keymer's Lodge
B.M.114·4

W

112

G.P

Keymer's Corner

15·410

TOTTINGTON VILLAGE

·906

Church meadows

984

5·903

683

G.Yd.

Vicarage

St. Andrew's
Church

390

council houses

1·107

227

Church Lane

Church meadows

397

Smith

409

2·303

Timber
Yd.

2 353

P.O.

Old School
or
Working Men's Club

181

was opened by the Rev. Matthew Dawson Duffield for upwards of 50 children who *"are by this means kept from idling away the Sabbath on the village green."* It was held at the Old School when I was young but later reverted to the Church. The Church bells would ring three times and the tune was normally *'Turn Again Whittington, Lord Mayor of London'*. After this a single bell tolled - when this started we knew we had to run to get there on time!

Tottington had good bell ringers to do justice to the six bells in the tower, the earliest two were made by John Brend II of Norwich in 1658, and Robard Gurney of Bury St. Edmunds in 1665. Three others were added from Lester and Pack of Whitechapel, London, in 1755 and another by Taylor of Loughborough in 1856. Of course these were removed in 1942; unfortunately the tenor bell was stolen from storage at West Tofts Church but the rest now have a home at St. Alphege, Seasalter, Kent since 1969.

Not everyone in the village attended church. Indeed many of the men, including my Father, didn't make an appearance except for special occasions, and the women probably went for all sorts of reasons other than mere worship. The Rev. Kent felt that villagers were suspicious of the Church, and *"Utterly indifferent to any form of religion. The struggle for life crushed it out of them."* (The labourer): *has no ill-feeling towards the church. It is his tradition to come occasionally, his wife is churched there, his children baptised - he has been married there and will be buried in the old churchyard. It is superstition that these things should be in the church.*
The Land of "the Babes in the Wood"   by Rev. Kent (1910)

However, my Mother and I loved the church and never missed the services. Most boys and girls were confirmed when they reached their early teens. For several weeks special lessons were given and the Vicar made sure that children knew the Ten Commandments and the Catechism. Confirmation wasn't held at the same church every year since one service was held for the children of several villages. When I was seventeen years old my own confirmation took place in Carbrooke Church. Either the Bishop of Norwich or the Bishop of Thetford would come in his finery and all the local Vicars attended. This taking of vows was considered important as people said one couldn't go to heaven if you weren't baptised and confirmed. Girls were dressed in white with a veil and the boys had to wear white shirts, but few parents were present. Men couldn't get off work except for a funeral and most Mothers had young children to look after; very few rode bicycles and hardly anyone could afford a motor-car in the 1920s. Weddings were not the grand, expensive occasions they are today. The Rev. Kent wrote that it was *"quite unusual for the Father of the bride to attend to give her away. The mother hardly ever comes to attend the wedding of her son or daughter"*. Rev. Crabbe, a Rector of Merton in the nineteenth century, wrote: *It is worthy of note that in the thirty years I have been at Merton I have had only had three weddings in which the father of the bride attended to give her away. On all other occasions only young people have attended from one to three couples at labourers' weddings.*

Most people turned out for funerals usually because everyone was related. I remember the funeral of Mrs Caroline Hancock, the Grandmother of my teenage sweetheart, Gordon Hancock. Aunt Carrie was my Grandmother's sister and was buried on my 18th birthday, 31st December 1930. The usual hymns were sung, 'Abide With Me' and 'On the Resurrection Morning'. The mourners walked for about three-quarters of a mile behind a horse-drawn hearse hired from Watton. I can still see the sad look on my cousin's face. In earlier years, my Father was a bearer at funerals but not for that one; he had to have permission to take time off work and afterwards had to get back to feed the horses. He told me that when Miss Crawford, the former School Governess, died of dropsy, the undertaker failed to drain and stop up the body. When the pall-bearers lifted the coffin, the excess fluid ran out over their suits. I doubt whether such an unusual and appalling incident could occur today. Uncle George Williams had a wagon from the farm to carry his coffin to the church. Sadly I was away from home down in London after 1931 so did not attend either of my Grandparents' funerals, in 1933 and 1936. If a child died before it was baptised it had to be buried at the back of the churchyard away from the other graves; a foolish man-made rule - how could an innocent child be sinful and not go to heaven?

Until recently the churchyard was somewhat dilapidated and slightly overgrown, with groups of gravestones surrounded by iron railings in front of which stands a high wire fence topped with three strands of barbed wire. This, along with the padlocked gate, gave the impression of a prisoner of war camp. Perhaps it was necessary since after the last War thieves stole some of the lead roof: in 1950 there was a court case where two Bury St Edmunds' men were sent down for a month for attempting to steal 3 cwt of sheet lead from the Church and lead piping from the Rectory House There used to be a three planked, white wooden fence which went all the way along the front with a white gate (beneath an old-fashioned oil lamp) leading to the south porch entrance.

Most of the villagers in Tottington and Sturston, including many of my direct ancestors are buried here but few of their gravestones exist, if indeed they ever had any. To the left as one comes through the present gates, lies the grave of my Grandparents with a headstone inscribed, "In Loving Memory of John and Frances Worby". Further back near the fence is the gravestone of Walter (1833-1922) and Emma Roseanna Hunt (nee Oldfield, 1849-1929), the parents of Arthur Hunt who married my Father's sister Rose Alice Worby. At the entrance to the south porch on the right hand side lie a number of Oldfields: Robert and Elizabeth (Cawley), and John (1844-1890) - my Grandfather's cousin - who married Ann Watson, and their children, Edith Louisa (1881-1899) and Arthur James Oldfield (1884-1890) plus, lying flat on the ground, the stone of Henry and Eliza Oldfield. Behind these are two gravestones: William Worby (1830-1912) and his wife Rebecca Lake (1834-1917); James Worby (1827-1910) and his wife Elizabeth Quantrell (1828-1897); both men were brothers of my Grandfather John Worby.

There are several graves of Macro(w) families including Henry (1821-1896) married to Mary Buckle (1826-1903) who were my Great-Grandparents on my Mother's side; and their son Henry James Macro (1863-1882). Of course there are others dotted around including some of the families who were all relatives: Dalton, Herring, Watson, Williams, Wright, etc, but many are barely readable as a result of weathering. In the north-east corner is the dilapidated cross-stone which marks the grave of Ernest Hastings Swann (and his wife Letitia) who was the Vicar of Tottington for thirty-four years before he died in April, 1909. In the south-east corner lies the body of Miss Lucilla Reeve, who was the Estate Agent for Lord Walsingham. Originally she was buried outside the consecrated ground as she took her own life in 1950, but since then the railings have been extended to accommodate her grave. There are very few early gravestones which isn't surprising. Restorations were carried out in the fifteenth century when the South Porch was added and the remains of stone coffin lids were incorporated into it. When the church fell into disrepair during the 17th and 18th centuries, extensive reconstruction took place. A wall was built around the churchyard and several ancient large coffin stones and carved crosses, which were previously over the graves of vicars and other religious persons, were laid on top of it. By 1819 this wall had disappeared along with the coffin-lids.

Many Norfolk Churches have been restored or cleaned and are well-maintained. Thousands of people visit them every year, not for any specific religious purpose but just to walk around, view the statues and monuments, admire the architecture, the roofs and the masonry, and generally appreciate the peace and serenity. Not so with our Church of St. Andrew's at Tottington. A thorough restoration took place in 1886 under the architect Edwards Preston Williams who also restored the church at East Dereham, and the stone fabric of the building remains today much as it was at the turn of the century, but after 1942 it fell into decay as no one appeared to want the responsibility of maintaining it. When we went to the Battle Area for a Reunion in 1993, my son peeled back a piece of the rusty corrugated iron sheeting which previously replaced the windows, to peep into the dark and desolate interior. Little could be seen except for the columns and part of the ceiling; water had seeped in through the roof and damaged the floors. Shortly afterwards the Church authorities authorised the Army to pay to have the roofs covered with coloured metal sheeting, the floors and windows to be repaired. Work began in October 1995 but local Council officers felt that original tiles should have been used to retain the architectural and historical integrity of the structure. Until recently it was not open to the public; getting access to the site was difficult enough let alone gaining permission to enter. Now the guided tours allow the public inside.

Until July 1996, the last time I had entered St. Andrew's was over fifty years ago so it was difficult to remember the layout of the church inside. However, that Reunion allowed a proper visit. There is a *Short History and Guide* by Roy Tricker, which describes the interior. St. Andrew's isn't that large: the nave measures 60 ft by 23 ft; the chancel is 32 ft by 19 ft; each aisle is 53 ft long and 11 ft wide. Upon entering through the South Porch one saw the 14th century octagonal font with its concave sides and a stem curving outwards at the top. This still resides inside the church, at the north-west corner of the nave. Most of the children of Sturston and Tottington were christened in its Babtismal water. Behind it was the Vestry where the hymn books and choiresters' surplices were kept. At the bottom of the tower in the north-east corner was a prominent staircase turret which went up to the level of the bell-chamber.

My cousin Tommy Spragg climbed this narrow staircase to the parapet to take the photograph of Tottington village which is now on display in the nissen hut at West Tofts Camp near Mundford.

TOTTINGTON CHURCH, NORFOLK.S.E.

Mrs Margaret Pory, died 1598.

"When we were boys the churches did not have to be locked and we often climbed the winding steps up to the belfry, lit only by the narrow slits in the tower walls, it was ghostly. On these narrow winding steps were the bodies of birds and rodents brought in and eaten by owls. It was always a bit thrilling to go up . . . as I imagined there might be something round the next unseen corner, something unknown. Sometimes a bird would fly out unexpectedly and give us a scare. When we got to the belfry we went up a ladder to a trapdoor . . . and out on to the lead roof of the tower where we leaned over the parapet to look at the waterspouts". (Freddie Bone)

The nave was separated from the north and south aisles by handsome 14th century arcades resting on the two rows of columns with their moulded capitals and bases. Both in the nave and the aisles, were oak pews leading to the pulpit and the wooden screen beyond which was the chancel and the altar. The church floor was of 18th century brick covered in strips of coconut matting placed where there weren't any graves. We always tried to walk round or stepped over such slabs as a mark of respect. There was a fine brass in the north aisle floor. Under the kneeling effigies of a woman and a child in prayer, was inscribed:

Here Lyeth Interred the Corpes of Margaret Pory, Whose Sovle the Father of Spirites Received Into Eternal Rest The 5th April An Dom. 1598 In The 54th Yere Of Her Age. This Monvment Was Erected By Lvke Vnger Her Second Husband In Token Of A Thankfvll And Loyal Mind.

On the little girl's coat were the letters E.U. probably indicating that she was Elizabeth Unger, the daughter of his second marriage. Most of the burial slabs in the church dated from the eighteenth century. Two of these, in black marble, were in the nave next to where the old reading desk stood:

Here lyeth the body of Margaret Knopwood ye wife of Robt Knopwood, who depd this life the 27th of Novemb 1729. Aged 67 years.

Here lyeth the body of Robert Knopwood, who departed this life the twenty-seventh day of May, in the year of our Lord one thousand seven hundred and twenty-three, and in the sixty-fifth year of his age.

There was a black slab to William Farrer (1714-1775) and his wife Mary Farrer (1715-1791):

In memory of William Farrer who departed this life April 22nd, 1775, aged 61 years. As I am now so must you be
Therefore prepare to follow me.
Also Mary the wife of the above William Farrer who departed this life April 6th, 1791, aged 76 years.

And one for their son William (1750-1808):

Sacred to the memory of Willm the son of Willm and Mary Farrer who died March 20th, 1808, aged 58 years.

These memorials remain in St. Andrew's along with two matching plaques of black marble bordered with free stone on the south aisle wall:

To the memory of Joseph Duffield, who departed this life June 21, 1758, in the 88th year of his age. To the memory also of Mary Duffield, wife of the said Joseph Duffield.

In memory of Thomas Duffield youngest son of Joseph Duffield and Mary his wife. He departed this life the 3rd of April 1770 aged 46.

Mary Duffield's funeral is recorded in the Parish Register; she came from Weasingham and ended up owning 39 acres in 33 different places around Tottington which she sold to Thomas de Grey in 1774. She was buried 7th March 1784 aged 96 years.

A large marble plaque on the north aisle wall commemorates Ann Hare (1838) and the Reverend Hugh Charles Hare (1847) who was Rector of Docking and Little Durham, before coming to Tottington. A ledger-slab in the floor nearby marks the place where Anne's ashes and Hugh's remains are buried. To the south of the chancel arch was a small plaque in memory of Frederick Worby, my Father's older brother, who was church Warden for several years before being killed (1915) in France whilst taking provisions to soldiers during the First World War.

On the wall above the back of the alter is an ornamental screen - a Reredos given by the Hon. John Augustus (7th Baronet - died 1927) and Elizabeth de Grey in 1896 in thanksgiving for their son's recovery from typhoid. The Creed, the Lord's Prayer, the Ten Commandments and five Biblical texts, were engraved on the stone plaques. Above this was a beautiful stained glass window.

The Reredos in St. Andrew's Church, 1998

There were some attractive windows in the church particularly in the chancel and both aisles. The South aisle was lighted by one window to the west and three to the south and one to the East which had the figure of an angel with wings and an outstretched arm, approaching a throne having these words on a scroll; *S C S SANCTUS S C S (Holy, Holy, Holy, Lord God of Sabath)*. The North aisle was lighted by one window to the west and three to the north all with fragments of coloured glass but the East Window had the figure of a lion bearing across its back a scroll with these letters; *ECCE : S P C : S C S*. There was also a female figure with a scroll inscribed *ECCE filius*.

When the Army moved in during 1942 a Mr. Dennis King was given permission to remove the glass, medieval pews, the wooden screen and the organ from St. Andrews. Unfortunately the glass disappeared and this precipitated a prolonged countrywide search of records and storehouses. After a five year treasure hunt, the glass was rediscovered loose on the floor of an attic in Merton Rectory. The two mid-fourteenth century tracery lights (measuring 20 inches by 22 inches and depicting the emblems of St. Matthew and St. Mark) were insured for £1000 and loaned to the European Exhibition of Gothic Art in Paris for two months in 1968. Now they reside in the Jesus Chapel of Norwich Cathedral.

In 1950 various items of furniture, taken from St. Andrew's, were transferred to Rockland St. Peter's Church to replace fittings destroyed in a serious fire there in 1948. On the 13th August 1993, my youngest son took me to Rockland where we borrowed the key from the lady of the house next to the Post Office, and made our way down a little lane to the church. It was a bright, sunny day and I was full of expectation, at seeing again after 50 years, items from the church that were familiar objects of my youth. St. Peter's isn't as large as St. Andrew's, there are no columns or aisles, but twenty of the pews are there seated in the narrow nave, plus the screen and the Jacobean pulpit, and the 17th century Reading desk. It brought back so many memories.

Tottington Church was always so cold even during the Summer. It had one fairly large, enclosed coal heater in the middle of the aisle. There were attractive brass, paraffin-oil lamps, (with large white glass globes over the chimneys), which hung from the ceiling, and other smaller lamps at either end of the choir stalls and on the pulpit. Sometimes when the wicks burnt low, these lamps smoked and smelt horrible. Everything was rather dark and dismal and dusty. What a contrast with the bright and airy interior of Rockland St. Peter's.

Sadly the pews looked in a poor state but then they weren't in very good condition at Tottington; most of them are suffering the ravages of time, with woodworm holes and broken carvings. The seats are open but very narrow; the highly ornamented, four-light, traceried panels end in popyheads of varying designs. There are carved animal arm-rests - mostly dogs - some facing forwards, others backwards. Few of these were intact even at the beginning of the 18th century, being worn down and damaged by centuries of use. We looked for the old inscriptions carved on the pews but found only one still existing on the back of the first seat on the left as one enters. This pew used to be on the north side of the aisle in St. Andrew's. It bears the following line:

1636 : THOMAS SALTER AND HIS WIFE JANE

A second seat had an inscription to Walter and Alice Salter during the reign of Richard III in the 1480s: *Orate pro Animabus Walteri Salter, et Alice Urovis eius et pro quibus tenentur*. A third seat in the north aisle used to have an inscription: *Su'ptu Ed'i Salter, et Bridgitt nup' vxor' eius: An'o D'ni. 1631*. A fourth seat had on the back:

THOMAS SALTER 1636

Sadly, these three no longer exist but they were evidence of the importance the Salter family had in the village for over two hundred years. They paid for the upkeep of the church; in 1529 an Edmund Salter gave ten pounds for the restoration of the north aisle. They owned the site of the rectory joined to the east part of Tottington churchyard plus the small manor known as Martham's or Macham's

190

Inside of Rockland St. Peter's Church with Tottington pews, pulpit and rood screen

lying to the north-west of the Church. There one can still find the remains of several ruined buildings which may have been the old Manor house owned by Edmund Salter who sold the land and the rectory to a Mr. Evesdon in 1714. Nevertheless descendents of the Salter family lived at Hall Farm right up to the nineteenth century before they emigrated to America. Indeed there are still people with that surname living in and around the nearby town of Watton. A few years ago some people came from the USA to do genealogical work on the Salter family.

Gone are those well-worn and tattered hassocks which were so hard to kneel on. None of the wooden seats ever had any cushions except for the front three. These had strips of red cloth to sit on. As in most churches important people exercised proprietory rights over certain pews. Lord and Lady Walsingham came in a carriage with two horses driven by a Mr. Dalton who wore a tall black hat. They always occupied the front seats on the left hand side in front of the pulpit, and the farmers sat on the right. My Aunt Field, who was once the school teacher, had her seat in the third row on the left-hand side; she came to church wearing a huge black hat with a veil and bobbles all round, looking just like a bee-keeper! Now, all these decades, later my son photographed me sitting in the same place where I had sat as a child with my Aunt and my Mother; it was a most nostalgic moment.

The pews reminded me of the Rector from Merton, Reverend Kent and his young wife, coming over in a pony and trap to the church services. He was very interested in the children and the choir and kept the Vicar on his toes. This was a Mr. Trownsell, who often had guests staying at the Vicarage; they sat in the two seats in the chancel the other side of the ancient wooden screen. Miss Reeve gives a child's eye view:

They always seemed tall folks and the women wore such dreadful hats - the men too would turn and stare at the rows of the Sunday School. The Vicar then used the reading -desk which faced us and was opposite the pews of the Squire, always filled with bored-looking children and foreign governess, with solemn maids in small black bonnets nearby.

She bemoaned the 'harmonium-cum-American organ which was installed in the chancel in 1914; *"a nasty-looking brown wooden object with smallish pipes"*. All I remember about this organ, which stood behind the pulpit, was that someone had to pump the bellows otherwise it wouldn't play a note! It was brought to Rockland but has since been replaced. The Jacobean wooden pulpit remains in very good condition, and is situated in a similar position to where it stood in St. Andrew's against the first pillar from the chancel. It had its own miniature staircase going up so the Vicar stood above the congregation to give his sermons. The old oil lamp has gone but the frieze of carved panels near the top still remains. This Rood Screen was a fine example, handsome and gilded, but it has long since lost its lustre and looks decayed and fragile. It still has three double panels each side at the base but the paint has faded and the designs are not discernable - although these used to be of Saints and Biblical figures. There were leaf designs, also a bird, a lion, an angel, and roses - one can still make these out upon close inspection. The open work above still shows that it had beautiful carved tracery and a central entrance arch, but the paint and gilt is faded and lost.

In Tottington Church people walked through the central archway of this screen, up the well-worn, carpeted steps into the chancel with its plain plaster ceiling. Wedding couples had to go through in single file when the Vicar took them off to the altar for a special prayer. Bearers at funerals had difficulty in getting the coffin through without hitting the screen. It was the centre piece of the church and as much a focal point for the congregation, as the altar which could be seen against the back of the chancel, surrounded by its three-sided communion rails.

Miss Reeve wrote an eloquent and evocative passage about 'THE SCREEN', again from the viewpoint of a child:

As ones eyes travelled higher up the screen the tracery arches became smaller and smaller and more and more beautifully carved . . . . But it was the shelf at the base of this final bit where one's eyes rested longest because of the row of candlesticks - one between each of the uprights . . . They were short and squat and just plain lead colour where the brass had just gone dull. . . . when you entered church on the evening of harvest festival or at Christmas, you stared and stared; for candles had been put in and they were alight! How lovely they looked, and with no greenery to hide the carving of the screen how it shone; and although they were at so great a height as to crick small necks in staring, one stared and stared - and even dared to whisper to best-beloved who had taken one to see them, that heaven must be like that.

Of course St. Peter's isn't the same as St. Andrew's but it is nice to see the old furnishings looked after and in use rather than as they were in 1947: . . . *in pieces hustled away to "safety" in the dour gloom of a church which was outside the battle-training area; stacked against the damp walls in the way of the cleaners.* (Miss Reeve). A great pity that more could not have been rescued; I wonder where the hymn books, the old Bible and the large Prayer Book, went to; where are the Communion cups, the silver patens, the crimson cloth and cushion for the pulpit? what did happen to that harmonium ? So many questions unanswered; everything occurred so quickly in 1942 and the villagers weren't informed.

One couldn't say that St. Andrew's was an ornate and very attractive church but it could look lovely with candles and oil lamps lit, and especially when the flowers were put in for Easter Sunday or the fruit and vegetables laid out for Harvest Festival; then it was a picture. There was an attempt to keep the church clean and tidy; sweeping, washing down, polishing the brass and fresh flowers for Sundays. Usually Farmers' wives and school teachers helped the Vicar's wife but someone was paid to do the actual cleaning. For a long time during the latter half of the nineteenth century, a Mrs Quantrell was paid to look after the church interior. It must have been a tough job what with all the dirty coconut matting on the brick floors, the woodwork and the stone or marble memorials on the walls; apart from trying to keep the windows clean! Before the Second World War, the daughters of

Mrs Noble who lived at the Vicarage did a lot for the Church and made some attractive drawings of the building. Tommy Spragg looked after the big coke stove and he filled the oil lamps; his sister Dolly cleaned the Church during the period 1930-1942 and acted as a Sunday School teacher.

My Uncle Fred Macro was the Churchwarden from 1899 to 1912, before emigrating to Australia. Although this position lost its status towards the end of the nineteenth century, as the villagers' lay representative, Fred kept his eye on the fabric of the Church and its possessions as well as on the parson, and he remained a most respected member of the community. The Tottington Churchwardens' Accounts 1855-1913 and Vestry Minutes 1889-1913 were discovered in the possession of a Mr. Jeffrey, the owner of a secondhand bookstall in Farringdon Road, London. Mr. Glenn Edy purchased, transcribed and donated them to the Norfolk Records Office in Norwich Library, 30th July 1987. They mention a touching event in recognition of Uncle Fred's work:

"A Vestry Meeting in Parish Hall, Oct 3rd 1912 received the resignation of F. Macro and appointed his successor. The Vicar on behalf of the Parishioners, in a suitable speech presented Mr. F. Macro with a silver 'Hunter Watch' and Mrs Macro with an oak writing desk, together with the names of the subscribers which besides a few friends included nearly every household in the Parish. The Vicar also on behalf of all wished them prosperity in their new home in Australia. Mr. Macro feelingly replied."

My Father's Uncle, John Wright the blacksmith and wheelwright, was *"to inspect Windows and Fences to see what repairs required"* There were discussions about income and costs. Often Lord Walsingham paid the total rate for parishioners. The amount was pitiful compared to the church tithes which left the village every year.

The rectory and parsonage tithes of Tottington were annexed as property by Samuell Harsnett, Archbishop of York, who endowed his free schools at Chigwell in Essex. An indenture dated 11th October 1624 between Sir Thomas Southwell, Thomas Hall and Henry Best of Norwich shows the latter paid £500 for the tithes and advowsen (right to appoint the vicar). Archbishop Harnsett (former Vicar of Chigwell and Bishop of Norwich) bought and leased them for twenty-one years at a rent of £60 a year: *all that Impropriate Rectorye & parsonage of Tottington ...... and the Advowsen ...... shall forever hereafter be*

In
Memory
of

ERNEST HASTINGS
SWANN.

34 YEARS VICAR OF THIS PARISH
DIED APRIL 1909.
AND LETITIA, HIS WIFE

ERECTED BY PARISHIONERS AND FRIENDS.

"FATHER IN THY GRACIOUS KEEPING."

Gravestone of
Rev. Hastings Swann

imployed for and towards the mainteynance of the said two Schoolemasters (Chigwell School Ordinances, 14th April 1629). Of the £60 a year income, the Latin Master received £20, the English Master £25, the clerk £1, with £10 going to the bread charity and the balance kept as a reserve. Whenever possible the Vicar of Tottington was to be a former pupil of the Latin School, or failing such, one born in Chigwell parish. In 1638 Samuel Chericus Spackman, Vicar of Chigwell, was at Tottington for a year, but the only known Chigwell old boy to become Vicar was Dr. William John Burford (1799-1850), although he appointed substitutes to be curates.

Archbishop Harnsett could not have anticipated the heavy fall in rents that coincided with the 1691 land tax, nor did he allow for the charges deducted: 7s 11½d. for the Archdeacon of Norwich's procuration fee, and the £3 6s 8d. towards the stipend of the Vicar of Tottington. All these factors caused the schoolmasters' salaries to become utterly inadequate during the next one hundred years. In 1773 the Lord Chief Justice, William de Grey, later to be Lord Walsingham, wrote to the School Governors suggesting they exchange their Tottington interests for lands near Chigwell. At a meeting in Batson's Coffee house in Cornhill, the governors decided to refuse the offer – an odd decision considering that land in Woodford or Loughton was bound to have rents rising more quickly than the remote sandy Breckland. In 1869 the governors did sell the advowsen, vicarial tithes and the glebe, to Thomas de Grey, the 5th Lord Walsingham for £500, but Tottington continued to send money for leases to Chigwell School.

As Miss Reeve wrote:

This was a great shame, and I doubt if anyone in my village has ever visited this school; and certainly there is no grant or scholarship open to any child of the village to go to the school in Essex which takes over four hundred pounds a year from the church and village. When as the land agent to the owner, I send each half year a cheque for this tithe I feel angry that such things should ever have been allowed to happen - or go on happening.

In 1936 by an Act of Parliament tithes were commuted and the school was awarded £6,635 3s worth of 3 per cent redemption stock from which £312 1s 2d. was diverted to the Norwich Diocesan Board of Finance in respect of the liability for chancel repairs to Tottington Church. Examination of the Chigwell leases' revenue during the three hundred years only serves to emphasise Miss Reeve's point that such money would have made an enormous difference to Tottington had the Merton Estate diverted it to the village and its inhabitants: to the upkeep of cottages, increasing farm labourers' wages and improving the education of their children.

Public access to St. Andrew's Church is strictly prohibited as the area is used for military training with live ammunition and trespassing is illegal. People wishing to visit have to apply for a special pass and are given a guided tour by the West Tofts Battle Area. Such a scenario could not have been imagined by the generations of villagers who, week after week, made their way to 'God's House' for acts of worship. It would have been inconceivable to my ancestors that the dominating structure of their village, which was hallowed by their prayers and hymn singing, where they were baptised, married and buried, would end up as a near ruin, its interior stripped bare of furnishings; a forlorn and neglected shell like some Victorian folly.

"I think of the church standing there through the changing seasons of 46 years. How ghastly it must seem on a moonlit . . . or wild stormy night with lightning flashing and thunder echoing round. I imagine it on sunny days with the sun slanting through the windows to shine on dusty silent pews and remember happy days when my sisters were married there and every Sunday knew music and singing where now all is silent. The time will come when the church will crumble and all who remember it will be gone." (Freddie Bone 1988)

Chigwell School revenue from Tottington leases 1629-1936

1628		21 years	£60 p.a.
1649	to Thomas Garrard	21 years	£60
1670		21 years	£60
1691	to Sir Nicholas Garrard	21 years	£30

(reduction in revenue due to fall in rents and land tax of 1691)

1712	to Sir Nicholas Garrard	21 years	£40
1733-36	to Mrs N. Garrard	not known	
1736	to Thomas de Grey		£39 15s 2d.
1736-42	to Thomas Speidell		£41
1746	to Thomas Speidell		£41
1768	to Mrs H. Speidell	21 years	£70
1789	to three tenants	12 years	£210

(increased revenue due to Enclosure in late 1770s)

1801	to Nettleship and Wiffen	14 years	£300
1815			£290
1818	to Woodford		£315
1829	to William Desforges	9 years	£340
1836	(Tithe Act of 1836 rent charges were fixed at		£414 11s 8d.
1859			£447
1862			£472 12s 5d.
1868	to Lord Walsingham		£457 7s 5d.
1880			£219

(decline in agricultural prosperity towards the last quarter of the nineteenth century led to a serious fall in income from the leases)

1901		£239 5s 3d.
1902		£277 4s 10d.
1908		£286
1930s		£400?

(abridged from, *A History of Chigwell School* by Godfrey Stott)

Assuming an average annual income of £300 from 1800 onwards the total, appropriated by Chigwell School from Tottington lands, amounts to over £40,000.

THE CHURCH VICARS

In Francis Blomefield's *'An Essay towards a Topographical History of the County of Norfolk'* (1805), there is a list of the Church Vicars from 1306 - 1665.

1306, 6 May	Roger de Helmingham.	The Prioress and Convent of
1354, 12 June	Richard Markant.	Campesse, in Suffolk, who
1361 6 Oct	John Brust of Hokwold	presented until their
1362, 16 Jan	John de Hillington.	dissolution

1404, 21 June Thomas Buschel, resigned.
1416, 17 Nov John Verjaunt, resigned.
1419, 12 June Thomas Wolde of Skulton.
1433, 6 Oct Roger-Full-of-Love of Quydenham, resigned.
1451, 19 Oct John Goodwin
1459 9 Aug John Boston, resigned
1466, 13 Aug John Knyght.
1469 30 Dec John Agges
1473 27 Jan Rob Bewafiz, died vicar
1502, 8 Sept John Hey, died vicar, buried in the Chancel
1521, 6 Oct Thomas Palmer, lapse, resign.
1533, 19 Mar Thomas Bele. last presented by Prioress. John Watson, died vicar.
1548, 14 Oct Alex Lee, was deprived. Sir Richard Southwell. Knt.
1554, 21 Mar George Prance, lapse.
1568, 11 Feb Henry Goldeston, lapse, reigned
1585, 22 July Tho. Ireland, resigned. Sir Robert Southwell, knt.
1587, 6 May Rob. Gittinges   ”   ”   ”   ”
1611 3 Feb Tho. Lammas, A.M. the King as Guardian to
1613, 13 Oct Henry Bury, resigned. Thomas Southwell.
1616, 10 Dec Clement Nurse, resigned.
1623, 8 July Peter Cockerell, A.M. Thomas Southwell, Knt.
1638, 22 Feb Chericus Spackman. Samuel Uty. S.T.P. Vicar, Chigwell in Essex.
1639, 14 Feb Thomas Mould. The King by lapse.
1648, Richard Tuck; he was the last ever instituted.
1662, the vicarage was void.
1665, 26 Feb John Blome, clerk, sequestrator from which time it was held by sequestration only.

As far as I can establish the following individuals were the vicars in the eighteenth century:

1711 (Curate) Samuel Rudland (died 21 February 1717).
1721-1750 John Verdon
1750-1778 William Clough (died 2oth Aug, bd. Saham Toney).
1778-1791 Thomas Scott (formerly the Curate).
1799-1850 Dr. William John Bursford from Chigwell School was Vicar he appointed substitutes.
1806 - 1812 The Rev. Henry Frankland. (Curate).
1812 - 1814 Charles Wodsworth (Curate).
1814 - 1815 Thomas Sayers (Curate)
1815 May-Dec Joseph Wilkinson (assistant minister).
1816 Gooch Fowell (Curate)
1812 - 1816 The Rev. George Bidwell.
1816- The Rev. Ralph Grenside, officiating in Nov.
1816 The Rev. William John Burford (Vicar) (Master of Chigwell Grammar School)
1817 - 1836 The Rev. Matthew Dawson Duffield (late of Caius College in Cambridge) ordained Curate 20 July.
1836 The Rev. W. J. Burford was at the vicarage. The Rev. Hugh Charles Hare (died 1847)
1850-1864 The Rev. Frederick W. Mant.

1869 the appointment of Vicars of Tottington came into the hands of Lord Walsingham (purchased the advowsen from Chigwell School)

1865 - 1883 The Rev. Samuel Cutler Hooley.
1883 - 1909 The Rev. Ernest Hastings Swann.
1912 The Rev. Mr. Trownsell was vicar of Thompson and Tottington followed by Rev. Matthews and then Rev. Robb whilst the Reverend Kent at Merton Rectory was in charge of all three Parishes.
1929 - 1930s The Rev. Thomas ran all three Parishes from Merton Rectory.

THE REVERENDS AND THE RECTORY

Tottington had a large number of Vicars during the Nineteenth Century, mostly curates of no great consequence. One who was important, the Reverend Hugh Charles Hare (died 3rd Nov 1847, aged 61) lies with his wife, Anne (died 21st April 1838, aged 54 – daughter of Isaac and Ann Bird of Burnham Norton) in the floor of the Church. In the latter half of the Nineteenth century, two other Vicars dominated church activities in the local area and were highly respected. The first was the Rev. Samuel Cutler Hooley (1865 - 1883) born in Nottingham, 1816, and married to Ann Lucilla who originated from Canada. They had travelled about since one son John Charles, was born in the Scilly Isles; two others, Samuel and Ellis were born in West Hackney; Claudius and Charles were born at Belchamp, Essex, whilst Marianne, William and Henry were born at Tottington. The second worthy was the Rev. Ernest Hastings Swann (1882 - 1909) born at Great Yarmouth in 1857 and buried at the back of Tottington churchyard. He was married to Letitia and they had two daughters, Alice and Helen, and two sons, Alfred and Victor, all baptised at Tottington. Although dead before I was born, the latter Vicar was well thought of and had imprinted himself in the memory of older people in the village.

Those who followed seemed to be men of lesser consequence but they still retained a certain position and residual authority within the village. In 1912 the Rector of all three Parishes of Merton, Thompson and Tottington was the Reverend Charles Kent who lived at Merton Rectory until 1928 and wrote a book about the area entitled, *In the Land of the 'Babes in the Wood'*. The Vicar of Tottington was the Rev. Charles Morris Trownsell, followed by a Rev. Matthews and then Rev. Richard John Robb in 1925. After 1929 a Rev. Thomas ran all three Parishes from Merton.

We called Reverend Kent 'The Rector' and he always seemed old to me. I suppose he was in his sixties. I don't know whether he had been married before but his wife was young, about thirty years old, maiden name of Cunningham. I believe she had been on the stage. At the time their marriage was considered a 'nine days wonder' but it's surprising how quickly things quieten down and are accepted. She was a very lively woman and always in plays as she was friendly with the Dramatic Society in Watton. When the Pageants were held at Merton Rectory, both the Rector and his wife took part; also the Delph's who were chemists, the Reeve's who kept the harness shop, the Harvey's who owned the newsagents, some young people named Trollop plus several other families from Watton. Rev. Kent had a pony and trap usually driven by a man called Arthur Crook who was also the gardener and continued working at the Rectory when Rev. Thomas took over. The Kent's were often at Tottington taking services at the Church, attending the Sunday School, and visiting the Day School. He was very keen on children singing in the choir.

I don't remember ever going into the Vicarage next to Tottington Church but my cousin, Dolly Spragg whose parents lived opposite for many years used to visit especially when the Noble sisters rented that property. She described it as a lovely house with large windows each containing six or eight panes of glass. Tall chimneys stood at either end of the roof. Inside were large Front and Dining rooms plus a long passageway into the kitchen at the back where there was another room for the laundry and boilers, etc. The bedrooms were spacious and well furnished. It had lots of trees and shrubs, and a number of sheds at the back, where her brother Tommy kept chickens and tended the beautiful gardens.

I came back home from London in the late Autumn of 1929. As it was near Christmas my parents suggested I wait until the New Year to find a job. This worried me as it meant living off them and not having any money; also my cousin, Minnie Hunt married Harry Street and as a bridesmaid I needed a new dress,etc. Fortunately, when Rev. Thomas

Tottington Vicarage

arrived from Douglas on the Isle of Man, he required domestic staff so in February 1930 I went to work at Merton Rectory about three miles away from Eastmere. It was a very pretty place consisting of a large house and out-buildings surrounded by flower and vegetable gardens, a rose garden, paddock and lawns where there was a tennis court. One lovely deep incline covered in flowers was called 'The Dell'. During my school days this was where we had our Pageants with the old Rector, Reverend. Kent. It was a heavenly place to me, surrounded by shrubs and little paths. I woke early to hear the birds singing especially the cuckoos upsetting the blackbirds which then made a sound like peas rattling in a bottle, 'mobbing' we called it. Across the paddock was a farm where we bought our milk, butter and eggs.

The Rectory was a lovely old red brick building with a conservatory at the front facing out onto lawns. All the rooms were large comprising a Drawing Room, Dining Room, study, a Hall with another room like a cloakroom and a door which went into the backyard. The kitchen was big enough for us maids to use it as our living room; it contained a big black Eagle stove with two ovens and a Donkey Stove to heat the water. Another door, used by maids and tradesmen, led from the backyard into the scullery with contained the sinks and a copper used for washing clothes. Next to this was a huge brick pantry containing food and crockery. In the front Hall there was a little room where at one time the

The back of Merton Rectory, 1931. Rev. Thomas' son, Peter

Hilda Worby with Rev. Thomas' children, Peter and Jocelyn

other maid washed the glasses and silver but when I was there we washed up together in the scullery.

Mrs Thomas, a very nice lady, did the cooking assisted by two maids and a governess for her six year old twins, Peter and Jocelyn. I did the household chores and helped her with the meals and there was a washer woman, Mrs Blanche, who walked about four miles to the Rectory to do the laundry on a Monday and ironed on a Tuesday; we helped her hang out the clothes in the paddock. This could be a pleasant task in summer but terrible on cold days; no washing machines and spin driers at that time! It took all day to do the washing and the old gardener, Arthur Crook, spent ages using a long-handled pump to get water into the house as well as bringing in sticks and wood to put under the copper to keep the water heated. All the fires were ordinary grates for wood and coal; it was my job to get up about 6.30 a.m. to light these fires, and the huge Eagle range.

When the other maid left Nora Fincham came from the village of Rockland; she was a nice friendly person and we got on well together. I was given the job of looking after the twins who were lovely but so mischievous. After lunch I took them for walks and we wandered for miles over the fields and meadows catching tadpoles and gathering flowers, etc. The children had a large twin pram and sometimes they persuaded me to take them out in it; one day it overturned and Peter cut his hand. Mrs Thomas was a kind and understanding as she knew just how artful her twins could be, but I never took them out in the pram again. Like their Mother, whose brother painted landscapes, the children were artistic and spent a lot of time drawing and painting; I still have some of their pictures.

At first I cycled to work daily but after a few weeks they asked me to live in, as there were lots of bedrooms. Some were never used but one was kept for storing apples and every night Nora and I raided it to pinch an apple last thing before retiring to our individual rooms. We often went out with the family to the seaside and for picnics. Nora and I played tennis with them and Rev. Thomas used to say I was a second Betty Nuttall, which was quite a compliment since she was one of the best women players at that time. Mind you he was fond of his beer although I never saw him tipsy. Once when there was an earth tremor at one o'clock in the morning he jumped into his Daimler and drove off. We laughed and said the Rev. Thomas was on his way to Heaven in his car never mind the rest of us! Strangely, he left the vehicle at the bottom of the drive and then walked back to the house.

Nora and I had one half day off a week plus every other Sunday and Mrs Thomas stayed with the children to let us go to church on a Sunday evening. Merton was about a mile from Watton and within easy cycling distance from Eastmere Farm. By the 1920s horses and carts were

Carting Hay at Merton Rectory. Tommy and Dolly Spragg with
Rev. Thomas' children, Jocelyn and Peter. c. 1932

fewer and motorcars had increased but the roads and lanes were very safe places. Not that I went very far and we had to be in by 10 p.m. There was a large wooden hut just outside the grounds which was used for meetings and social gatherings and we often went there for dances. Sometimes when I went home, Dad would cycle back with me. Then I acquired a young man, a third cousin, Gordon Hancock, and he cycled with me. We both had fair hair and were often taken for brother and sister. I think Dad was a bit put out; if I didn't go to church on a Sunday he came over on his bike to see me; maids were not allowed to have boyfriends to visit - and quite right too!

Rev. Thomas and his family spent their holidays on the Isle of Man. In 1931 they let the Rectory to a Rev. Blackburn from up North; he had several grown up daughters and sons, and a huge Great Dane dog. It was the wettest July I ever knew. My Father fell off the long cart and hurt his ribs and Mother became ill so I had to look after her. Nora, who was a little older than me, was going steady with a young man from Watton. Whilst the Thomas's were away we both decided to leave and handed in a month's notice. Nora went off to be married, and my restless feet took me back into service in Hampstead, London. Later my boyfriend, Gordon, joined the Norfolk Regiment and Phyllis Leeder, (the eldest daughter of George Leeder and Alice Maud Williams), took my job at Merton Rectory. I had been there two years and it was one of the happiest times of my life.

The Methodist Chapel next to the New School

THE METHODIST CHAPEL

The non-conformist element in Norfolk was very strong, but the widespread, positive effect of the Primitive Methodists only began in the 1830s when they came from Lincolnshire. Congregations slowly formed in parishes all over Norfolk, but more so in the open villages than closed ones like Tottington.

Landowners, important farmers and professional people attended the Anglican Church but not the Chapel whereas most villagers who were religious attended both. There wasn't a clear division of allegiance as existed between Protestants and Catholics. The Rev. Kent wrote that the villager *"liked the praying and preaching of the Chapel; he felt at ease, at home, comfortable"*. Partly this was because of the democratic nature of Methodism. At St. Andrews Church ordinary people were made to feel inferior and to show deference by bowing and curtsying; Lord Walsingham would tell a person off for not toucing his hat to him. In the Chapel everyone was equal, illiterate men and women could develop their own brand of public speaking, and by expressing their thoughts aloud they gained an independence of spirit. The language may have been crude, even offensive but such discussion enhanced villagers learning and self-respect.

To some extent this activity was an affront to the local Vicar and the gentry, even more so when Methodist Ministers were in the fore-front of championing farm workers' rights. The Chapel became a centre for social forces opposed to both the Anglican Church, the landowner and the public house. As a result Chapels were opposed by landowners in many areas; indeed it wasn't until 1922 that a proper, unpretentious, brick-built Methodist chapel was erected in Tottington next to the New School - before this a little green tin hut served its purpose. The new structure had several foundation stones lain in the bottom wall dedicated to different people who had subscribed money for the building. A pity that it couldn't have been saved after the Battle Area was established. For us it meant a long walk into the village so sometimes we went to Little Cressingham Chapel instead as this was also about two miles away.

Chapels were busy, comforting, social centres where members often met up during the week. A number of people attended regularly and a Vicar came from Watton for the services. The atmosphere was friendly, active and exciting, the sermons lively and entertaining, There was the usual yearly Anniversary Service where nearly all the village joined in with songs and recitations ; the liittle harmonium seemed more homely than the church organ being pumped by some poor little boy. My friend Nesta Sculfer and I often sang a hymn called 'Little Mary'. Also the Harvest Festival, when there would be a party with cakes, jellies, blamanges, tea and lemonade; all the produce given went to the hospital in the same way as that from the Church.

Once the Tottington Church no longer had its own Vicar and services were less frequent, the villagers attended Chapel. The Fisher's and the Bone family were Chapel people. Ethel Bone told me that whilst her sisters and brothers were baptised in St. Andrew's, her's took place at the Chapel. When it came to confirmation, the Anglican Rector in charge of Merton, Thompson and Tottington, would not believe she had been baptised since she wasn't on the Anglican Register. Nevertheless she was confirmed at Ashill whereas mine took place at Carbrooke, being the places visited by the Bishop of Norwich on his circuit.

St. Andrew's Church with new roof, 1998

THE WAR MEMORIAL

One could claim that there were few more patriotic villages in England than Tottington and Sturston. Before the First World War there were about 150 males in the villages; many of these were too young or too old to go to war, and some like my Father weren't fit enough to be accepted; yet 59 able-bodied men went off to serve and 15 of these, including my Uncle Fred Worby, never came back. Those men fought for an England of their own countryside, their village commnunity - for a rural tradition which was radically altered by the War itself.

The large numbers of Norfolk lads who joined up for service mixed with others from all over the country. They travelled, lived in towns, went abroad and met people with different accents, attitudes, ideas and behaviour. Such contact and mobility offered an alternative lifestyle whilst the actual conflict destroyed bodies, minds and many established beliefs. A whole generation died and many who were lucky enough to survive, had no wish to return to the confines of village life.

Throughout England, villages sought to commemorate the Great Patriotic War; Tottington was no exception. The relatives and friends of servicemen, whom the villages were justly proud of, collected money to erect a memorial to their memory. In her book, *The Earth No Longer Bare*, Miss Reeve noted that the villagers,

The War Memorial in front of the Reading Room

Defied the all-powerful vicar by insisting that the memorial to our dead should be in the centre of the village, and not a tablet on the wall of the church . . .those great days after 1918 when we raised quite a lot of money with cricket matches for our War Memorial. We sold tons of soft drinks, vegetables, fruit and vegetables and heaps of other things . .the winning team capped round . . the losing eleven were fined! How hard we had to work to raise enough money to get a plain stone memorial to erect in proud and grateful memory to the men who had died in what we hoped was a war to end war.

It was unveiled on a Sunday in 1919 outside the Reading Room, *"where they could place flowers or say a prayer".* Many of the men had been Nonconformists and Reverend Robb obviously disagreed with so public a display: *"the vicar called himself a man of God; but sometimes we thought of him as an envoy of the devil. He had abused us and said if we had our way over this matter disasters would fall on our fair village, and our memorial become a 'cockshott for passers-by'."*

Well, Rev. Robb's prediction certainly came true but I don't think God was offended by our monument recording the names of those who fought and died in the First World War. The War Memorial bears the following inscription:

ERECTED
IN PROUD AND GRATEFUL MEMORY
OF THE GALLANT SONS
OF STURSTON AND TOTTINGTON
WHO FOUGHT FOR THEIR COUNTRY
IN THE GREAT WAR , 1914-1918.
THEIR NAME LIVETH FOR EVERMORE.
THESE DIED THAT WE MIGHT LIVE.

FREDERICK BONE	CHARLES RAE
ROWLAND FLATT	WALTER RAYNER
WILLIAM FLATT	WILLIAM THOMPSON
WALTER FRISTON	ARTHUR THORPE
HERBERT HANCOCK	ALBERT WOOLSEY
HERBERT KENNY	FREDERICK WORBY
PHILLIP MOORE	EDWIN WRIGHT

WILLIAMS PERKINS

Such a tragedy and a waste of young men who had everything to live for. It was repeated in villages and towns all over Britain. To some extent nothing was the same thereafter; people went on with their lives yet many were haunted by the memory of those who did not return. It wasn't just individual family grief but a whole community loss since so many of the dead were related to one another. We can only imagine what life would have held in store for them and the effect they might have had on society.

My own Father was fortunate not to go but his two brothers, Frederick and Jack were called up. Sadly, Uncle Frederick Ernest Worby (born 15. 5.1881) died in France, 24th October 1915, whilst driving provisions for the soldiers. He was a very popular man and great pals with my Father. Like all the Worby men he was big and tall with large hands; he had a strong jaw line and wore a slight moustache. At the beginning of the Great War, I was two years old but I retain this faint memory of him in his uniform coming to Eastmere to say goodbye before going off to the trenches. His body lies in a war grave in France. He was mourned and missed by all who knew him.

Those who returned continued a roll call of village families:

W.	ADLEY	Albert	OLDFIELD
Joseph	BALLS	Arthur	OLDFIELD
Jack	BELHAM	Ernest	OLDFIELD
A	COOKE	George	OLDFIELD
Tom	COOKE	John	OLDFIELD
William	COOKE	William	OLDFIELD
Daniel	FISHER	Fred	PERKINS
Elija	FISHER	Archie	RANDS
Geoffrey	RAE	Herbert	REEVE
Walter	FLATT	Alfred	SWANN
W.	GATHERCOLE	Fred	TUDDENHAM
Robert	HERRING	Herbert	TUDDENHAM
Charles	HANCOCK	Jack	TUDDENHAM
Scarfe	HUNT	W.	LEDDON
George	WEEDS	Fred	WILLIAMS
George	LEEDER	C .	WATSON
Sidney	LEEDER	Will	WATSON
Robert	LEFFLEY	Arthur	MACRO
Robert	WOODS	Edward	WOOLSEY
John	WORBY	Fred	WOOLSEY
S.	WRIGHT		

John George Warby, or Uncle Jack as he was called, survived the War; he was at Gallipoli when aged nineteen. I think he was in the Norfolk Regiment which afterwards became the Royal Norfolks. Once he told me of a time when he was in the trenches and the Turks ran along the top, shouting and screaming, with someone's head on a bayonet. It must have been a terrible experience for someone who had led such a sheltered life and was made such a fuss of by his mother and sisters. My own Father would probably have taken it in his stride but not Uncle Jack. I believe he was wounded in the leg but in any case he had an awful time and was lucky to survive.

He was a tall, dark, handsome man with a bonny face and blue-grey eyes plus a mop of black curly hair which would never lay down. Nevertheless it was always neat and tidily brushed backwards. Everyone loved Jack and I was very fond of him too which only makes me wonder what Uncle Fred would have been like had he survived. Upon returning home Jack lodged with his sister Gertie who married his pal Alfred Simpson. Both men worked in Burrell's Engine firm at Thetford for a short while but Jack left for London and passed the entrance examination into the Metropolitan Police. Whilst stationed in Islington he met and married on 1st July 1925, the daughter of an undertaker, Martha Florence Hawke. Aunt Doll, as we called her, never felt comfortable with Grandmother nor with her sister-in-laws, although she became good friends with Emmeline.

Being in London they often visited one another on John's days off. Sometimes both families travelled up together to visit Grandmother. We looked forward to their visits at Eastmere as we all went for long walks on a Sunday; a tribe of cousins tagged along with them and it made a good cricket match with everyone joining in. When I first went to London aged fourteen, I lived with Aunt Emmeline in Barnes but saw a lot of Uncle Jack and Aunt Doll. Sometimes I went to stay with them at their flat in Arlington Square, which was on the third floor, consisting of a kitchen, bedroom and small landing yet their front room was on the second floor, and they had to share the bathroom. Jack drove a squad car but owned a motor-bike and sidecar, later he had an Austin 7, and came up to Norfolk as often as he could.

Doll was a nice lady, about average height and sturdy build. We became great friends and I spent a lot of time with them when I went back to London aged nineteen. When he retired from the police after the Second World War, Jack came up to Norfolk and lived with Aunt Blanche and Walter for a while. He worked for Mr. Timothy White's family as a handyman where he did the garden and sometimes acted as

Uncle John in uniform, 1917

Uncle Frederick in uniform, 1914

212

Aunt Doll and Uncle John Worby

Butler. They had a pretty little lodge opposite the gates of Salle Hall, but the ceilings were very low and it seemed a depressing place inside. Their little Ford car enabled them to get around and visit all the families. Like Aunt Emm, they didn't have any children but Jack was fond of other people's and made a great fuss of my own two boys. Doll was disappointed I didn't call the second one after him.

When Jack became ill with pain in his chest the Doctor said he had fibrocitus but Aunt Emm's husband took him to see his physician who diagnosed cancer of the lung and gave Jack a few weeks to live. He went into Whitlingham Hospital and lasted six weeks before dying aged 59 on the 18th August 1956. He was buried in Salle churchyard just inside the wicker gates. His death was a great shock and loss to Doll who returned to London to live with her relatives in Islington where she died aged 75 from a haemorrhage of the brain. Her body was brought up to Salle and buried with Jack in 1980. Sadly such graves are neglected and forgotten but my son and I sometimes visit and put flowers on their tombstone in remembrance.

That other stone memorial, on which the name of John Worby and many of his relatives was inscribed seventy-six years ago, IN HONOUR OF THE RETURNED from the 1914-1918 War, stands isolated. It was removed to Merton Wood Corner on the way to Thompson village after the Army requisitioned the Battle Area. When the the Hon, Richard de Grey died in January 1984 he left a net estate worth between £25,000 and £40,000, and income from £200 left to the Trustees was meant to pay someone to keep the Memorial tidy. However, for a long time it was left forlorn and neglected; its names growing less and less visible each year, unseen and unknown by passers-by. Thankfully, in 1997 it was cleaned up.

THE VILLAGE SHOP

Mrs. Edith Balls ran the shop, assisted by her daughter Gladys. People seemed a bit in awe of her as she could be sharp and didn't put up with any nonsense. She always wore these spectacles on the end of her nose, and looked over the top of them as you entered the shop; it was enough to put us kids off. Several girls from the village worked there as soon as they left school: Gladys Thompson, Dolly Fisher and Gladys Williams. The shop was a busy little place situated between the Old School and the timber yard owned by Charles Wright the carpenter; on the Watton Road at the beginning of the village just after Church Lane. The premises were part of a house; the front doorway was all cobbled with a little porch over the top to keep out the rain, and to its right was a small window. The door was left open for the customers to enter; a passage-way (absolutely packed with all kinds of things, some even hanging from the ceiling) went into the living quarters but the actual shop was on the right hand side.

It was a small room with a brick floor covered in coconut matting, and shelves on the walls stacked with all and sundry - a bit like Aladdin's Cave. Mrs Balls sold anything and everything, *'from a needle to a haystack'* as the saying goes. What she didn't have she would always get for us. Under the window, were two little, upright wooden chairs where people could sit to wait and chat. On the wooden counter was a set of brass scales with proper weights. Sugar, sweets, butter, fruit and vegetables, were weighed, even loose tobacco and 'twist' (a block of baccy which was chewed like gum). You could buy a 1d worth of aniseed balls and pay ½d for a bar of chocolate. We didn't have nicely wrapped food in the first decades of this century, not like the pre-weighed, cellophaned-wrapped foodstuffs from the supermarket. Had we been able to peep into the future and seen the disappearance of the village shop and the growth of superstores, as well as the prices, we would never have believed it possible in our lifetime.

The shop sold newspapers and was also the village Post Office. One could buy daily papers like the E.D.P. and the Mirror but our family took the weekly 'Thetford and Watton Times'; Mother had a weekly magazine 'The Home Companion' and as children we took a comic called 'Playtime'. Later on, newspapers were also delivered by a boy on a bicycle from a shop in Watton, called Edwards and Son. This still exists but has grown enormously. Mrs. Balls stayed open until 8 p.m. and the last post was at 10 p.m., taken to Thetford by a red mail van from Watton which returned at 4 a.m. The Postman would be on his bicycle round by 6 a.m. and we received letters at Eastmere by 7 a.m. and then again about 3 p.m. Watton was the nearest money order and telegraphic office.

Several shop carts came into the village usually from Watton. In my early years a butcher called Mr. Sharman came on a Saturday morning in his horse and cart. Mr. Sharman ceased coming round in the early 1920s but Mother had a man call on a Tuesday and Friday from another butcher in Watton, named Walter Whalebelly, the same family which hired Mortimer Farm from Lord Walsingham. I can see Mum going to the gate with her round meat dish, the dog following and the two cats running expectantly with their tails in the air. I still posess that old meat dish! Mother couldn't afford much, although we ate bacon and of course we had rabbits and the occasional pheasant. People weren't vegetarian by choice in those days, just too poor to eat meat that often. A small round joint of beef, for Sunday, cost about 2/-, but Mother might buy a portion of shin to make the meat puddings in a basin for Saturday dinner, or sausages, or 'fry' (offal) or a biggish piece of suet, and some bones for the dog. Even after the War in 1946 we could buy a small leg of lamb for 2/6. Mother kept the suet fresh in her large flour bin; there was no such thing as a fridge or an ice box and milk had to be boiled directly we fetched it home in the summer time. In the late 1920s, villagers were able to get milk and butter from at least four farms.

The Village Shop

Three bakers called on the village. Mr. Payne had one shop in Watton and a man called Eric Chilvers brought the bread round. When Mr. Payne died, Eric set up on his own at Ellingham and Mother carried on trading with him. He called on a Tuesday and Friday and during the winter it was often dark when he came with a light on his pony and cart. He also sold flour in 14lb bags, chicken food, yeast and no doubt cakes. The chicken food was maize and 'supas'- very much like fine bran and as children we often ate some raw but didn't take any harm. Normally it was mixed with boiled potatoes and peelings for the chickens' tea; their first meal in the morning was just corn. The other two bakers didn't come up to our farm at Eastmere. A Mr. Cross eventually took over from Mr Payne and employed a boy called Rex Jolly and the other baker was a Mr. Hazel who took over Mr. Ludkin's business. In the 1930s motor cars and vans replaced the old horse and carts.

Groceries were obtained from stores like George Durrants' "Great Shop", the Merchant and Milliner and Tea Dealer in Watton. Orders were placed one Thursday and delivered the next by a man called Mr. Goodrum. He would take out his book and write down Mother's order; after every item he would say "Thank you Mrs Worby". This tickled my brother and I pink so we ended up calling him just that. It was very convenient because as well as grocery we could order any drapery on approval. Later on a younger man came with a motor van and we called him "Hubby" Lancaster. There was an International Stores nearly next door to Durrant's which started coming round in the 1930s and Mother got a few things off them. They only sold grocery but they had a large slab of cake on their van which was quite cheap and came in very handy when packing up for the men on the fields and for harvest teas. D. Dunnett, another important store on the north side of the High Street in Watton, sold grocery provisions, hosiery, family drapery, boots and shoe, but didn't deliver in Tottington. Bicycles became more common so people could get into Watton easier and a bus went there on a Wednesday.

The insurance man came on his bicycle every Saturday morning, to collect the weekly premiums. There were two companies, 'The Pearl' and 'The Prudential'; Mother paid into the latter. On a Friday afternoon an oil cart came to the other Eastmere Cottage on the Cressingham road. Mother walked about a quarter of a mile to meet this man. He came from a firm called 'Butcher's' and sold oil and candles, etc. Mother took her oil cans to have them filled with paraffin for our lamps, and later an oil stove which she used for cooking and heating. These stoves became quite popular and could be used to boil a kettle on for a quick 'cuppa'. The Butcher's cart was covered over with canvas and he carried a lot of extra stock such as brushes, pails and all things connected with hardware. There were some firms which came around with clothes; these were called *"Talli men"* but my Father was very strict about having things on 'tic' (as we called it). If we couldn't afford anything we just didn't have it; *"Neither a lender nor a borrower be"* as the saying goes.

THE SHOEMAKER and POSTMAN

On the right hand side of Mrs. Balls' premises was another shop used by her brother Wilfred Herring as a shoemaker's. 'Tippy' as he was known was also the village Postman. Somehow the children aggravated and cheeked him, and he would chase them away from his window. He made and mended most people's boots and shoes whilst sitting on a stool wearing his old leather apron. The door of his shop was at the back and was split in half like a stable door so if we went round he simply opened up the top half to speak to us.

Tippy Herring was the last in a long line of shoesmiths. The surname was well known in Norfolk dating back many hundreds of years. In 1327 one Johanne Heryng is listed in Thompson, and during the eighteenth centuries there were Herring families in Merton and Tottington. William Herring (1744-1824), a cordwainer from Buckenham Parva and West Tofts married three times and had fifteen children. One of these, William (1787-1866) was also a cordwainer and Parish Clerk for Tottington. He ran a business which employed two men and two boys. His second wife Mary Crook bore him three sons who were all shoemakers: John Herring (1816-1870) who married Sarah Fox (1818-1887) at Tottington in 1844; Henry (b.1818) who married a widow called Mary Ann Macrow (nee Walker); and Robert (b. 1823) who married another Mary Ann Macrow. John's eldest son, William John Herring (b.1844) left the village to become a teacher in Oldham and gave rise to several Herring families in and around Manchester.

Many of Henry's children died early, but Robert was the Father of Wilfred Victor (b.1866) and Edith (b1862). Robert is listed in the Kelly's Directory for Norfolk 1881 as grocer, shoemaker and Postmaster, having taken over this from Edmund Macrow. Mary Herring acted as sub-Post Mistress and Edith, who married a Walter William Balls from Bury St. Edmunds, inherited the store. Edith had three children, Elsie, Gladys and Joseph (who was a blacksmith and

Postman for a while before Walter Wyett, the caretaker of the Working Men's Club, took over). Joe married Ethel Perkins and had three sons, one of whom, Donald Balls, was the Postman in Eccles near Quidenham after they left the village in 1942.

This slight digression into a family history serves to highlight the continuity in village life of trades which were often handed down from Father to son. It also illustrates the intricate web of relationships which permeated the families in Tottington. My Mother always said we were related to the Herring's and the Balls and my son's genealogical research has proved this to be the case. My Great-Grandfather, Henry Macrow (1821-1896) was a cousin of Wilfred and Edith's Mother, Mary Ann Macrow (b.1832) so they had Grand-parents in common, John Mackrow (1767-1848) married to Mary Mackrow (1776-1845). Village life depended upon this continuity of employment and the family inter-relationships built up over centuries. It was the destruction of this by the takeover in 1942 which was so sad and unfortunate. Once removed, people lost contact, old allegiences faded and family links were forgotten.

THE WHEELWRIGHT CARPENTER and BLACKSMITH

There was a little bank and some railings by the side of Tippy Herring's and a gate which went into a big yard belonging to Mr. John Wright, the blacksmith, and his son Charles, the carpenter. The large shed and buildings stood well back from the road so it was a quiet place for horses to be shod. This site had been used by wheelwrights, blacksmiths and carpenters for a very long time, being known as the 'Smithy', with a Timber Yard by the side of it. This yard was large (Tommy Spragg hired one of the sheds to keep his car in) and always had farm implements lying around waiting to be mended.

For centuries the wheelwright was a most important and indispensable craftsman of the village. He needed carpentry skills and cooperation with the blacksmith who made the iron items, from nails and hinges to hoes and scythes, from metal tyre rims for wooden wheels to coulters and plough shares. Sometimes one man practised all the crafts but more often they were shared by brothers, or a Father and son, or two families. A large Smithy would employ several workers and apprentices, all types of vehicles and machinery were built and maintained: wagons, ploughs, harrows, rolls, horse-hoes, cultivators, grass cutters, binders, threshing-machines, etc.

218

This is well ilustrated by the Chilvers family which dominated these crafts for most of the nineteenth century in Tottington. In the 1830s and 1840s John Chilvers (1771-1846), who married Kerenhappuch Kennedy from Watton, was a farmer and a wheelwright; and from the 1850s to the 1890s their son, John Chilvers (b.1811) was a blacksmith and wheelwright, employing five men, including Edward and Arthur Watson, plus James and William Cook; (another son William Chilvers b. 1814, became a shoemaker). The original John had three brothers: William (b. 1776) was a shoemaker who married Charlotte Balls, and their sons, William, James and John Chilvers were also shoemakers; Samuel (1778-1833) became a butcher; Robert (1790-1853) was a farmer and carpenter as was his eldest son, George (b. 1822) whilst his youngest son, Abraham (b. 1828) became a blacksmith. Strangely enough, by the time of the 1871 Census this very important Tottington family of craftsmen had all but disappeared from the village, leaving John Chilvers the wheelwright with his son Robert (b.1854) as the blacksmith. John Wright (1852-1936) came from Caston and married my Grandfather's sister, Sarah Ann Worby (1849-1904). Their son Charles (b. 1878) was my Father's cousin and very good friend, playing cricket and going hand-bell ringing together. John was apprenticed at the Smithy to John Chilvers and eventually took over the business. By 1904 John Wright was the village blacksmith and wheelwright. The 1912 Kelly's Directory of Norfolk also lists him as cart and wagon builder, and for a while he acted as the village undertaker, arranging the pall-bearers. John always walked in front of the coffin at burial services and after he died the village had to use undertakers from Watton.

Almost every member of the community called upon a village blacksmith who could provide a grate for the fire, door hinges, flat irons or the heaters for box irons; repair household items like frying pans, kettles with broken handles, or holed coppers; and make gardening tools. Charlie Wright made a lot of handles for all sorts of tools in the village. My Father and brother had their own special spade and fork, as did many of the workmen. Small items of furniture could be ordered. When we were quite small Father had two wooden stools made for my brother and myself; mine is still in use at home. Also we had two nice picture frames and I had a pastry board made. It may seem odd but wood for making things was in very short supply even though the Estate abounded in trees. We were not allowed to cut down anything which was flourishing, only dead wood and that was for the fire. Once I wanted a small bookcase and Father tried to make me one. All he could find for the job was wood from an old orange box. He didn't have any nails so you can imagine what it loked like. I didn't like it one bit!

I remember Father's huge wheel-barrow made of solid wood. It was painted green on the outside and pink inside and was so heavy we children couldn't move it - a far cry from the lightweight alloy barrows of today. When we were older and stronger it was still tricky as like all barrows things had to balance in the middle or over it went. There was a fairly large wheel and a tail or dash board at the back which could be removed to allow us to put a shovel in and empty it. Barrows, used on the farm for shifting manure from the stables, were made of metal, similar to those found on building sites to move cement. I guess they were made at the Smithy as well but when I've no idea. People kept tools and equipment for generations so there were things being used in the village that were very old.

Wagons weren't expensive to make; from £10 in the 1890s to about £25 in 1920. It depended on the type, shape and size, the wood used and the decoration. When properly serviced - greased, cleaned, painted and maintained - they lasted forever. I don't remember John Wright and Charlie ever making a complete wagon but there were wheels to re-tyre and mend. Each wheelwright selected the wood himself from local trees in the forest; Charlie Wright had some sheds on the left of the Smithy Yard where such wood was stored for a couple of years. Nearby was a saw-pit about six feet deep where the wood was cut. I remember seeing shavings lying in the bottom after Charlie had been sawing wood for a coffin. The pit-saw, what we called a 'cross-cut', was a long, large-toothed blade which required two men to operate. A log was placed on struts or rollers and the more skilled sawyer straddled it above the pit pushing a 'tiller' handle to make the downward cut. The bottom sawyer stood in the pit to help the upward stroke and keep the saw oiled. The resulting planks were stacked with spacers to allow air to circulate and season the wood.

The Smithy was much more than a garage for making and maintaining carts and wagons. In Tottington it was one of the main meeting places for men to mardle (gossip) and exchange news, especially since there was no pub in the village after the turn of the century. The forge always had an audience of onlookers standing around watching the work in progress. The fierce flames of the blazing furnace kept red hot by someone pumping the wheezing bellows, and the shoes being nailed to horses hoofs, as well as all the various tools and implements, provided a ready source of entertainment and topics for discussion. Passers by were drawn by the clang of white-hot metal, beaten by a hammer on the anvil, plunged into cold water causing a furious hiss of steam.

There were lots of horses on the Tottington farms even up to the Second World War and since some of them might travel forty miles in a day their shoes were soon 'burned up'. It was fascinating to watch my Great Uncle replacing shoes, 'roughing' or 'turning' them in Winter and making new ones. Of course these weren't machine made; they were heated and hammered out of a measured length of raw metal, and 'fitted' to each horse individually. Shoeing was hard work; taking off the nail heads and removing the old shoe, cleaning up the hoof with a knife and being careful not to cut the frog (the horny elastic pad in the centre), when levelling off the surface with the hoof-parer. The horse-shoe was shaped to the hoof and placed on whilst still hot causing a lot of smoking and a sizzing sound through burning which left a pungent smell in the air. As a child I used to feel sorry for the horse but I gather this caused no pain as the hoof is horny and not sensitive. Occasionally things went wrong: there was a horse called 'Depper' at Eastmere which died from blood poisoning after being shod - but this was unusual. The blacksmith was more likely to be hurt especially if the horse kicked or leaned on him. After several trials the 'shoe' was fixed with nails driven through holes in the metal. Sometimes the owner would have all four shoes replaced but more often an old one was used to replace a shoe that was badly worn, or a piece of steel might be welded onto a weak spot to increase the life expectancy of a set. Not that this was an expensive job. Blacksmith ledgers in Suffolk show that in the 1820s the charge was 6d a shoe and this remained fixed for a long time. In 1900 it was only 8d but after the 1914-18 War the price did shoot up to 2s. 3d and by the time John Wright died in 1936, the charge was about 9s for a set of four shoes.

The children of Tottington liked John Wright; he would make funny noises and pull wierd faces and make us laugh. At the time I didn't realise he was my Great Uncle but now I can appreciate the complexity of his work and his importance to the village. He was one of the last of his kind. Unfortunately, Charlie died soon after his Father, and Joe Balls took over the blacksmith's business. When John Wright's first wife died he married a much younger woman, Laura Parkes. They had a son named Maurice who worked in Eastmere barns for Mr Madoc who kept bees. Laura and Maurice moved to Saham in 1942. Sadly Maurice passed away in 1996.

OUR DOCTORS MEDICINE

There were two Doctors for the village, both lived in Watton four miles away; Dr. Panting lived in Back Street and served the poorer people, a very nice old man who would come out at a moment's notice, and Dr. Boag who lived in Middle street and dealt with the better off. The residence and surgery of Drs. Panting, Subonodiere, Plumbley and Shenks, was a huge three-storied, Georgian residence called Harvey House built in 1720, named after its original owners, the Harvey Family, who were well-known Norfolk wool merchants. Both Doctors had pony and traps but in the 1920s they drove everywhere in cars. Dr. Boag had a black vehicle which looked like an old fashioned London Taxi cab.

The stock response to any inquiry about one's state of health was "Fair ter midlin' " or "I'm feelin' a sight bet-er terday". People who were sick felt 'quare' and to 'look right lantern-jawed' meant being ill; if they had a cough it was a 'tizzick' ; if feverish they had the 'dudders' (shivers); and to be treated meant being 'under the doctor'. Most people tried to take care of themselves as best they could; many were frightened of having the Doctor call because of the expensive bills and therefore did not seek proper treatment for illness let alone have any sort of check up before the Health Service came into being in 1947. Minor illnesses were treated by local remedies handed down from generation to generation, such as using brown paper soaked in vinegar for headaches, or a stocking wrapped around the neck for a sore throat - of course the longer you had worn it the better! When the weather was bad or there was a cold wind people wore a thick piece of brown paper across their chests beneath their coats. Trying to avoid a cold was very important: they used camphorated oil (a stimulant embrocation for sprains, bruises, chilblains, etc) and white oils for sore throats and chest complaints but my Father used his horse linament. Mother would boil some treacle, honey, sugar and vinegar for us to drink a little of the hot mixture. For a cold, salt in water was used to gargle with, but a good 'corf' remedy for children was to cut up a raw onion, cover it with treacle and soak overnight beneath a saucer, and then drink the liquid. Onions were used for gruel for colds and eaten raw with the packed food. Along with the treacle and sulphur, onions are said to be good for the blood.

At a time when chamber pots (guzunders) were commonly used - people didn't go outside to the garden privy in the cold of night - another remedy for chilblains was to bathe the foot in urine which doesn't sound too pleasant now but it was effective. I remember Mother used to treat her chilblains in Winter by rubbing snow on them. If people got wet feet, which was quite often, they soaked them in mustard baths (good for rheumatic pains in the joints). The Steward of Eastmere Farm did this and fell asleep only to wake up in stone cold water - a lot of good that did him! Of course these baths were the old tin variety with handles either end used for washing clothes in as well. They were easy to carry and often placed in front of the fire on which kettles of water were boiled to fill the bath. This could be a long and tedious business so many families used to share each other's water rather than have to empty and refill the bath. It was the era before running hot water, and of course people couldn't take a bath whenever they felt like it or have a shower every day to freshen up. One Sunday Mr. Bone was washing his feet (a weekly chore) and decided to clip his toe nails with his long-handled barber's strap razor, and nearly cut his toe off! Miss. Lucilla Reeve who lived close by had to get on her motor-bike right quick and fetch the Doctor from Watton.

Father carried an onion around in case he was stung by a wasp or a bee, but if it happened to us, we ran for the 'blue bag'. Usually Mother would have a partly used blue square in a cloth and we would wet this and put it on the sting; also vinegar, or soda, and of course dock leaves were used for nettle stings. Farm workers often carried a potato in their pocket as a remedy for rheumatism; when it went hard they replaced it with another one. Backache was quite common and this was eased by taking one drop of oil of juniper on a sugar lump every other day. People did all sorts of things to remove warts; putting raw meat on them for instance. These 'remedies' were part of the folk lore; some might consider them 'old wives' tales' but they often worked. There were medicines; Sedlitz powders were given for headache and stomach upsets. People suffered a lot from indigestion in those days - no doubt from the tough bread and the vegetables as well as the lifestyle. Beacham pills, bicarbonate of soda, and liquorice powders were taken as laxatives; magnesia was given for indigestion. When aspirin pills came on the scene they were widely used for all sorts of aches and pains which gave 'jip' (aggravation).

The Doctor was called as a last resort but there were no antibiotics or injections so one had to grin and bear the 'misery' (severe pain). When I was four years old I cut my right index finger badly on a glass honey jar. It should have been stitched but Mother bandaged it up tightly. Unfortunately, unwinding and bathing left the finger badly scarred. At twelve a thorn poisoned the middle finger on the same hand but this time I went on Wednesday by bus to Watton to have it lanced. However, it became worse and on the Sunday Father and I cycled to Watton to have it lanced again by Dr. Panting; without any local anaesthetic! In the early days there were no telephones in the village nor any cars so if one wanted a doctor, either a pony and trap was used or people just had to walk until bicycles became common. Once the Dr. had called we would have to go the four miles to Watton to fetch any medicine. No wonder people tried to do without the Doctor! Of course, the Dr. might not understand the patient's meaning; one story concerns a woman who said, *"I want some med'cine for my little 'un. Pore little booy, he suffer suthin' terrible from stoppages"*. Thinking the malady must be constipation the Dr. prescribed a laxative. A week later the woman returned: *"Doctor, that there med'cine ent dun him a mite o' good. All that fare to du is gripe him."* Only then did the Dr. discover that *'stoppages'* was the Norfolk term for epileptic fits.

Every year my Grandmother would eat too many runner beans and the Doctor had to be fetched in the night. There would be a tap on my parents' bedroom window; someone would come up the two miles from Grandma's house and off Dad would go to fetch Dr. Panting. Sadly some of the more serious illnesses, like pneumonia, and bronchitis, took their toll as a result. Tuberculosis (often referred to as consumption) was a killer: there was a fourteen year old girl called Grey who had to live in a hut in her parents' garden to breathe as much fresh air as possible, but like many others she died. One lady, a Mrs. Worledge, aged about forty, died in childbirth as a result of scarlet fever which was feared when I grew up but which had been eliminated in Britain since the Second World War due to innoculation. Measles and scarlet fever were very contagious and seemed to strike as an epidemic - if one child at school was affected so were most of the others. Polio wasn't a problem until after the Second World War - one of my cousins in Thetford had an eight year old child die of it - but now that seems to have been eliminated also. The damp and the cold affected many of us badly and my chest is still weak as a result.

There was a Club called 'The Odd Fellows' which some men belonged to; they had to pay their dues in Watton and were seen to by Dr. Boag, but most of the working men joined a club called 'The Foresters' which is still in existence. The men paid so much per week into a fund and this entitled them to a little money to cover medical care if they were ill or sick. It didn't cover family expenses or bills and there wasn't a Social Security system like today when one can sign on and receive a giro-cheque every fortnight to cash at Post Office. It was a type of insurance; the fee had to be paid on a Saturday night at an inn called Thompson Chequers, a three mile walk away. Of course, being a pub, some of the men would have a 'skin full' and then would sing all the way home. My Father didn't always go so he gave his money to an Uncle George Williams who lived at Westmere. George would pay in Dad's money but often had a little too much to drink.

He had to come home by a plantation called Clay Acre that was supposed to be haunted. It was on a hill one side of the Cressingham Road, with a pit surrounded by trees on the other side. It seemed pretty awesome on a moonlit night and evidently Uncle George was scarred stiff of the place. It frightened me too and I can remember trying to cycle up the hill as fast as possible and being out of breath upon reaching the top. My first bike was a fixed wheel which meant there was no stopping the pedals once they were turning, i.e. there was no free wheel although it did have a brake. This could be tricky going downhill because the pedals could turn faster than your legs, so we used to sit tight on the seat and splay our legs out to let the pedals go round freely. Nevertheless it was a relief to be able to glide down the slope of the road from Clay Acre towards the village.

One tragic incident occurred when Dr. Panting, whilst driving his pony and trap, accidently killed a little boy. His wife was with him and it upset her so much that she would never go out again and became an invalid. A driver called Arthur Sturman was hired and he later became the chauffeur driving Dr. Panting's Model 'T' Ford. After Lord Walsingham took over Westmere Farm he was instrumental in obtaining a district Nurse by the name of Miss Abrahams, who lived in Merton. She came by bike, and was a great boon to the village people being practically as good as a Doctor, and acting as a midwife (there wasn't a great demand for this service but some of the women did need to be looked after having a baby). Once, when my Father fell off the long cart he put some turpentine on his ribs and nearly took all the skin off. Nurse Abrahams had to come and bandage him up everyday. I don't know how she was paid but her services were free to the village and she served the whole Estate. This would be about 1926 by which time the workmen had insurance cards for sickness but still didn't receive any unemployment benefit.

LAW AND ORDER

Whilst I was growing up the local 'Bobby' was a man named P.C. Legge who lived at a village called Caston about five miles away, the other side of Thompson and Stow Bedon. Sometimes when we came out of school he would be standing at the cross-roads corner leaning on his bicycle talking to his superior the sergeant from the town of Watton. He always rode an upright, black bicycle with a gear case, made by the firm of Raleigh unlike our fixed-wheel bikes. When my brother left school and earned enough money be bought one of those bikes. How proud he was of it, and every young lad in the village wanted to have a ride. Whenever we left a dance P.C. Legge would be waiting outside to pick up any offenders riding without lights. He always seemed to be around even when the sheep were being dipped. He was an accepted and integral part of the rural scenery. It was amazing how he got about on his bike and controlled the surrounding villages; and we often had to be on the alert. The Headquarters were at Watton. The police station being on the corner of the Thetford to Watton road called New Inn after the public house opposite. Today the station is at the bottom end of the High Street in Watton, a much more grand building. After a certain time of day the police have to come out from Dereham or Thetford to the local villages. The notion of a 'Village Bobby' has gone forever and seldom is a policeman seen walking the local streets let alone riding a bicycle.

The Worby Family has long had connections with the Police. My Uncle John served in the police force in London and my brother Eddie was a village policeman in Norfolk. When he was sixteen he joined the Grenadier Guards for three-and-a-half years but then decided to do seven. Most of the time he was stationed at Caterham in Surrey and really looked something in his uniform of black trousers, red jacket and busby. After I went to work in London we saw a lot of each other on our days off; he was mad on bands and walked me off my feet following them for miles. We spent several of his leaves from duty together at Eastmere with Mum and Dad. The barracks were next door to a Mental Hospital, and Eddie got to know one of the nurses, an Irish girl named Catherine O'Rourke. He left the Guards and joined the Norfolk Police being stationed at Cromer on the coast. They were married 19th June 1937 whereupon he was sent to Hethersett near Norwich where I now live. When War broke out in 1939, Eddie was called back to the Guards being on reserve, but this was only for a few months. He returned to Hethersett and then went to a village called

Gressenhall. Kath had two children, a daughter called Bridget (b. 1938) and a son named Edmund (b.1942). Later on Eddie was transferred to Walpole St. Andrew near Kings Lynn remaining a village Bobby until he retired. He lived to be sixty-five but died on 8th April 1976; having caught a cold he couldn't stop coughing, and when taken to hospital they diagnosed leukaemia, but next day he had a heart attack and never recovered.

Eddie would have been very proud of his son, 'Big' Edmund, who joined the Police as a cadet after leaving school and had a successful career rising to Chief Superintendant, retiring, aged fifty in 1992. He married Pat Ledell and they had twin daughters, Sarah and Joanne Worby (born 1969) both of whom went to Wymondham College and then to University, exactly as my youngest son 'Little' Edmund had done twenty years previously. Eddie's daughter, Bridget, married Ron Baker, but died of cancer, on 29th December 1985, leaving a son Michael; she was only 46 years old - so sad for all the family.

Somehow ordinary people stood very much in awe of the Police before the Second World War. In general we were honest, as part of a Christian upbringing: maybe we were afraid, or had guilty consciences but certainly we were brought up to respect the law and not to steal or do wrong things. Part of our education was being guided by homely maxims such as 'Honesty is the best policy'. The young people of the village did get up to various japes - sometimes we rode our bikes at night without lights, or we stole someone's apples or Mr. Pearson's turnips and swedes on the way home from school - but nothing serious or hurtful to anyone else. Yet the fear of being in the wrong has always stayed with me and whenever I see a policeman knocking on a door, I always think of trouble and never appreciate how much the Police do to help people. Today children seem unafraid of the police and perhaps this is a shame as often they don't respect other people or their property and take the view that anything goes as long as they can get away with it. The news is full of juvenile crime without adequate punishment for the offenders. Perhaps it is the television or the breakdown in the family, or just the greed of people, but so many illegal acts are committed nowadays that would never have occurred in a village like Tottington where everyone knew each other or were related. The thought of someone murdering a young girl in Watton, as happened recently, and remaining undiscoved, or the molestation of elderly women, would have been incomprehensible to most villagers. Ours was a controlled, law-abiding community. Like everywhere else, husbands and wives went astray but usually it was a nine days wonder, not something which meant divorce and the neglect of children, as seems to be the case today. Relatives held families together and people could not afford financially to separate; there was no running to the Social Security office for a weekly handout, or to have one's rent paid. Our gardens were full of fruit and vegetables so, usually, we had enough to eat and were thankful for what we received. We worked hard, people helped one another, nothing was wasted, clothes were passed on, wood was freely available. Most people were reasonably content and poverty was no excuse to resort to crime. Poaching had its place but foxes were the biggest criminals stealing the poultry at night!

One story comes to mind which illustrates the nature of the society I grew up in. At Christmas, Mother took us to Watton to see the shops and buy some presents for the family. Time came for us to walk home, already being dark, we kept to the main road. There were very few cars or traffic. A boy from the village called George Moore, walked with us but when we had gone quite a way on our journey Mother realized she had left one of her bags of shopping outside a shop back in Watton. George kindly offered to run back and was fortunate enough to find the bag just where Mother had left it. That shows how honest people were then. Seldom did we lock our doors or windows. Sheds were left open, they didn't even have locks on. Bicycles could be left anywhere. When we were older we left our bicycles in the Baker's Yard on the edge of Watton Town and never heard of one being stolen. Sadly today everything has to be placed under lock and key and you never know what will happen next. A few years ago, my cousin, Bernard Woolsey, the son of Walter Woolsey and Blanche (Worby), went to open the garage of his house in Brancaster only to find the cupboard was bare, someone had broken in and stolen everything!

Eddie Worby in police uniform

A DAY'S OUTING

What excitement when we knew we were off to the seaside.
Normally it was to Yarmouth by coach, but I can remember when very
young going by train to Hunstanton. No doubt we changed at Dereham
or Kings Lynn to get there. We had to put our names down beforehand,
who was going and how many parents would accompany us (usually
our Mothers who paid for themselves). The money for the outing was
collected by holding Dances and Socials or having a play at school. A
coach was hired and we would all meet opposite the village shop as this
was more convenient for everyone than going up to the school. Of
course it would be summer time and we left about 8 a.m. It took a while
to load up with push carts, etc, and then we were off. The children were
shouting and the grown ups talking - what a din! As it was a forty mile
ride it took about two hours. The coaches never went very quickly and
we usually stopped somewhere on the way for people to go to the loo
and take refreshments.

Upon reaching Yarmouth we received instructions where to meet for
tea plus the time and place for the departure homewards. Then
everyone went their separate ways: some Mothers toured the shops but
most people made for the beach, where there were clusters of wooden
bathing huts on four wheels in which people could change, and the
children, with buckets and spades, enjoyed the water and the sand. You
could hire a carriage to go for a ride around town but Yarmouth wasn't
anything like it is now. The North Denes was quite wild and
undeveloped, a mass of grass and sand dunes without any caravans.
The entertainment wasn't the same either. I can only remember the
barrel organ, slot machines, the Punch & Judy show and the donkey
rides along the beach. The old South town had its hotels, boarding
houses, shops and the fun-fair, but no neon lights and disco music; we
would have been amazed by the new Marina Leisure Centre, the giant
roller-coaster rides and the amusement arcades. Going down the main
promenade were electric trams with open top decks, plus horses and
carriages, and there was a tower which we could go up and look over
the town.

Nearly everyone took sandwiches and some would have fish and
chips and no doubt ice-cream (a cornet was about 2d), and there were
all sorts of sweets (chocolate and Yarmouth rock was priced at 2d, 4d
or 6d). Once we walking down Kings Street and lots of oranges rolled
off a stall and the children picked them up to eat. At 4 p.m. we met up
at a certain restaurant for tea. A proper meal ranged from 1s to 1/6 but

Mrs Williams and Mrs Worby at Yarmouth, 1934

a cup of tea off the stalls could be bought for a 1d. Afterwards, another quick look at the sea and then we queued for the coach and our journey home. On one occasion the sun shone in our driver's eyes all the way home; it was a beautiful evening and there was a good sing-song on the coach which stopped at the half-way point for the adults to have a drink. By the time we reached Tottington, it was around 8 p.m. and everyone was very tired. Usually, the Fathers met Mothers and children at the drop off points, good nights were said and people went their way home. Some lived quite near but others like us had to walk two miles. In later years most children had bicycles and it wasn't so bad, but Mothers still had to wheel their push chairs. Such trips happened at least twice a year; one outing from the Sunday School and one from the Day School. In the early days school children were taken to Fetes, etc, in waggons with two horses. We used to sit on the side ledges and forms. The different villages held their own dances and whist drives, and this brought people together; they would meet mostly at Watton when there would be all sorts of sports. Maypole dancing by different children every year took place on the 24th May, Empire Day.

Watton was a popular place especially on a Saturday night where families met up for a drink and local gossip. There wasn't a public house at Tottington. Originally there were two, one called 'The Green Man', the other 'The Cock', but not in my lifetime. The nearest pub was 'Thompson Chequers' and Stanford had 'The Cock'. A Mr. Perkins always drank there. He drove a horse and cart and once, whilst drunk, ended up in a pit on his way home. Usually he was brought back every Sunday dinner time by a man from The Cock in his motor- bike and side-car.

When we were old enough, we thought nothing of cycling to Thetford even though it was ten miles from where I lived. On a Saturday night about ten of us used to go there to the cinema or to a dance. In 1933, my cousin, Gordon Hancock, who was in the Norfolk Regiment and home on leave, cycled with me to a dance. He was in uniform and looked so smart, and I remember wearing a brown dress with a wide red belt. We seldom went to the local capital Norwich even though this was a major shopping centre. There were Sunday trips to London by train from Norwich to Liverpool Street for 5 shillings return. People from the village did take advantage of this but it meant an eight mile journey to the Thetford station. My Mother came to visit me in London whilst I was in service and sometimes I came home on the train to Thetford. That station has left lasting memories. I can still feel the thrill experienced as a child standing on the platform waiting for the train to Yorkshire; seeing the smoke in the distance and hearing the roar of the steam engine with its whistle blowing as it came round the bend. Then our trunk being put in the luggage van and us bundled onto the carriage seats; off to visit Mother's relatives in Sheffield. What an adventure!

EMPIRE DAY: This meant a lot to all the folk of the various villages. No matter what day the 24th fell on we always celebrated it on a Thursday because it was half day closing in Watton. It was also Queen Alexander's birthday. Waggons were provided from Eastmere or Westmere Farm; although my Father's horses were used he would never drive waggons with children in them. His Uncle George Williams and his cousin Ted Williams, would usually drive. Each waggon had two horses which looked smart with their platted manes and tails trimmed with red, blue and white ribbons. We all met up at the village shop; Mothers and their young children came as well as the school children. Watton was over four miles from Tottington and it took us nearly an hour to get there as the horses didn't walk very quickly. The celebrations started at 2 p.m. on the large meadow, behind the sale yard in Watton, now known as Charles Avenue. It was entered by a short lane and a large five-barred gate. On arriving there we were soon organised. As several villages took part numerous waggons and horses were arranged around the edge of the meadow. The horses were tethered to the back of each wagon to be fed with oats from their nose bags, which were made of material like strong, thick coconut matting bound with leather and looped over the horse's head.

In the middle of the meadow a ring was roped off with a platform for the band and for important people to sit, like Lord and Lady Walsingtham, who generally opened the celebrations. Children wore their Girl Guide, Brownie or Boy Scout uniforms. All the school children had to get into formation and march around the ring, carrying a Union Jack and other banners, to the playing of the Watton Town Band. Someone would give a speech about our Empire and we sang a song which went like this:

Unfurl the Empire's standard
And sing aloud today
One great glad song of triumph
That echoes far away
For God, for King , for country
Thus ever so to be
True servants of our Empire,
In faith and unity.

Then the sports would start; the children competed in all sorts of races. We had one family in our village, the Leeders, who ran like hares and often won the prizes. There were flat races, jumping, 3-legged plus egg & spoon; girls would bring their skipping ropes and compete. Sports activities would go on until about 4 p.m. when we would be given tea. Forms and seats were laid out near the Refreshment Tent and we would have tea and lemonade with sandwiches and cakes. The free food was much appreciated by the children.

There were several stalls for people to spend their money at, such as a coconut shy, bowling into holes to get the highest score and win the pig, throwing balls to win prizes; there were pony and donkey rides and a gypsy fortune teller, as well as a small roundabout for young children, swing-boats and swings. After tea everyone went back to gather round the ring and children from one school were chosen to dance around the flower-decked Maypole. Children would practise for weeks beforehand and sometimes performed other country dances. Our school had a team of four boys and four girls who were often chosen. When I was a member the others were usually Dorothy Macro, Gordon Hancock, Cyril Leeder, Frederick Spragg, Esther Thompson, Albert Spragg and

232

Nesta Sculfer, not that we were the best dancers in the school but we were all the same height! There was also a fancy dress competition. which brought out some very odd outfits.after tea it was the parents turn to take part. The Fathers came along after they had finished work on the farms. The different villages took part in a tug of war. which lasted a long time. About 7 o'clock there would be a sing-song followed by 'God Save the King'.

The waggons were loaded up and we arrived home just after 8 p.m. very tired after a most enjoyable day which would be a talking point for many weeks. It was fun coming home, with children and Mothers having a good natter. As the waggons came from Eastmere Farm we were fortunate to have a ride all the way whereas others would be dropped off and still have some distance to walk, pushing prams etc.

WATTON SHOW DAY: Another event we looked forward to was Watton Show Day, sometimes referred to as the Wayland Exhibition, and in later years as the Wayland Agricultural Show. This was held between the 10th and 22nd September, depending on the anticipated ending of the harvest, but always on a Wednesday which was Market Day; Lord Walsingham was the Show 's President. Everyone went but not necessarily to the show itself as there were three Fairgrounds and the streets were full of stalls with 'Smart Alec's' and 'Cheap Jacks' and other attractions. On one market stall a Chinaman used to sell watches and I remember him saying "*If you vant to vy a vatch vy a vatch some people charge you 15 thillings but I charge you one thilling only. Come and vy*".

Children wanted to go to the Fairgrounds with the lit-up horses on the roundabouts, other rides and more stalls. Everyone would manage to win a coconut and buy sticks of rock from the fair grounds. Of course the pubs did a good trade as did West's, the fish and chip shop in the middle of the High Street, with fish at 3d and 4d and chips 1d a bag; not forgetting the lovely little currant buns we bought for a ½d from Moore's Bakery Shop. We always visited a tiny sweet shop at the bottom end of the town. Everyone loved this landmark, run by a dear old lady called Mrs Chamberlain who sold everything in the sweet line, especially little knick-knacks for children. The Showground was at the far end of Watton, where the Library and the Police Station now are. It was like a small version of the present Norfolk Show. All sorts of animals werc shown and prizes awarded, Farmers came from miles around with their best livestock. People brought their pets, vegetables and flowers. My Mother always treated herself to some whelks; I could never stomach the things.

To look at them was bad enough let alone eat them!

Somehow it often managed to rain and thousands of people tramping around churned the ground up into a mud plot. We had to make our own way to Watton and usually walked through the Park. Once it rained nearly all day. My Mother, Nesta Sculfer and I got absolutely soaked. Mother wanted to turn back but we were so persuasive she gave in to our whims. Luckily Nesta's brother came and fetched us home in their horse and cart. Later on we were able to cycle to such events. Watton was a great meeting place, especially on a Saturday night. Once a year Watton had a weekly Carnival with something happening each day. On the Thursday there was a Parade through the town with decorated floats, a collection for Norfolk and Norwich Hospital. (even though there was a small cottage hospital in Watton at that time). On the Saturday there was a Fete and sports events on the meadow at the back of the sale ground. By about 1920 buses were running through Watton to Norwich every day and on a Wednesday being Market Day, a small bus would run through the village about 11 o'clock and return around 3 p.m. so people were back in time to meet the children out of school and have tea.

Village Cricket Team before WWI

Albert Worby (captain) first on left of the back row.
John Worby, ..., John Wright and his son Charlie, Ernie Oldfield
Fred and John Williams, George Leeder.

234

XMAS and NEW YEAR: It always seemed to snow at Christmas and most of the Winter time when I was young. Now some Winters we hardly see any snow, and if we do it doesn't lay very long. Like all children we looked forward to Christmas. It meant a fortnight's holiday from school and Mother would get extra things in and make the puddings, mincemeat and cake. One year our dog Floss ate the cake which Mum had put in a tin under the bed. I've no idea how she managed to get the lid off the tin! We would go into the woods with my Father to cut down a tree which was large enough to fill the end bedroom. When we were small my brother slept in one room with my Father and I slept with my Mother, as the house was so damp and cold. Later on when the house was repaired we did have our own bedrooms. The tree was planted in a large pail of soil and put in the bedroom where we would decorate it with a fairy on top and lots of silver tinsell. We had to be careful not to break the little decorations. Also there were little clip-on candlesticks and when their candles were lit the whole affair was very pretty. Sugar mice, apples and oranges were tied on along with small presents and crackers. There were little packets of Neopolitan chocoloates, five oblongs of red, white and blue, tied on with ribbon or rafia plus chocolate animals in silver paper.

We had the extra treat of a party at the Day School and another at Sunday School, both with decorated trees, and it was at this time of the year when we would be given presents and any prizes we had won. Xmas night we hung up out stockings - must have been Mother's - and this was the only occasion my brother and I slept in the same room so as to be able to open our presents together. We would try and stay awake as long as possible to see Father Christmas. My brother Eddie would always say there wasn't such a person and it was Dad who brought the presents. Come morning our stockings would be full of nuts and apples and oranges, sugar mice, a chocolate shape, one of the Neapolitan bundles of chocolates, and of course our presents. Compared to what children receive today our little bundles weren't much to talk about but we were well pleased with everything. We didn't have much pocket money but usually made some little present for our parents. In 1926, when my brother started to earn money he bought me a work box. Although the lid has come off, I still treaure it sixty-six years later. Christmas Day was spent at home with the usual Xmas Dinner. Most people had chicken and of course Christmas pudding and custard afterwards. Mother always made another one for my birthday on 31st December, a date I didn't like, it being so near Xmas when my parents couldn't afford much extra in the way of presents.

Unless Boxing Day fell on a Sunday there was always a social in the evening from about 7.30 to 12 p.m. or 1 a.m. As my Mother supplied the music we always went with her. Lots of people entertained themselves by singing songs and giving recitations between the dances. The latter were the old favourites: the Barn Dance, Veleta, Boston Two-Step and the Lancers. Sometimes, when the young men became too boisterous they would swing the girls off their feet as they all joined arms and went round in a circle. The clergymen used to arrive and throw sweets for the children. Sometimes the old Lord Walsingham, who owned Merton Estate, would put in an appearance and sing for the children. Usually it was his favourite song about a pear tree in a field:

All in a beautiful field there stands a pretty pear tree, pretty pear tree with leaves.
What is there on the tree? a very pretty bough, bough on a tree, tree in the ground.
All in a beautiful field there stands a pretty pear tree, pretty pear tree with leaves.
What is there on the bough? a very pretty branch, branch on a bough, bough on the tree, tree in the ground
All in a beautiful field there stands a pretty pear tree, pretty pear tree with leaves.
What is there on the branch? a very pretty twig, twig on a branch, branch on a bough, bough on a tree, tree in the ground.
All in a beautiful field there stands a pretty pear tree, pretty pear tree with leaves.
What is there on the twig? a very pretty nest, nest on a twig, twig on a branch, branch on a bough, bough on a tree, tree in the ground
All in a beautiful field there stands a pretty pear tree, pretty pear tree with leaves.
What is in the nest? a very pretty egg, egg in a nest, nest on a twig, twig on a branch, branch on a bough, bough on a tree, tree in the ground.
All in a beautiful field there stands a pretty pear tree, pretty pear tree with leaves.
What is there on the egg? a very pretty bird, bird on the egg, egg in the nest, nest on a twig, twig on a branch, branch on a bough, bough on a tree, tree in the ground.
All in a beautiful field there stands a pretty pear tree, pretty pear tree with leaves.

The children loved him and he got them to join in. Sadly he died in 1927 and no one took his place for entertainment. Col. George de Grey, the new Lord Walsingham didn't mix in the same way, although he had his good points and joined in parades and church celebrations.

NATURE AWAKENING

People living in towns have no idea of the variety of animal sounds especially in the morning with the cock crowing and the ducks quacking. Cuckoos rise early upsetting birds in their nests; blackbirds make such a noise like pees rattling in a jar; sparrows create an awful racket in the hedgerows when it's going to rain. We all have our favourite times of day and whereas most people prefer the dampness of the dawn with the rising sun and the sweet chorus of birds, I loved the dusk, when we came out of our doorway at Eastmere and looked towards the farm buildings and "the hills" to see the moon coming up from behind the trees like a huge orange ball. My brother used to say it " got up from the floor". It was like magic gradually rising higher and higher. Nowadays few people have the time or inclination to watch the moon rising and the stars slowly come out. A few appeared fairly low in the sky and then graduallly, on a clear night, the dark canopy overhead became sprinkled with sparkling gems.

In the late evening as I walked up the garden path with the scent of all Mother's flowers filling the air, on through the iron gate into the meadow, I would be greeted by the low flying big black beetles and the brown mid-summer does which thudded against one's head or face. They didn't sting but if you picked them up they wrapped their strong legs round your fingers which was really painul. These insects lived in the huge manure piles which lay all over the meadow and as the twilight settled they burst into life. The rooks and the starlings were all lined up like so many miniature aeroplanes about to fly home to roost. Their rookeries were high up in the trees usually by a church, and the noise was terrific; starlings only added to the cacophany of sound. Swifts came away from their nests on the farm buildings and flew about catching insects, narrowly missing our heads. Bats joined in the feast and flew into our houses which made women nervous because of the rumour that if they got tangled in your hair they can't be got out. One night we had a bat fly in attracted by the lamp light and my Father, wielding a rolling pin, tried to catch it, whilst Mother sat in the corner with her head in a towel. It was very funny but I got told off for laughing.

In the distance we often heard the cuckoo having his last song before retiring and the pheasants would be hollering (as we called it) usually a warning of thunder in the distance. It was said that in the First World War they hollered when they heard the guns firing over in Belgium. Pheasants have wonderful hearing but I doubt that story. Ducks and

Geese are as good as any watchdogs. We had a few ducks near the garden on the meadow and often when I came home late at night they would kick up such a din that I hurredly said goodnight to my escort and went inside. It was peaceful how one by one things settled down. The pee-wits would be calling their last "pee-wit, pee-wit" and many a night after we were in bed the curlew would be giving forth its call. All seemed right with the world as light faded out of the evening sky but as a child I was afraid of the dark.

OUR SUMMER HOLIDAY FROM SCHOOL

The days seemed almost endless
Skies were ever blue.
Up early in the mornings
Lots of things to do.
Hours spent in the harvest fields
Helping with the corn.
Chasing rabbits, sharing food.
How lovely to be born.
In the evenings there was cricket
Our dog fetched all the balls.
When there was the hide and seek
She'd answer all our calls.
After fetching home the cows,
Safely put the hens to bed,
Out came the flying insects
Dived and hit us on the head.
The sky was red and glorious
As the sun sank in the West
The bats all started flying
And swallows went to rest.

Oh, what happy days they were
So carefree and such good fun.
To be brought up on a farm
Where all the work was done.

Hilda Perry

238

RELATIVES AND FRIENDS:

These natives are a sturdy folk, worthy of all admiration. They are much more sober and thrifty than the Shire folk, ... The women-folk are, many of them, of the stout Dutch type with fair hair and florid complexions, while their children are specially noticeable for their flaxen hair and rosy cheeks.
The Land of the "The Babes in the Wood" by Rev. Charles Kent

A history of a lost village would be nothing without reminiscences about the families which inhabited that place and how they lived. Crumbling ruins leave some impression of their lifestyle, museum artifacts conjure up their daily round, faded photographs portray buildings and people, but the past lives on in the memories of those who survive as witnesses. Once the latter are gone only the disfigured gravestones and the written word bear testimony to their existence. It is the documents, journals, letters and books which illustrate events, thoughts and feelings. Traditional village life revolved around the extended family and the tribal relationships of several generations: Grandparents, Fathers and Mothers, brothers and sisters; Aunts and Uncles; cousins and in-laws. Large numbers of off-spring resulted in numerous distinctions and interactions; an intricate web of family connections, often dimly remembered and only faintly understood yet fundamental to the social fabric. Whilst not as important economically as the tenant farmers or the land owner Lord Walsingham, nevertheless most of the villagers in Tottington were my relatives and part of the purpose of writing this book was to remember and commemorate their lives since their story is the history and identity of the village.

I have written about my Grandparents and Parents, plus some Uncles and Aunts, farmers, teachers and clergymen elsewhere, but it would be remiss of me to neglect several other relatives and family friends who played an important role in my life and were part and parcel of the village.

HENRIETTA ELIZABETH WORBY: (8. 7.1885 - 19. 7.1930) was a tall, slim lady who lived at Little Cressingham after she married William Jones on 22nd October 1906. They had seven children: Grace, Sydney, Frederick, William, Mabel, Cecil, and Lily. Henrietta used to walk the six miles to Tottington pushing a pram to see her parents. My Mother was very fond of her and during the holidays she, Eddie and I walked the four miles from Eastmere to spend the day with Henrietta.

They lived in a row of houses quite a way from the main road. At the back there was a largish meadow with a deep canal. I was terrified of this and it was dangerous; children become fascinated by water and go too close with the risk of drowning. Aunt Henrietta didn't enjoy good health. Once I overheard Mother mentioning that the Doctor said if Aunt Henrietta had another baby it might cleanse her blood. She did have another girl but died soon afterwards from breast cancer. I recall the day of her death, July 23rd 1930: I was eighteen at the time and we were celebrating Sports Day in Watton and one of my cousins came up and told me she had died at the relatively early age of forty-four.

Henrietta Elizabeth Worby

Thereafter, my cousin Mabel, stayed at home and brought up the children. Grace married a well-off antique dealer, and Freddie joined the Grenadier Guards. William Jones died 14th May 1938 aged sixty, and Mabel passed away from cancer in Wayland Hospital in 1982. Only three of my Jones cousins, William, Cecil and Lily are still alive in 1994.

BLANCHE ANNIE WORBY: It is peculiar how in a large family one child seems destined to stay home and look after the parents and other members of the family. Blanche (29.0.1886 - 11.02.1975) assumed this role just as Dolly Spragg did in her sister's family, and Alice Oldfield in hers. All the other girls went away into domestic service, usually to London, which was a good life if one gained the right position, as food and shelter were provided and enough money to get by on. At the turn of the century many of the young girls in the village pursued this course as there was no work for them anywhere else. In those days men didn't do much of the housework but there were a lot of chores to complete when bringing up a large family. Each day the household had to be organised and everyone given their separate tasks. Once I asked my

Father what Grandmother did when her husband went to work catching rabbits at 4 in the morning. He said she did needle-work in bed by candle-light. Yet she must have had her hands full what with the cooking, the laundry, the cleaning, etc. Blanche's role was to help with the bringing up of the four youngest children and they looked upon her as a second Mother. She was fairly tall, slim, and always smartly dressed. To me she seemed a very straight-laced woman who looked down on all sorts of people she considered inferior. As grandchildren we were a bit in awe of her.

The brothers and sisters were very close and often came home to Grandmother's for holidays; Blanche was especially fond of Emmeline. As each sister married. Blanche would be the one to come and help out when they had children. She was a great asset to her eldest sister Florrie who had ten children including two lots of twins. Actually my own Mother didn't like Aunt Blanche very much in the early days, nor did Uncle John's wife, Doll. It was as if the sisters thought their brothers' wives weren't good enough, and the latter felt this disapproval. Such differences evened out in later years and judgements altered. I used to think my Father's family thought more of my brother Eddie than of me, but again matters changed as we grew older.

Emmeline and Blanche Worby became Mrs Jeeves and Mrs Woolsey

Gertrude Worby with husband Alfred Simpson plus children Kenneth and Winnie

Until 1924 when Lord Walsingham took over Westmere Farm and introduced a large dairy herd, the only farm which sold milk to the village was Grange Farm, where a family called Woolsey came to live. Blanche became friendly with the youngest son Walter (15. 4.1898 - 8. 5.1986) and they married 8th December 1923; their son Bernard was born 11th January 1924. Blanche was a strong-willed woman who dominated her husband, a meek and mild man twelve years her junior. Walter had a quiet, somewhat shy, softly spoken manner and was often to be seen wringing his hands when he spoke to anyone. Blanche's marriage meant she moved to a little farm at Bagmere so Grandmother had to manage on her own for a while. Walter had a much older brother, Frederick William who married a woman called Maud and lived at Merton village - they had four children: Doris, Phyllis Edna, Vera, and Sylvia. Of the other brothers, Albert died in the First World War, and John (known as Jack) married Kathleen May Sculfer in October 1923.

Blanche lived to a grand old age of 88 and died at Docking, 11th February 1975. Walter lived on to the same age and died at Brancaster, also on the north Norfolk coast, 8th May 1986, where he lived near his son. Bernard married Gertrude Purdy on 28th July 1945 and now lives in Heacham just south of Hunstanton. They have two sons: Roger Woolsey (10. 5.1945) and Richard Woolsey (18. 6.1948) who have married and produced six children. In such fashion there is change and continuity: the Worby name dies out to become Woolsey; large, extended families of the past give way to the small nuclear families of the present; descendants of Tottington villagers have moved to far flung places and gradually lost contact with one another.

EMMELINE FRANCES WORBY: Many of those girls who left Tottington to go into service didn't return except for odd visits, but Aunt Emmeline (15. 9.1888 - 1. 8.1965), who went to London and married Herbert Jeeves on the 26th August 1913, often came back to Norfolk to stay with the family and never wanted to return to the big city. Sometimes her husband, Uncle Bert, came with her and they visited all the families. We loved to see them at Eastmere where we could get together and have a game of cricket. Uncle Bert was a golf professional, he and Emmeline dressed so smartly that everyone thought they were better off than they were. He had a weakness for gambling and would have a flutter on the horses sometimes but he didn't have any luck. They used to give us a few pennies when they went away. On one occasion she gave me a silver sixpence which in those days was a lot of money to a child. Unfortunately, I lost it and was

Blanche, Albert, Gertrude, John &
Frances Worby, Emmeline

so frightened to go home in case I got into trouble with my Mother. Rather artfully I hung about the gate until Father came home before I told her, knowing full well she wouldn't scold me so much in front of him!

Emmeline didn't have any children of her own but she was happy to have a nephew or niece stay on holiday in London. When I was thirteen, she took me to stay with her during the late Summer. They lived at Barnes, then a very pretty place, and were very kind showing me around London which was a great eye-opener. We sailed on the river Thames from Westminster to Richmond and walked on the towpath at Hammersmith and along where the Boat-Race is held from Putney to Mortlake. I stayed for six weeks which took me into the term so I had to attend the local School. At Tottington only the boys were allowed to take Art as a subject, the girls had to do sewing but at Barnes I was asked to draw a bunch of grapes and had to explain that I had never done any Art before. Still the teacher thought my picture was a good effort.

Leaving school aged 14 and working for the de Grey Family at Westmere Farmhouse was a big change but going down to London was a totally new experience. How many parents today would dream of allowing their young teenage daughter to go off to the metropolis to work, yet in the 1920s it was considered quite normal; hundreds of thousands of girls left the countryside to work in service or in factories. Uncle Bert found me a job at the headquarters of Lyons, Spike House opposite Cadby Hall in Kensington. Barnes was about half-an-hour's ride from Kensington, and there were 'Pirate' buses which raced along to get to the bus stops before the general buses so as to pick up all the passengers. Usually these were open-topped and it was pleasant riding along in the fresh air on a fine, clear morning. They drove across Barnes Common and then over a lovely old bridge called Hammersmith on the way to the Hospital. After a while Bert and

Emmeline moved to East Sheen, a place next to Barnes, which meant going though Roehampron to get to work and the scenery was so interesting and attractive. There were many young boys and girls employed at Lyons. I had to check the slips from the 'nippies' (waitresses) who worked in the numerous Lyons Tea-Houses. On our desks we had twenty-six pigeon holes, A to Z . All the bills which came in had different letters on so we sorted them out and put each one in its proper pigeon hole. Then we had to be sure they were added up correctly. Some of the supervisors were hard task-masters who made us stick to the time-schedules for completing the 'shops'.

I was nearly fifteen and all these experiences had a huge impact upon me having been brought up in the quiet of the countryside with its slow pace and placid rhythms. All the buildings seemed so big, the hustle and bustle of city life frightened me especially when I had to go to night school at Holland Park to learn shorthand, typing and book-keeping. It didn't suit me and became quite a strain. I started at ten shillings a week which was quite a good wage in 1927. On my sixteenth birthday I received an increase to twelve shillings and sixpence a week of which Aunt Emmeline took ten bob, another two went on bus fares, leaving me a mere sixpence a week to spend! I didn't realise that Auntie had so little money and this was made worse when Uncle Bert lost his job. I needed a new outfit for the office and had to ask Dad to send me the money. He had so little anyway that it broke my heart to think I was a burden on my parents when I should be earning my own living. I stayed two years but left after Emmeline and Bert caught German measles. They felt I had brought it home from the Office and there was a slight controversy so my Father said come home to Eastmere which I did in the early Autumn of 1929. There was no discord: Emmeline saw me off at the station, we remained good friends and saw a lot of one another when I returned to London in 1931 to work in service.

Uncle Bert lost his job coaching golf and after the War they came up to Norfolk to live for a while with Aunt Blanche. Eventually they went back to London where both died: Emmeline lived to be 77 years old and Bert, despite his weak heart lived to the ripe age of 96.

GERTRUDE MARY WORBY: Aunt Gertie (17. 1.1890 - 7.12.1946) was also a tall, slim lady who married an engine driver, Alfred Simpson, and went to live in Thetford. They had five children, Kenneth, Winnifred, Ethel, Gordon and Joan. Uncle Alf and Uncle John Worby were in the army together and then worked at Burrells the engine firm in Thetford. About 1920, Uncle John joined the Metropolitan Police and became a squad car driver in London, whilst some years later Alf went to work for the Electricity Board.

When we were small we often went to stay with the Simpsons at Thetford as it was about twelve miles south from Eastmere. Aunt Gertie and Alf cycled the eight miles to Tottington most Sundays to see her parents. Thetford had a railway station where we left to go to London when older so either we called in or they came to see us off. During the Second World War, Aunt Gertie worked very hard and fell terminally ill. Her youngest son, Gordon, abroad in the army, was allowed home to see her but sadly she died of cancer aged fifty-six on 7th December 1946. Gordon married after the War and went to live with his Father who was a very kind and gentle man. Kenneth and Winnie both died young but were married with families. Gordon's twin sister, Ethel married and went to live up north as did Joan the youngest daughter.

MABEL HILDA WORBY: Because she was away in service in London when I was young, Mabel (8.6.1892 - 14.3.1947) wasn't as well known to me as the other Worby Aunts. She was unlike them in being shorter and more stout, and her lot in life was to be more arduous. In some ways her life-story illustrates the difficulties many village folk encountered when they went out into the wider world. The sentimental view of traditional village life ignores the reasons why so many fled to seek a future elsewhere, in the cities and abroad. Apart from the harsh privations of rural poverty, family loyalties and restrictions made life claustrophobic for those who sought independence or privacy. Many of the youngsters who went off to the Army or into service were ill-prepared for the changes and challenges of adult life; the cruel ups and downs of urban existence left their scars; who knows how many villagers came to grief in the outside world? In writing about Mabel so candidly I wish no criticism, only compassion for the sadness of her situation.

Many village women married whilst teenagers and had children before they were twenty but when a woman became pregnant and didn't marry she was labelled as immoral, and often it left a certain stigma. To some extent that remains true today with 'Single Mothers' but before the First World War it was viewed as a personal and family disgrace. However, a double-standard was at work: if one checks the Parish Register for births in Tottington during the nineteenth century, many brides went to the altar already pregnant. It isn't that surprising;

Mabel Hilda Worby   Percy Worby married Irene Davis

children were a necessity so no labourer would enter into wedlock without some assurance that his future wife would be fruitful. Moreover sexuality hasn't changed and since there were scarcely ever more than two bedrooms in the cottages, children of large families were brought up together with little privacy or delicacy of feeling. Of course there were the controlling influences of Christian morality, especially amongst the Methodists, but surrounded by nature and so many animals they could scarcely be unaware of 'the birds and the bees'.

Mabel was twenty-one when she gave birth to a son named Percy on the 13th June 1913, less than six months after I was born. He was brought up by her parents and older sister Blanche. Percy wasn't denied love or attention but Mabel was working away from home for the next thirteen years and that must have created problems for him. Ten years later Mabel had another child by a man called Charles Drew. This son was born 19th May 1923 at Queen Charlotte's Hospital, London, and christened Charles. Evidently Mabel had hoped to marry Drew but he deserted her. She went to court and obtained an affiliation order but after three payments these ceased and Drew disappeared. A warrant was issued but no further details are known. Mabel found it difficult to pay fostering fees to a family which was looking after Charles. Her employer's Father was the solicitor and close friend of Dr. Barnardo,

246

whose organisation was approached and made a contribution towards the cost.

Young Charles was admitted to Barnardo's, 19th July 1926 but by 28th August he was sent back to the foster home at Waltham Abbey where he remained until leaving age. Nothing is known about his childhood before he took a job as an errand boy at a local grocery shop. During the Second World War he joined the Fife and Forfars Tank Regiment but sadly, on 28th June 1944 aged 21, he died in Frnace of severe burns and shock after rescuing his friend trapped in a tank. It is a tragedy that he never knew his real Mother or the large number of relatives, many of whom were unaware of his existence.

Before Charles died he had known Agnes Joan Scales from Hornsea, London and this resulted in a baby girl, Diana Joan Scales born 21.9.1941. Later he had a relationship with Edith Phyllis Hodgson (married name Packer) and this resulted in a daughter, Lorraine Phyllis Packer born 11.10.1944. Diana was not told about her real Father and Lorraine did not know until she was eighteen. All families hide their 'skeletons in cupboards' and these facts regarding Mabel and Charles were shrouded in secrecey and not discussed. They came to light as a result of Lorraine searching the records and getting in touch with Barnardo's who forwarded all the above information, but whether Mabel ever knew what happened to her son Charles cannot be ascertained.

In June 1926, Mabel married James Nash, a gardener by trade who had been badly gassed in the First World War and who could only work occasionally. They had a girl child called Hilda born 19th September 1926, and settled in Sturston close to Tottington in a house near Aunt Blanche's who lived at Bagmere. The country air was a great benefit to James' condition but it couldn't provide a cure and he died 29th April 1929. With a young daughter to care for and very little income, Mabel came home to live with her parents in Tottington. In a sense this was a reunion since her Mother and Aunt Blanche had brought up Mabel's first son Percy, who, by then, was sixteen. Until her parents died, (John in 1933 and Frances in 1936), Mabel devoted herself to looking after them and bringing up Hilda, who was terrified of her Grandmother.

The property was rented from the Estate owner, Lord Walsingham, and it passed to Mabel's eldest sister Florence married to Thomas Spragg. Aunt Mabel, Hilda and Percy had to find alternative accommodation, which seemed unfair except that the Spragg's had a large family and could use the extra space. The Estate offered Mabel an isolated house in the middle of the woods near Thompson Watering, called the 'Madhouses'. This wasn't a pleasant place and being a fair distance from the village it meant Hilda, who was only ten years old, had a long and lonely journey walking to school. It made everything worse for a young girl who only had her Mother's love, affection and reassurance to rely on.

When Tottington was taken over in 1942, Mabel and Hilda went to Saham Toney in a dreadful little place, one room up and down. Eventually they moved to Griston where Mabel died on 14th March 1947. The Barnardo's Report, speaks of Mabel as "hard-working, trustworthy and unfailingly amiable". She was well-known for her knitting skills, something her daughter Hilda inherited; she worked hard in looking after her parents and the children as well as helping out with her sister's needs. Unfortunately they always seemed to treat her as if she was beneath them socially. When Mabel died, Blanche walked in and took some of the things which had belonged to their Mother. This caused ill-feeling with Percy.

The 'Madhouses' near Thompson Watering in 1942

John Percival Worby , known as Percy, joined the Army before the Second World War broke out. He came home safe from the War but tended to keep himself to himself and detached from the rest of the family. After moving from place to place he married Irene Phyllis Davis from Shipdham and had two children: Christine Elizabeth who married Timothy Wisken and have three children, Colin, Ian and Simon; plus Clive Worby who married Susan and has two children, Wendy and John George Worby. At least the family name continues in another branch.

Percy Worby with Albert Worby, John Worby and
Tommy Spragg, 1931

Hilda Nash lost touch with her half-brother Percy for many years but managed to contact him again through the Salvation Army not long before he died near Peterborough in June 1991. She married Frederick Holden and had two children: Pauline (born 1946) who married Tony McNeil and has two children, Hayley and Lyndon; and Peter (born 1949). Later Hilda married John Wallace and now lives in Thetford. Recently we have become good friends, renewing contact after such a long time apart.

THE WILLIAMS FAMILY: Grandmother's Family were related to the Barrett, Howling and Chinnery families who had lived in the village during the nineteenth century. She was one of eight children born to George Williams (1.3.1823 - 7.10.1900) who married Marie Howling (29.11.1829 - 8.2.1894) on the 4th November 1848.

Henrietta 15.12.1849 - married James Brightwell Coates
William John 8. 6.1853 - married Ann Macrow
Frances Ann 5. 5.1856 - 11. 9.1930 married John Worby
Eliza 15. 7.1859 - 2. 1.1951 married Henry Oldfield
Caroline 15. 7.1862 - 28.12.1933 married William Hancock
George 12.11.1865 - 3. 7.1926 married Elizabeth Laura Quantrell
Herbert James 7. 1.1869 - 18.11.1878
Anna-Marie 31. 8.1871 - married Alfred Reynolds

Trying to unravel the ancestry of George Williams has been difficult since he was the illegitimate son of a Frances Williams who appears to have been the daughter of George Williams and Hannah Rout (married 1786). Whether she was the sister of the shepherd John Williams, married to Sarah Haystead in 1812, with several children including a George Williams who became a tailor, is mere speculation.

Marie Howling, had a somewhat chequered upbringing since she was the daughter of Samuel Howlin (1799 - 1829) who married Mary Ann Barrett (1797 - 1859) in 1822, resulting in four other children, Mary Ann, John, Elizabeth, and James (all of whom died very young). After Samuel's death, Mary Ann married James Chinnery (1800 - 1872) from South Lopham, and had three other children, Elizabeth, Mary Ann and James. Marie Howling's step-sister, Mary Ann Chennery married an Isaac Boughen (from an old and well-known family of the area) in 1860 and had a number of children; Nathan, George, Tipphany, Augusta and Lucy.

Four of George Williams and Maria's children lived in Tottington (Frances, Eliza, Caroline and George), whilst the others lived at Caston. William John Williams, who married Ann Macrow in 1873 had three children, Elizabeth Maria, Emma Rosetta and Herbert James. After marrying Elizabeth Quantrill in 1887 and moving to Merton, George the younger ended up as Teamman along with my Father for Mr. Wace in 1912, living in the other small cottage on Eastmere Farm. Elizabeth gave birth to five children who were all my Father's cousins:

1. *Alice Maud* (born 1887) - married George Leeder in 1911 and had six children (Phyllis Ivy, Cyril George, Lena Doris, Douglas Wilfred, Edith May and William John Leeder) who were all living on Westmere Farm until 1942.
2. *Ethel Maria* (born 1884) - married Frederick Buckle and had two children, Joyce and Frederick.
3. *Lilian Ellen* (born 1889) - married John Whalebelly in 1909, went to live in Watton, and had two sons William and George Frederick.
4. *Frederick George* (born 1897) - marrried Harriet Violet Mace in 1919 and took over his Father's job and cottage at Eastmere. They had six children (Evelyn Joyce, Lily, Gladys Maud, Sylvia Joan Frederick George, and Shirley Hilda Williams).
5. *William John* (born 1862) - married Maud Garrod and had a son, George Williams.

Such is the intricate web of relationships created by numerous children and their marriages. I still try to keep in touch with Sylvia who married Ronald Game and lives on the Bowthorpe Estate just outside Norwich.

The Williams Family, 1960s
Gladys, Frederick, Shirley, Father Frederick, Mother Violet (nee Mace),
Lillian and Sylvia

251

THE HANCOCK FAMILY: Caroline Williams (15. 7.1862 - 28.12.1933), my Grandmother's sister, married Walter Hancock (1864 - 3.5.1903) on 11th February 1882. He came from the village of Ovington, one of five children born to William Hancock (1820 - 1899) and Maria (1826 -1907) from Carbrooke. Walter had published Marriage Banns with Mary Priscilla Cator in 1877 but for some reason didn't go through with it. Caroline was a tiny person but very active - she thought nothing of walking to Watton right up until the time she died - quite different from my Grandmother. She had eight children all born at Tottington towards the end of the nineteenth century.

1. *Edith Alice* (13.12.1882) - had a child called Daisy May (born 26.12.1900) who died after six weeks. She married John William Lake in December 1907 and they had a daughter named Daisy Lake.
2. *Charles Edward* (8. 4.1884) - nicknamed 'Brassy'.
3. *William John* (21. 7.1896) - married Evelyn Maud Mace from Saham Toney and lived at Sturston. They had six children in the 1930s: Olive Elsie, Donald John, William, Gordon Phillip, Shirley June, Derek Harold.
4. *Violet Maria* (13. 3.1887) - also married a man called Lake.
5. *Emma Elizabeth* (18. 5.1889) - married a man surnamed Carr and had a daughter, Elsie May in 1908 who married Charles Thomas Howlett in September 1927 and adopted a girl called Barbara.
6. *Georgianna May* (9. 5.1891 - 12. 2.1917) - had a son, Walter Gordon Hancock (13. 3.1913) who married a cousin Olive Sear of Caston and had three children, Anthony, Margaret and Malcolm.
7. *Amy Caroline* (16. 6.1895 - 1990) - whose son Kenneth George (16. 5.1919) who was killed in the Second World War.
8. *Herbert George* (16. 5.1897) was killed in the First World War.

The Hancocks were a large family well known in Tottington and their men had a liking for beer. Before she was married, Edith had a daughter in 1900, called Daisy May, who only lived to be six weeks old; Georgianna's son Gordon, and Amy's son Kenneth were brought up by their Grandmother, my Aunt Cary, whose other daughter Emma lived at home for years as did Violet until she married. The Hancocks kept lots of chickens and they roamed all over the place and into the lane. One of the cockerells was a terror and would pick anyone and anything; I still have the scars where it picked my knee. Aunt Cary often had indigestion and when she was aged 68 it led to a terrible pain on her chest. The Doctor arrived and diagnosed wind round the heart, and this caused her death that same night. I still remember the sad look on the face of my cousin, Gordon Hancock, at the funeral of his Grandmother which took place on my 18th birthday, 31st December 1930. The usual hymns were sung 'Abide With Me' and 'On the Resurrection Morning'. The mourners walked for about three-quarters of a mile behind a horse-drawn hearse hired from Watton. Her daughter Violet looked after everyone thereafter including a lodger called Stephen Wright.

Gordon was a very generous boy but spent a lot of his money on drink, for himself and others. He would take me to a dance and then go off with the boys - to the pub and come back the worse for drink. It used to worry my Dad. Gordon promised he would give it up after we married but my wise old Dad said, "If he wouldn't give it up before you are married, he certainly won't when you are married." I used to think about that. My Aunt Emeline said we shouldn't go together because, being cousins, if we had any children they might not be quite right. I said that to him once and he replied, *"They'll be as right as ever she is!"*

Gordon and I corresponded when I was in London and he used to come up by train on the 5/- Sunday excursions. After he joined the Royal Norfolk Regiment and was stationed at Aldershott we would meet and go home together as we did for Christmas and New Year 1933. My 21st birthday was on 31st december which was a Sunday and we went for a walk in the snow in Merton Park. He sang a song to me called "Linger a little longer in the Twilight with Me" which was so romantic in the moonlight. Also we cycled ten miles to a dance in Thetford. After all these years it's marvellous how the memories linger. After Gordon had been abroad for a while in India I broke off the engagement having met the man who was to become my husband, Geoffrey Perry, who delivered the groceries to the house where I worked in London.

Most of the boys in the village were called up at the outbreak of war but as far as I know the only one who lost his life was Gordon's cousin, Kenneth Hancock. It was a far cry from the sacrifice made during the First world War. When Gordon came home again after the War he met and married a girl called Olive Sears who lived at Caston and they had three children. Dolly Spragg told me that he used to ride a big motorbike all over the place, still spent a lot of time in the pubs, and remained as popular as ever: sadly he died in 1989.

Percy Worby, Cyril Leeder, Gordon Hancock, Albert Spragg, Basil Pawsey
and George Moore taken at Keymer's corner 1932

Charlie Belham, Tom Pie, Vivien Hunt, ...and Frank Hunt with Merton
Hall in the background 1931

THE OLDFIELD FAMILY: By the time I was born none of the original family of Oldfield lived in Tottington but if one goes back through the Parish Register and the Village Census counts, the name occurs time and again. They were connected with my family generation after generation. William Warby married an Elizabeth Oldfield in 1774, and his daughter, Elizabeth Warby (1787 - 1866) married George Oldfield (1781 - 1852), a vermin killer in Tottington. George's brother, John Oldfield (1784 - 1815) married Hannah Lake (1781 - 1860) on the 12th October 1802 and their daughter Hannah married my Great-Grandfather John Worby in 1825. Hannah's brother James Oldfield (1810 - 1881) married Hannah Sturgeon (1815 - 1852) and had ten children: one daughter, Charlotte Oldfield married Thomas Leffley and their children married into the Watson and Woods families; another named Sarah Ann married Matthew Rands and their son Archie married Annie Oldfield; a son, John Oldfield married Ann Watson; and Emma Rose married Walter Hunt. This created an intricate network of family relationships approaching Biblical proportions and we considered ourselves related to these people and their descendants.

Oldfield is a very common name in the Breckland area, to be found in Watton, Thetford and many of the villages nearby. The man who married my Grandmother's other sister Eliza in 1878, doesn't seem to be directly connected with the original Tottington Oldfields. His name was Henry Oldfield (1849 - 1926) the second son of Henry Oldfield (1810 - 1896) from Saham Toney and his wife Elizabeth, who took over Grange Farm. This younger Henry and his brother Bob Oldfield owned the threshing engine kept near the Crossways in Tottington and during harvest time they toured the farms for miles around. At the Crossways near the New School there was a building containing three houses occupied by Henry and Eliza Oldfield, Mrs Pryke and Mrs Leffley; later on, the Bone Family came to live in the middle house.

My Father's Aunt Eliza and Uncle Henry Oldfield had nine children:
1. *William Charles* born 12. 5.1880 who married Mary Ann Ling in 1903 and had Horace William, Irene Rebecca, and Doris Annie Alice Oldfield.
2. *Ernest* born 9. 7.1885 who married Mary Howard in 1913.
3. *Henry George* born 7. 7.1881 who married Agnes Annie Park in 1903 and had Elsie Ellen Agnes, Ivy (married John Kohler 12.8.1931) and George Oldfield (married Dorothy Robinson 1.6.1931).

4. *Annie Elizabeth* (26. 8.1889 - 7. 1.1971) who married Archie Rands (1886 - 1976) in 1920 and had Frederick Harvey (1920), Derek Arnold (1924), and Vera Gwendolene (1928).
5. *Arthur* born 17. 1.1892 who married Lilian Lucy Belham in 1927 and had Phyllis (1928).
6. *Frederick* born 30. 3.1895 and died 10. 5.1899.
7. *Alice Maud* born 9.10.1896 and married Jack Belham.
8. *Albert* (17. 2.1899 - 25. 6.1967) who married Ivy Helen Robinson (1902 - 1988) from Ovington in 1923 and had Doris Rosalind (1927), Gladys Marie (1924), Dulcie Joyce (1934) and Patricia Pearl Oldfield (1942).

Most of these people were at Tottington when it was evacuated in 1942. Alice stayed at home and looked after her Mother. My Father was very fond of his cousin Arthur and they were in the village cricket team, played quoits and went hand bell ringing together. Before I was born people visited each other's houses for singing and get togethers so there was more contact. By 1910 the old school had become a Village Hall and these small parties seemed to disappear. Nevertheless most of the relatives kept in regular contact with one another.

THE BONE FAMILY: Edward Robert Bone was born at Blakeney on the north Norfolk coast and married Elizabeth Mabel Park in 1908; she came from the village of Hockham, and was related to Agnes Annie Park who had married Henry George Oldfield in 1903. Edward had been married previously to Mabel's cousin who died in childbirth; their son, Frederick Bone, was brought up by the cousin's sister, Laura who married my Uncle John Wright. Sadly Frederick died in the First World War. Edward had been in the Royal Navy and came to live on the Meadows near St. Andrew's Church in Tottington. A girl called Elizabeth was born but died quite early. No one knew why; she stretched out her arms to be picked up from the pram and just fell back dead. After this Mabel had six children:

1. *Elizabeth ('Betty')* (28. 6.1910 - 1998), married William Frank Gulliver in 1934 and had Michael (1938) and Barbara (1946).
2. *Reginald ('Reggie')* (1911 - 1963), married Ada Buttle in 1939 and had Margaret (1942) and Marjorie (1944).
3. *Robert ('Bob') Edward* (9. 7.1914 - 1996) , married Alice Croxford in 1938 and had Doreen (1939) and Alan (1949).

4. *Ethel Maud* born 26. 6.1916, married to Harold James Spinks in 1941 and had Susan (1942) and Frederick (1947).
5. *Allan John* (1922 - 1963), married Jassie Hatchley in 1946, and had Tony (1947), Judy (1951), and Valerie (1959).
6. *Frederick ('Freddie') Gerald* (1928 - 1988), married Doris Grinling in 1951 had Linda (1953) and Jane (1956).

Betty and Ethel had long auburn coloured hair which they inherited from their Father who was a biggish man working on Eastmere and Westmere Farms. Before I was born they lived next to my parents on the Meadows and our families have remained friends ever since. Reggie and I were christened together at Tottington church; Mr and Mrs Bone were my Godparents and my Mum and Dad were Reggie's. After some years they went to live in a house at the Crossroads near the school where Mrs Bone became the caretaker. She was a tiny woman who worked very hard and was loved by everyone; a generous and kind-hearted soul, always making excuses for people who did wrong. For some unknown reason Mr Bone always called me 'Jimmie'.

Betty left home and went into service in London where her Mother's sister, Jemima, lived. Ethel also went but didn't like it and returned to work near home. Reggie worked on the railway in London whereas Bob had two jobs close by; working first for the District nurse (a Miss Abraham at Merton), and then as a gardener for Lord Walsingham; later he went to London into private service. All the boys went into the Army: Reggie served some time in Ireland; Bob ended up in munitions; Allan and Freddie, being younger, were called up and went into the Navy.

In 1942, Mr and Mrs Bone plus Ethel and her husband

Edward and Mabel Bone

257

Mr Spinks with children, Arthur, Walter, William and Mary with Harold on
Mrs Spinks' knee.

Harold Spinks, went to Tuddenham St. Mary near Mildenhall. Harold
was born in 1914 and had an interesting pedigree. 'Spinks' is a
common name in the Breckland area particularly in the villages of
Bodney, Hilborough, and Cressingham. Several families emigrated and
there are descendants in Canada and Tasmania. Harold was the son of
Frederick Charles Spinks (1872 - 1931) who married Hannah Oldfield
(1871) the daughter of William Oldfield (1844 - 1917) and Ann
Downes (1840). That made Harold a distant relative of mine since
William was the grandson of William, a younger brother of the George
Oldfield who married Elizabeth Warby, and Ann was sister to Sarah
Downes, the wife of William Spragg, and mother of Thomas Spragg
who married my Aunt Florence Worby. It sound rather convoluted but
that is how peculiar the relationships of different families were.

Mr Bone lived to be over eighty; he had a brother who used to travel
around Norfolk in a donkey and cart and was well known even
appearing on television. Mrs Bone lived to be a Great-Grandmother, a
sweet old lady who died in 1981 aged 98 all bar two days. However,
the family has suffered great heartache. Allan and Ethel went into
hospital for cancer treatment. His son, Tony, upon hearing his Father
was dying of a terminal illness, passed away broken hearted in 1962,
three months before Allan. Ethel survived but Reggie died in 1963.
Betty's husband William died of a heart attack in 1964 and the

258

youngest son Freddie went nearly blind. My Godmother was very stoical and only said, "Why couldn't it have been me, being so much older, I've had my life." Her daughter, Ethel, has had her share of troubles. Despite suffering from sugar-diabetes and angina, she nursed Harold for over ten years after he suffered a stroke which left him badly paralysed. She had to do everything for him up until he died in 1988, followed soon afterwards by her brother Freddie whose own daughter Jane died in 1982 aged 26; life often seems unfair and unjust. Bob lived in Eastbourne but passed away in 1996; Betty died in Brighton, 1998.

THE FISHER FAMILY:

Rose and Dan Fisher were well known and much liked, becoming an integral part of Tottington village life although no relation to us or any of the other families. Where they came from I don't know but they lived in a nice place with two dwellings. Charlie Wright, my Father's cousin, lived next door but he died fairly young leaving an adopted son called James Dunham. Mother taught him to play the piano and he became quite good at it.

Dan worked at Hall Farm for years but when Mr Bob Childerhouse took over the farm and Mortimer and Sturston in the early thirties, the family moved to Sturston Farm House. Mr. Childerhouse lived at Hall Farm and then moved to Mortimer. As Hilda Rose Fisher, the youngest daughter, had married his son Joe Childerhouse, they and the Fisher family moved into Hall Farm. A Mr. and Mrs Mansfield moved to Sturston Farm. Rose and Dan were small thick-set people and she always had a rosy face. They had eight children: Elijah went into the Navy; Alice Margaret married Arthur Buckfield in 1925; Ivy went into service; Herbert Sydney worked on the land and married Emma Elizabeth Goss from Stanford in 1939; Joan (Lily) also went into service; William James, also an agricultural labourer, married Emmeline May Baker in 1933; Dolly May worked in the village shop until she married William Gordon Wyer an ironmonger from Watton in 1934; and Hilda Rose.

MISS LUCILLA REEVE:

It would be remiss of me not to include a section about this extraordinary woman who held a responsible and important position as the Agent of the Merton Estate comprising 8000 acres, four villages and several farms belonging to Lord Walsingham. It was very unusual in the first half of this century for a woman to do such a job which meant she had to see to all the hiring of the farms, the houses and their rents, keeping them in repair by the use of the Estate's own bricklayers and carpenters as well as maintaining and improving the numerous fields, woods and plantations.

According to the Tottington Parish Register, Lucilla was born (at Hunstanton) 28th March 1889 to Polly Reeve (b.1868) but her Father isn't recorded. She came from a working labourer's family which had lived in Tottington for some time. Reeve is a common surname of the area but not all of them were related. Lucilla's Mother was one of seven children born between 1865 and 1877 to Christopher Reeve and his second wife Susan. His first wife was an Ann Macrow and it is interesting to note how many times these two families intermarried. I am descended from John and Mary Macrow; their son Thomas married an Ann Reeve in 1827 (giving rise to Mary, James, Sarah Charles and Christopher Reeve Macrow); their daughter Sophia married a William Reeve (giving rise to Sarah, Anne and Mary Reeve). Their other son Henry Macrow had two sons: Robert (1825-1855) who married Mary Reeve (1827-1852) in 1849 and had five children (Edwin, Clare Ann, Blanche Ann, Robert and Ellen Macrow); and Nathan (who married Sarah Ann Reeve in 1834 and had four children (Alfred, Anna, Frederick and Clara Macrow). As such Lucilla was related to a number of families in the village, but always remained apart by virtue of her different upbringing, position and personality.

She was brought up by her Grandmother, Susan, but left Tottington school at fourteen and went to London, possibly working in domestic service. She must have continued her education because it became obvious to all that Miss Reeve was well-read, artistic and musical as well as possessing the commercial and accountancy skills necessary to become secretary to Mr Hipwell who was the Agent to the Estate when I was very young. He had an office in Home Farm at Merton, the only farm directly operated by the old Lord Walsingham. Lucilla returned to live in the village with her Granny in a cottage called Braesma on a meadow belonging to Mortimer Farm. Rumours abounded that she had an affair with Mr. Hipwell, a married man. About 1920 he left under a cloud of scandal and went to Newmarket whilst Miss Reeve took over his job as Estate Agent.

I first remember seeing her on a bicycle whilst on my way to school. Often she rode a horse, astride not side-saddle, and went around in riding breeches. Standing about 5 ft 4 inches tall and dressed in a dark blue or black, well-cut jacket, a white, starched blouse buttoned to the neck, a tweed skirt and stout brogue shoes, Miss Reeve was an imposing figure. Moreover she had her hair cut short almost like a man's Eton crop - something unheard of for a woman in those days; it quite upset the later Lady Walsingham, Hyacinth de Grey.

In this book I have quoted extensively from her three works: *'The Earth No Longer Bare'* , *'Farming on the Battleground'* , and *'The Pheasants Had No Tails'*, written after the Second World about her experiences from 1938 to 1947 at Bagmore Farm south of Stanford. Although interesting in themselves and containing several historical asides with many comments and opinions there is little specifically about Tottington. Nevertheless, it was her village, and she was undoubtedly fond of the place; in one passage, describing the avenue of cedar trees lining the road entering the village from Thetford, she thought it "more beautiful than Dedham in Suffolk's Constable country".

In 1927 the old Lord Walsingham, who lived at a house called "The Hassocks" in Merton, died and Mr. Wace who had rented Eastmere, retired. The new Lord George de Grey, who lived at Westmere Farm, took over Eastmere and as the farmhouse was empty, Miss Reeve was given the large front room as an Office. This she became most fond of, and my Mother often lit her fire in the morning and tidied up, until a young chap called Harold Spinks (the future husband of my good friend Ethel Bone) came from Sturston to work for her. He was followed by my cousisn Albert Spragg who drove Miss Reeve aound in her red, two-seater, racing car. She loved speed and often drove so fast herself that behind her back people nicknamed her 'madcap'. In the early 1920s, the old Lady Walsingham was head of the Girl guides and Miss Reeve was her Lieutenant. We used to meet up once a week in the Reading Room behind the War Memorial. Girls from Thompson Village also attended and we paraded at the major events like Armistice Sunday, when the whole village turned out. Watton Town Band led us from the Memorial to St. Andrew's Church, along with ex-service men, the Old Blokes, nurses, Brownies and Boy Scouts, etc.

Nothing went on without Miss Reeve knowing about it, and she had a wealth of information about the villages and the history of the local area. As to her own personal life there is little to go on since no one seems to have kept her letters or papers, or to have written about her. Most of what is known stems from articles she wrote for the the EDP and the Farmers Weekly many of which are collected together in her books. If she kept a Diary, it does not appear to have survived which is a great shame since all that I have written about occurred whilst she was in charge of the whole Estate. She had an insider's knowledge about the important events for the two decades from 1926 to 1946 as well as the facts and figures about the Merton Estate which I do not have access to. Moreover she was privy to much personal detail since her opinion was often sought after as she was very strong-minded about lots of things and not afraid to express it. She had a habit of being blunt and often called 'a spade a spade'. Sadly, in later years, people dismissed her as being somewhat of a crank or at the very best eccentric. Even in her own day she was considered unconventional, a bit of a local character. Indeed she was a bundle of contrasts: born out of wedlock, daughter of a village working-class Mother, yet well-educated and cultured; physically short and wiry, tough and resiliant, she didn't pretend lady-like refinements; she was as capable of manual work as any farm labourer, handling the machinery and looking after the animals; she could ride a horse, shoot a gun, and practise the skills of a businesswoman in her position as Agent for the Merton Estate; she had a strong sense of fair play and a secure belief in God, insisting upon

The Land Agent at her desk

her fields being blessed; she tried to be kind even towards those soldiers who ruined her fields with their exercises and took down the netting she erected to keep out the rabbits. She may have been sentimental and a little superstitious, holding a belief in witchcraft, ghosts and dowsing, but her love of the earth, of animals, of all nature, shines through strongly in her writing and in one senses she was ahead of her time with her concern for afforestation and protction of the countryside.

Before the Second World War Miss Reeve became interested in National Socialism and Oswald Mosley's 'Blackshirts' ; she attended their meeting during the Norfolk Campaign 'Britain for the British'. Today people tend to forget that many important individuals, including the Prince of Wales who became Edward VIII, held sympathies for the Fascists and even admired Hitler for what he appeared to being doing in Germany. 'National Socialism' was not seen to be the dreadful ogre it is today with our hindsight of the appalling atrocities, the murders and genocide of the concentration camps. No doubt Miss Reeve's political opinions displeased Lord Walsingham who was a rank Conservative and thought all who worked for him should vote accordingly. Certainly a number of the village folk felt uncomfortable with her views and some even called her a traitor. It made Albert Spragg a little wary so he went to work in London. She never fully recovered from the stigma.

When Bagmere near Sturston beame empty at Michaelmas 1938 she couldn't let the farm so decided to run it herself, turning the buildings into a guest house in 1940 but it was never successful, even though she installed a bathroom and toilet. Her book, 'The Earth No Longer Bare' describes her trials and tribulations at Bagmere. Despite severe financial restraints she rennovated the dilapidated buildings which were totally overgrown with bracken and ragwort and overrun with rabbits. It was a marvel how she managed to keep going; one has to admire her integrity and industry. During 1942 she was working sixteen hours a day and her life seemed to be filled with committee meetings:

There were miles of walking to select timber for the nation's needs, over and above the usual estate work. More and more meetings of the R.D.C. and the usual Guardians' Committee three times a month. Then there were always military or services people calling about requisitions and more meetings than usual of school managers and parish meetings. Later there were to be constant meetings of Food Control Committees, Invasion Committees and the like. As the Agent I had enough work but was still looked to as the only person capable of being in charge of these posts for not only my own village of Tottington but for Stanford with West and Buckenham Tofts.

This never left her much time for herself or Bagmere: *I often only saw the farm in early mornings and late evenings for Sunday would mean a day of book keeping or income tax returns.* Unfortunately, after putting up several wire fences to keep out rabbits out, reclaiming the land and planting numerous small woods of young beech, oak and elm, her farm was taken over by the Army on the 13th June 1941 for tank and troop training. Miss Reeve didn't own the land so received no compensation for her crops except for the two worst fields but tried to continue with the harvest. Owing £600 to the bank and unable to repay she risked going bankrupt, so sold her livestock to two farmer friends. Along with the rest of us, the creation of the Battle Area in 1942 deprived her of her home. She was a real trooper and didn't complain but tried hard to help people find places to live, only to end up with nowhere herself. She was turned out of her farm with promises of another one but that never materialised. Her horses, Ben and Beauty, were sold at Thornber's Sale which also auctioned most of the machinery and livestock at Eastmere Farm.

She bought the large plucking shed from Thornber's at Eastmere Farm plus three other poultry huts on sale in South Norfolk and had them re-erected in Merton Woods. All her belongings were transported there by a succession of trips in her little car:

I drove my car down Frogshall Hill
The hour was late, the earth was still.
The trees look'd down with pitying eye,
To see the laden car go by.
My heart was sad and bowed my neck
Four years of work and planning wreck,
Behind me lay, across spring Breck.

She tried to make a little farm there and being on the edge of the Battle Area often met up with troops suddenly descending upon her and ruining her fences. Also in October 1942, she took over the thirty-two acres of Broadmarsh Farm at Gt. Ellingham where two previous farmers had died strangely; one by shooting and the other by hanging himself in the barn. For a woman who believed in ghosts as 'real people' and who claimed to have seen "the Grey Lady" whilst walking around Merton Park, it was an odd choice. She kept sixty cattle, fourteen sheep and twenty eight pigs and as usual gave most of them personal names. However, this wasn't that successful either so on 13th November 1944 she let Broadmarsh and decided to concentrate upon farming sixteen acres near her huts.

Miss Reeve retained a wonderful dream that one day she would have a nice farm away from it all. She had given up her job as Estate Agent to concentrate upon her farming but this was not successful She planted thousands of trees, in various places known as Princess Elizabeth, Silver Belt, the 'de Greys' , etc, and no doubt many of these still stand as a monument to her foresight. Her ideal was for the Merton Estate to be prosperous farming area producing a variety of crops, timber, as well as heathland for sheep rather than a shooting park. However, the strain of work, and the loss of all that she had striven for, eventually took its toll. One only has to read her books to realise how difficult everything was for her during the War and afterwards; the setbacks and disappointments and the Government's 'broken promise', hit her deeply. By 1943 her home at Bagmore lay in ruins after being shelled by tanks, the many trees and shrubs she had planted so assiduously were destroyed. On Remembrance Day, 11th November 1945 Lucilla went to Tottington and,

" *seen the ruin and desolation of a village I had, only seven years ago decribed as lovely. . . . . . . The dead and staring eyes of the cottage windows where once the geraniums bloomed, and the spotless curtains fluttered, look out on a scene of desolation. The sides of the once tidy road are full of holes made by tanks roaring through . . . . and the once lovely hedges of privet, lilac, thorn and wild roses are mangled and torn. A silence as of night broods over all"*. She cycled on *"to see the ruins of what had been my home. It was gutted by fire following shelling of tanks in August last year . . . . It was a sad sight but I shed no tears as I walked round past the one wall still standing"*.

Living alone in Merton Woods in an old wooden plucking shed must have been cold, uncomfortable and depressing, especially after she crippled her hand with a reef hook. In the end it all became too much and Miss Reeve took her own life on 30th October, 1950; a sad comment upon, and indictment of, the Army's takeover of the Battle Area. Originally her body was buried outside the churchyard of St. Andrew's in unconsecrated ground, as was often the practice when someone committed suicide, it being considered a grave sin by the Christian Church. Now that the metal fence has been altered to incorporate her grave inside the churchyard, may she rest in peace.

1942 THE BATTLE AREA

In 1942 about 220 people lived in Tottington, with a dozen young men in the Armed Forces; of the 39 houses in the parish, 30 were occupied by ex-servicemen of the 1914-18 War or their widows. The community was busily engaged in supporting the war effort by trying to cultivate more fields and grow as much food as possible. The Breckland was a perfect training area with its wide open spaces and flat land: there was an Air Force base at Mildenhall and an Army camp at Bodney and Czech servicemen were stationed at East Wretham. Around the Merton Estate signs of military activity intensified and soldiers were regularly seen from 1939 onwards. On Friday, 13th June 1941, Miss Lucilla Reeve, Lord Walsingham's Estate Agent, was informed that certain parts of some of the fields on her farm at Bagmore and others at Waterloo Farm near Stanford, were wanted by the army for military purposes; a loss of nearly ninety acres of cultivated land. Relays of army officers came to look around, and netting she had erected to keep out the rabbits was taken down by the troops. There was constant troop and air training with bombing practices, and enemy planes coming over most nights. Miss Reeve suspected the Army would take all the land south of the Tottington - Stanford road towards Thetford, but much worse was to come.

By 1942 the War Department had decided that it needed a larger area where troops could train under realistic war conditions, even at the risk of casualties from live bullets, bombs and shells. Obviously this violent activity would be extremely dangerous for either civilians or farm stock to remain in the vicinity; such a 'Battle Area' would have to be cleared. The Army had made up its mind to requisition the centre of the Breckland. Apart from Miss Lucilla Reeve in her book, *'Farming on a Battleground'*, very little has been written about the events in 1942 which the general public has access to. No doubt those evacuated from the Battle Area have written letters with views and opinions and mentioned interesting details - each family has its own memories and sad moments. Newspaper articles are few and far between: there was hardly anything in the Thetford & Watton Times and the Journal; the Eastern Daily Press carried a few reports in 1942 but nothing much for the rest of the War period. Although there were a spate of articles in 1946-48, these are mainly factual accounts of the meetings and activities held to regain the land and the villages. However, Tottington was a very small and obscure village in the wilds of Norfolk, and only one of many in the three areas taken over by the War Department for troop training purposes (the others being Ashdown Forest in the Lake District and Maiden Castle). It was also a question of military secrecy, and of course during the War there were more pressing issues to be considered.

I was away visiting my husband, who was stationed at Stratford-upon-Avon, when I received a letter from Mother, the contents of which came as a shock. Along with most of the other villagers, she attended a meeting at the Blacksmith's yard in the evening. Returning home she wrote a letter to catch the 10 p.m. post, to say we all had to leave Tottington, by July 19th, 1942. The Eastern Daily Press carried an article, Saturday 20th June, reporting events. On the previous Thursday, 18th June, all the villagers - the local tenant farmers, trades people, farm workers and their families - had gathered in the open air of the local smithy's yard to listen to Lt. Gen. Anderson, Army G.O.C-in-C, Eastern Command. He explained the reasons for the decision and said it would affect 18,000 acres (about 30 farms, 150 houses and cottages, 3 schools, 2 pubs, 34 miles of roadway) and about 800 people.

"There is little you will want to hear in the way of sympathy and the last thing anyone wants to do is turn Englishmen from their homes . . . . I don't deny we are causing a lot of grief , pain and trouble and I am deeply sorry for it but this is one of the places where the disturbance will be least felt. . . . .it is essential that certain areas be reserved wholly for military purpose and therefore entirely evacuated by the civil population." Lt. Gen. Anderson, *"gave an assurance there would be no wanton damage and everything would be done to protect homes and churches and other places of interest from destruction'.*

According to the reporter, his speech was listened to in silence and afterwards there was a burst of applause. However, those who were present have told me that this isn't so; there were interruptions and questions but people were ignored. Lord Walsingham, who chaired the Meeting, described the situation as a calamity but hoped the training would shorten the war; *"My word I am proud to belong to an area where such people live."*

Lord Cranbrook, the Deputy Regional Commissioner and a War Dept Valuer explained the procedure for evacuation and compensation: people were given a month to leave; crop value less estimated harvesting costs would be paid; the War Dept would pay the fees of private valuers; War Agricultural Committees would arrange for the offer of alternative accommodation to farmers; if necessary, costs of stock removal and furniture storage were to be met by the military. Where people could not make private arrangements, vehicles would be provided for removal of personal possessions and livestock. Efforts would be made to rehouse the workers in new areas and where that was not possible billets provided. Elderly people who did not want to go to friends or relatives would probably be given separate rooms in a large country house.

Villagers who were there have talked about that infamous day ever since. Miss Reeve wrote, *"It was indeed a blow. . . . . I'd never dreamed they would take the whole of Tottington village and parts of Thompson and Merton."* The truth is that the area was only half the size the Army had asked for! Most people were too worried about what they were going to do, to argue or quibble with the authorities. Thomas Spragg, whose sons Albert and Clifford were in the Army, said that if it was going to shorten the war then they would just have to accept it. Others did feel a grievance and thought Lord Walsingham had sold them out. Some villagers felt that the meetings were a waste of time; the Army had made its decision and that was that.

" In my view they were wrong . . . . . . an insult to the people who were being turned out. Were we a load of nit-wits and ignorant, uneducated folk who didn't know there was a war on? . . . damn it, even if we did grumble . . . we knew how to take a knock decently. You'd have thought we were in darkest Africa and had to be given a few beads to keep us quiet! . . . I very reluctantly went to the meeting held in Tottington and it made me so hopping mad I nearly created the only row there would have been . . . it made me sick. As many fully armed officers and plain clothes civil force as they were come to quell a mob of rioters in Ireland. God forgive them for their ignorance and their lies and stupid promises - soothing syrup for people who were ashamed of them." (Miss Reeve)

Personally I feel this is a harsh and unfair indictment of men who felt they had a responsibility to the nation's war effort and a job to do, however unpleasant. People may not have liked their visits and speeches but it was more courteous than a letter or a public notice in the local newspaper. There was an additional meeting for the inhabitants of Stanford, Langford, Tottington, and Buckenham Tofts at West Tofts.

Miss Reeve quotes an ex-service farmer who went to that meeting:

"I wish I hadn't gone . . . . Did you see the silly fools? One officer near me even flourished his revolver, just in case! I had hard work to keep from taking it away from him. What the hell were they scared of? I'm so ashamed of it all . . . and what a pity one of us couldn't have got up and told them just what we thought about them; do they think us chaps don't know what discipline is?" she claimed, *"that was just what most of us felt. The leaders of our country sank right down in our estimation and the memory of those meetings will never be erased from the minds of people who were talked at"*

The E.D.P. of Monday, 29th July, carried an article quoting Mr. Hudson, Minister of Agriculture, speaking at a War Agricultural Executive Committee Meeting at Kelsale near Saxmundham, East Suffolk, on Saturday 27th: *"I know this means individual hardship but so are many things that have to be done if we are to win this War. I fully sympathise with all those who have to leave their farms and homes. . . . . I do want the men and women affected to remember that they are making. . . . a necessary contribution and an inevitable sacrifice to the cause for which we are all fighting and that they can still carry on the fight to good purpose in other areas."* The Government didn't give the people much time or opportunity to move. Miss Reeve wrote, *"we were told on the 13th and requisition took place on the 20th - seven days, and they actually thought we could all be moved in that time! Eventually we were given until the 18th of July; and I can only think of those five weeks as hell let loose."*

She hints that the local powers didn't take the threat seriously and thought some other area would be requisitioned. The villages themselves were stunned by the news and some didn't accept the reality and a few people felt that the decision could be reversed: *"one of the worst things about that first week was the rumour that it wasn't going to happen after all . . . I am afraid until some of them got the requisition notices they did not believe it was true. . . . .A lot of the early time we had was wasted in going round with a petition which was to be sent to the King. I hated the idea of us doing this, because if it was necessary for winning the war to take over our homes we should not have asked his Majesty to interfere . . . .He didn't of course."*

I don't remember there being a petition. My parents didn't sign it and in any case we didn't have any spare time to waste. My Father had Eastmere Farm to see to with many responsibilities. Most people were too busy for quibbling or recriminations. It was a tall order to go looking for a new place to live and another job when one had work to do every day, a home to look after and children to care for, gardens to attend to. Even more so when people lacked mobility - there were few cars available. It was hardest for the elderly who had hoped to live out the rest of their lives in cottages they had occupied for years. One has to remember that some people had lived in the village, in the same house, all their lives and were surrounded by relatives and friends they had grown up with; brothers, cousins, uncles, worked together on the same farms. My own Father had been born in Tottington and we had lived at Eastmere Farm Cottage for thirty years. Such an upheaval caused much emotional distress. Many people had similar disturbing experiences to this lady:

"When we were told we had to go and find somewhere else to live I did not do anything about it at first. You see I had been at Stanford all my life. But my husband made me realise it was true. We were offered part of a house in another parish. There were goslings on the kitchen table and there had been tar in the copper. When I looked out of the window and saw goats climbing into our car that decided me against the place. You know how precious a car was in war time. Later we found a lonely cottage and had a rough life there for ten years. There was no well and when the war was over we were snowed up in that bad winter of 1947, and then half the tiles blew off in a gale." (E.D.P. 2nd November 1962)

People rallied round and took villagers to look at different places. Most of the inhabitants were relatives so it was a very sad time for everyone, the breaking of relations and family, the ending of an era. Some villagers moved far away, to other counties but most tried to find homes just outside the Battle Area (see Appendix). We had a hard time with Mother who was bitter about the whole thing, and didn't like the places we were taken to by volunteers in their cars. A Lady Albermarle drove us one night to a village called Sporle and I remember saying to Father that we would have a long way to come to fetch out 'taters' which amused him in that elite company. Another cottage had the cattle yard next to the back door so we didn't go there. Eventually my Father got a job on a farm at the village of Hingham fifteen miles away,

270

belonging to a Captain Denny. We had a nice little cottage even though the wall-paper in the sitting-room was flapping off the wall. It was in the middle of a meadow at the end of a long lane. Mother was quite happy there and when Father retired in 1954 they were given a new Council house in Hingham along the Watton road.

As one by one the villagers departed, we were among the last to leave. All the farmstock and implements were Auctioned off on Thursday 17th July; the sale of animals. particularly the horses, was very distressing. My Father and I waited until the very end feeding them but lots of people never had a chance to say goodbye. One of my saddest heartaches was having most of our pets put down. The RSPCA men came round and caught all the stray cats. It left a deep impression since animals seem to know what will happen. I'll never forget the reproach in my cat's eyes. He was called Jimmie and trusted me; I tried taking him to the van in a box on the back of my bike but he escaped and ran home, so the R.S.P.C.A. man drove up to the farm and caught him and a number of wild kittens that roamed the farm buildings. Fortunately Jumbo went with my parents to Hingham and was Mother's faithful friend. I think the last animal left was the bull. Dad had to feed him before we went - we could hear him stamping his feet and roaring. One can imagine how he felt left alone after being with seventy heifers!

We moved on Saturday 19th; Mother burnt the milk that morning - it had to be boiled because of the warm weather - but the men still drank it in their tea. One of the duck hands helped us to load our possessions; we took as much as possible including the bikes and our huge wooden barrow. Many people had to travel in open lorries as few furniture vans were available; Father, Mother, myself and Jumbo had to sit with the driver up front. It was very wet and Mother worried about the beds becoming damp. All her beautiful flowers had to be left as it was Summer, unripe fruit hung on the trees and vegetables remained in the gardens. Thus our beloved Eastmere came to an end and we all had sad hearts and lumps in out throats, even Jumbo seemed to know. It wasn't so bad for me as I had been away in London and only came back in 1940 when my husband was called up, but for those people who had lived in Tottington all their lives, it was a catastrophe as bad as if their homes had been destroyed in the Blitz. The Army moved in immediately and their manoeuvres began a destruction which continued for the rest of the War and afterwards.

We did go back to Tottington one Sunday in 1942, cycling 15 miles each way. Many people found that soldiers had either taken or destroyed their belongings and gardens had been run over by vehicles. All Mother's beautiful flowers had been left as it was July but luckily these had survived. She loaded up so many plants that when she mounted the saddle, the bike wobbled, overbalanced and ended up in the ditch. My Father was angry but I laughed so much he had to laugh once he found that Mother was okay. They often amused me when they were cross with one another; Dad would shake himself and say "Oh, Alice!" and Mum would say "Oh, Albert!". Sadly Mum had to leave most of her flowers in that ditch. Not everything could be moved and some villagers left furniture and other items in their houses or sheds. There must be a lot of treasures laying around as people threw so much in what would be called their 'gutter holes'.

The Army moved in immediately and their manoeuvres didn't exactly make it easy for people; Miss Reeve gives an illustrative story:

"One day I really lost my temper . . . . We were high busy baling the hay and three times did a large car drive up and an official get out and knock at the door to ask if we were going on all right . . . . . and was there anything they could do. The third time I snapped, "Yes, take your coats off and work!" . . You can imagine how angry it made us to see so many folk running around and almost getting in the way." Ever since that time there have been accusations of deliberate vandalism by the troops who smashed their way through fences and hedges even before the people left their homes. This is difficult to substantiate even though people claim to remember minor incidents. Miss Reeve was adamant about the behaviour of some of the troops: *"No sooner would a family take away one load of furniture, and these hooligans would go into the house and loot and even befoul it before the people came back for the rest of their things. Doors were broken off, windows smashed, and some houses almost wrecked. . . . . There seemed to be absolutely no discipline in the army we saw in the weeks of that summer."*

Perhaps this was true but it has to be remembered that the troops were just young lads, many of them from towns and cities, unused to country ways. To begin with no one seemed to know the exact extent of the Battle Area; it wasn't clearly marked and so many troops were difficult to supervise.They did take away Miss Reeve's netting along the side of the Stanford-Tottington road, and drove lorries all over the small beech, ash, pine and fir trees she had planted. Women worked hard to scrub clean and leave their homes neat and tidy - just as if new tenants were expected - and to have their homes and work despoiled made people angry and sad, especially since they thought they were were coming back. The Army and outsiders had different ideas; in one sense the village houses were like war booty open to be pillaged. Miss Reeve wrote about incidents which happened after she had relocated to Merton woods:

"There were long spells when no training was being done, and very often I would be disturbed those nights by lorries and cars breaking the barrier and going into the area to loot. They took such things as coppers, ovens, doors, and anything else they could move . . . . and I expect troops were blamed for much damage they had not done."

Those who had access to the Battle Area during the War have said that they saw some of the buildings destroyed by shellfire. However, when this and allegations of vandalism were raised in Parliament four years later, Lord Pakenham, Under-Secretary for War in the Lords replied: *"No one resents more than the ordinary Army officer the suggestion that he is a vandal blind to the beauties of the countryside."* Moreover, at the Wayland R.D.C. Meeting on Saturday, 31st May 1947, Mr. S. George said that a Committee had toured the Battle Area:

"We visited all the Churches and many houses and we noticed that that the houses were not damaged at all by gun-fire. They were practically perfect. One or two council houses in Stanford had a tile or two missing but that was due to the gale. The trouble in the houses is dry rot. The rectories are in a terrible condition by reason of dry rot." (Thetford and Watton Journal, May 1947).

People who read the newspapers at the time and listened to rumours gained the impression that everyone was to be fully compensated, but there wasn't an act in force whereby villagers could be paid for the crops or found homes and farms, etc. Not until the 4th August 1942 was this issue debated in the House of Commons and the War Compensation Act passed to allow people to receive money for the garden produce and fruit left behind, for the jobs they had lost, and to pay no more rent in the future than they had been at Tottington, etc. The reality of the situation was different from that which people were given to understand. For a start there were no farms available and the local R.D.C.s had to hunt up poor old cottages which had been condemned for years, and hurredly try to do a few repairs. According to Miss.

Reeve, anxious farmers sat around tables and filled in forms to give particulars but only one was found a new farm. Nor were they told what was to become of their livestock and farm implements, in the meantime. If they sold everything then how could they equip a new farm? Many were in debt so they would not be able to afford to start again. The truth quickly dawned and the farmers realised they had to give up. Thornber's had an auction at Eastmere and sold everything. Miss Reeve, had nothing but praise for the fairness and efficiency of the valuers, even though she was to be deprived of her home, her livelihood and all the work she had put in planting trees and reclaiming land on Bagmere Farm. She asked Thornber's for an old plucking hut at Eastmere Farm which was dismantled and then erected at a site in

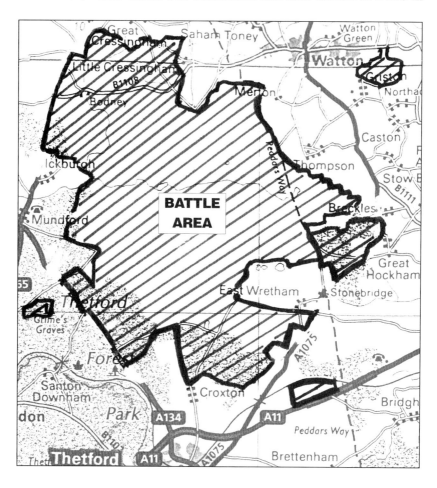

274

Merton Woods near Thompson, along with three poultry huts she bought from south Norfolk and a tin hut from her home, Braysmead. Lord Walsingham had the whole farmhouse at Westmere dismantled and rebuilt in Merton Woods.

There were about 2000 acres of cereals left inside the Battle Area in July 1942. It wasn't harvested by the farmers and their workers who had moved elsewhere but boys from Repton and Norwich Grammar Schools worked with the soldiers in gathering crops of barley, oats, wheat and rye. Mr. D.H. Sanderson, who had farmed in the area, was placed in charge and sixteen combine harvesters were brought in along with threshers and bailers to complete the work. Mr. J. C. Mann of the War Agricultural Committee directed the proceeds to the Treasury and compensation was paid according to the estimates of crop value minus cost of harvesting as agreed previously. On the 16th October 1942 there was a second "Armistice" to harvest the following acreage: 500 of sugar-beet, 70 of mangolds and swedes, 60 of carrots, 30 of potatoes, 16 of parsnips, and a few of red beet and clover seed. By that time all the people who had lived in the villages were gone. Tottington had ceased to exist as a thriving community and had become an empty shell. As an E.D.P. reporter wrote:

"There is not a civilian within miles but garden gates were closed and orchards and holdings still much as they had been left when the local folk moved out in their great victory contribution."

Church with Council houses boarded up

A BROKEN PROMISE

After WWII, various groups expected that land requisitioned for training and defence would be returned to its owners. As such Tottington wasn't a specific issue, only part of a debate concerning the post-war use and ownership of land. (about 9,505,000 acres out of 11,400,000 were returned). Those who advocated a return argued the issue of food production, housing, and the principle of a *"broken promise"*. It was understood by all from the Stanford Battle Area, who had read the newspapers and attended the meetings held in 1942, that the Government of the day gave a promise to allow people to return after the War. The Lords Cranbrook, Cranworth, and Walsingham pressed this case in the Upper Chamber and the Leader of the Opposition gave a pledge that they would not let the matter rest. Lord Nathan, Under-Secretary to the War Office, explained the difficult position but assured people that the Government still held themselves bound by the promise of their predecessors to return the training areas to their former occupants. Nevertheless, two factors have to be appreciated about the post-war period: the Labour Party's socialist ideology advocated state ownership not just of major industries but also of land, and the War Department wanted to retain certain places as permanent training areas. As a result in 1946 about 500,000 acres across the country were still in military hands.

In 1946, the Norfolk County Council's "Review of the Facts" documented the extent of the initial requisition. It concluded that: *"The owners of the property . . . were promised by the Regional Commissioners that the area would be returned to them after the War. . . . . three whole villages have been deprived of existence and in terms of human happiness, apart from all economic considerations this is a serious loss"*

As I have tried to describe, Tottington, and the other villages, were small but unique communities which were literally destroyed overnight by the creation of the Battle Area in 1942. During the Second World War they still existed, they were not 'physically lost', the structure remained. However, they were 'spiritually lost' in that the relationships between families, to the land and animals, to their work and their homes, was broken. Whether communities can be re-established let alone resurrected in their previous form is a moot point, even today. Firstly the question, of whether the land around Stanford and Tottington was worth farming or the houses capable of being lived in, became an important practical issue. Obviously the land had deteriorated and needed much work; it had only been kept productive by constant application of farmyard manure and intensive folding, and the ploughing in of green crops. Less than 8000 of the 18000 acres was farmland in 1942 - some of it was heathland ploughed up at the beginning of the War. In peace time about 2000 acres was arable with only 1000 acres under crops. 13000 was heath and woodland used for the shooting of pheasants, partridges and rabbits. Was it worthwhile to return this land to proper cultivation? Where was the money and the manpower to come from to renovate everything?

An article in the E.D.P. 8th May 1946, wasn't very positive or supportive: *These people seem to visualise a certain day practically as soon as the release is made on which the displaced persons will march back into their former homes, flags flying and bands playing and hordes of tractors ploughing and everything in a month or so just as it was before. It cannot happen .* . Such a comment was hardly fair or correct. Many people had created new lives for themselves, living in better accommodation in other villages and working for different employers. They didn't want to return, certainly not to a dangerous place which had to be cleared of shells, bombs and mortars, where the housing had been damaged or destroyed, the fences knocked down, the fields full of weeds like canker, ragwort and brachen, and of course rabbits. The E.D.P. writer made a case for not allowing people back: *ammunition is everywhere . . . . . Death lurks not only in the woods and on the farmlands but in the cottage gardens . . . . . How long would it take to clear death from the whole of 18000 acres? The problem has to be looked at from a national angle and what is best for the future welfare of the land. It involves the people as a whole for the cost has to be borne by everyone of us.*

There was the problem of the damage caused by the training and firing. The Army have long held that no real destruction of homes took place as a result of the exercises, but there is evidence to contradict this. Houses were destoyed by shellfire, and by soldiers knocking bricks out of walls for gun placements. Indeed, four years had taken their toll as the E.D.P. writer went on to admit: *Attempts have been made to keep some places in repair but it hasn't amounted to much because of the constant firing or exercises. . . . Brick floors are uprooted by rabbits and wood was eaten by the rats. Clay lump walls have gone in and thatched roofs sagged. Brick houses have been shaken and fungi grow on walls. Gardens are no more, all fruit trees are ruined, and in many cases tanks have gone through fences and walls . . . . most of the wells are polluted and in some cases filled with petrol tins, etc.*

The E.D.P. article stated there were two courses of action: *(a) to go on using the land as a Battle Area, or (b) clear it and use a small part for farming or small holdings, or as a Government Training Area for both farming and forestry, and the rest could be a National Park.*

Nevertheless it would have been physically possible to re-establish Tottington and the other villages. The real issue was the requirement by the Army for a large training area as opposed to those who wanted to return to their former property and livelihood. In the Parliamentary debate on Requisitions of Land for Training Purposes (20th Dec. 1946), Mr. Sidney Dye, Labour M.P. for S.W. Norfolk, said that the country didn't need the Stanford Training Area, it was more important to open it up for food production. In January 1947 the Norfolk War Agricultural Committee, visited the Stanford Battle Area and reported that the 6000 acres formerly in cultivation had become *"veritable forests of ragwort"* but most of the buildings appeared to be in good condition. On February 25th 1947 Mr. Tom Williams, Minister of Agriculture (in a written reply to Mr. Dye) declared that the War Dept had given permission for about 2000 acres or practically the whole of the arable land within the safety belt of the Stanford B. A. to be cultivated in the following year. At the same time it became apparent that the War Dept. intended to hang onto the remaining 16,000 acres.

Troops in Battle Exercise Waterloo Farm in Background

278

Meanwhile various bodies in Norfolk began to organise. Wayland R.D.C. unanimously agreed to do everything possible to secure the release of the Battle Area. Lord Walsingham pointed out that 1100 people had been affected in 1942, and there were at present 75 houses in the Wayland area which could be occupied and in the Swaffham district about 125 houses. At a later Meeting, Mr. G. W. Trollope said that in Tottington there were scores of houses that could be put into habitable condition at very little cost and so relieve the housing shortage (E.D.P. 29th January).

In March, a Joint Committee of the Breckland (representing the important naturalist and archeological associations in Norfolk and Suffolk), made representations to the Ministry of Town and Country Planning against the War Dept proposal to retain the Battle Area as a permanent military training ground. *which was a gross violation of the specific promise made in public to return the battle training area after the War and to reinstate the inhabitants and farmers and others then evicted.* A host of arguments were put forward: *the loss of food production badly needed after the War and the effect of weeds and vermin on adjacent agricultural land; serious interference with forestry, transport, scenic beauty, natural history and archeology; the area had unique flora and fauna not found elsewhere in Britain, meres of rare and special beauty plus 353 acres at East Wretham surrounding Langmere acquired by the Norfolk Naturalist Trust.* (E.D.P. 26th March 1947)

The War Dept. had no intention of relinquishing the area and changed the goal posts. In April their proposals for the permanent acquisition of 28,000 acres of the Breckland came before the Inter-Departmental Committee on Services' Requirements. It intended to make Eastern Command the main infantry command with Stanford B. A. the chief training area. Far from returning land already taken, the War Dept. wanted to take over areas where former inhabitants of the six villages (Stanford, Sturston, Tottington, Langford, West Tofts and Buckenham Tofts) had now settled. It was to stretch from Buckenham Tofts Park to Gooderstone Warren and Hilborough in the north, three-quarters of a mile short of Foulden to the NW, to Croxton on the SE and Thetford-Swaffham Railway on the east up to Wretham Park, including the safety belt and the lakes at East Wretham. Limited cultivation would be permitted and tenants could claim compensation for damage to crops. It was a shock to say the least. On April 16th a meeting in Norwich of interested parties passed resolutions protesting against the proposals and calling for the immediuate release of the land. Major J.

C. T. Mills of Hilborough Hall said: *The Government have . . . . broken the promise to allow these people to return to their homes after the war . . . it seems they are to be hounded out again and deprived of their livelihood.* The National Farmers Union was opposed to the plan; Lady Walsingham raised the issue of compensation claims; Mr. Harry Hopkins, the County Planning Officer, said the County Council had presented a case to the I . D. Committee urging that a Public Inquiry be held. The A.G.M. of Swaffham R.D.C. (April 21st), expressed its grave concern in a letter sent directly to Prime Minister Clem. Attlee and the I. D. Committee. At the May Meeting of the Wayland R.D.C. Mr. J. R. Ware said, *"we have not made any protest about the Battle Area during the last fours years because of the promises . . . . Now we want those promises honoured"*.

Interestingly, no one bothered to survey by questionnaire or seek a referendum of ex-residents, to find out if they wanted to return. Few of the former inhabitants had owned their own house, not even the farmers. Villagers had been rent paying tenants with no claim to property. It was the larger landowners and various organisations which pressed the matter. Past promises were one thing, practicalities another. Even gaining access to the Battle Area was difficult and few people returned to visit unless they lived nearby. In 1947 some official visits were allowed during May and August 1st to September 15th, but on all other dates military units were carrying out training using live ammunition. Major B. Langley, Public Relations Officer, Eastern Command, announced this to the N.C. Agricultural Executive Committee at a meeting in Colchester, 30th April. *"Any member of the public not holding a pass (from the W.D. or the C.A.E.C.) will be liable for prosecution"*. The Thetford - Watton road was closed from May 4th onwards.

Mr. Lewis Silken, Minister of Town & Country Planning, told Norfolk M.P.s who sought an interview to discuss the proposals, that such a meeting would be of little value. In a letter, he tried to reassure them and clear up a misunderstanding: *if the provisional conclusions are that the proposals should be adhered to, a Public Inquiry will most certainly be held before a final decision is reached . . . . the War Office do not propose to extend the existing Stanford Battle Area. .* The Norfolk Council for the Preservation of Rural England (C.P.R.E.), forced into inactivity in 1940, was revived at Suckling Hall, Norwich, 10th May 1947. Its Secretary, Mr. A. P. D. Penrose said he did not think enough had been made of the specific and definite promise of return given when people were evicted. *"This is the kind of new morality we have got to stand out against . . .A promise is a promise - at least it used to be in Norfolk".* At their General Meeting, (7th June 1947), the Norfolk & Norwich Archeological Society reported that its Committee having inspected the farms, churches and houses (at Tottington, Stanford, West Tofts and Langford) could see very little damage done by firing but it was a sad sight. There were interesting houses and cottages in the area going to pieces.

"The ravages of nature, gale and rabbit damage had to be seen to be believed . . . All churches are of interest and if they were to be maintained it was only satisfactory if they were put to their proper use. So long as they were in the Battle Area they were cut off and nobody in the ordinary way could see them. They were subject to some neglect and the Army authorities had of course no special interest in keeping the buildings in repair.

THE PETITION: Mr. C. R. F. Allen Meyrick, Managing Director of Meyrick Ridmore Farms Ltd, Wretham, formed a Committee to organise a Petition to Parliament about the return of the Battle Area to its former inhabitants. The Wayland and Swaffham R.D.C.s and Thetford Town Council joined together to promote it. Lord Walsingham hoped members of the Councils would take copies, which covered all points, to their parishes and get it signed. Mr. Dye, the M.P. presented the Petition in June. On the 15th August he spoke to the three Norfolk local authorities at a Meeting in Attleborough and told them that a Report of the Committee of Public Petitions was of the opinion that some of the signatures were in the same handwriting, *"better if there had been 3000 genuine . . . . than 6000 that were not". "As far as the Petition is concerned it is finished".* Lord Walsingham referred to the 'bogus signatures' saying that probably what happened was the head of the household told someone to sign it for them and that the names of the whole household would be written down by the lady of the house; *"they are not bogus signatures I am quite certain that is what happened". "What we are trying to get back involves the lives of over 1000 people who were turned out".* Unfortunately many of the former inhabitants had moved far away and were not contacted. My own parents were living at Hingham, a mere eighteen miles away, and to the best of my knowledge they were never approached nor did they sign the Petition.

W. D. SERVICES' LAND REQUIREMENTS: On 14th Oct. 1947, the leader writer of the E.D.P. stated that there was a suspicion that the War Office contemplated the use of about 60,000 acres in a sort of Salisbury Plain in East Anglia. The W.D. had intentions on the lands of Elveden Estate, Lakenheath, Eriswell, Mildenhall, Icklingham, Barton Mills to Tuddenham including a further 23,430 acres of farm, heath and woodland SW of Thetford. The W. D. had tried to minimise the agricultural value of the land and picture it as a barren waste with a few thousand acres of poor farmland on the fringe of it. Whether this was a genuine proposal or merely a threat to call the bluff of those who were demanding the return of the existing Battle Area, remains unproven, but it raised a blackmail situation - if the West Tofts, Stanford,Tottington area was returned then other land in East Anglia would be required as a Training Area.

At a Conference in London arranged by the C.P.R.E. in conjunction with the Town & Country Planning Association (Nov. 1947), Gen. C. B. Callender (Director of Military Training, W.O.) replied to a question from Major H. W. Wilby (Chairman of Wayland R.D.C.) describing the Stanford area as a particularly difficult case, *". . one knows about it only too well"*. In a sense he was dismissive of any demands for a return stating that once the Territorial Army got going the land would be thoroughly used. Many people had argued that the Battle Area wasn't used in 1947 and on 3rd Dec. the E.D.P. printed a letter from Mr. Merrick to this effect. Indeed at that time the 160 acres of heath, known as Black Rabbit Warren, half-a-mile from Tottington were being reclaimed by Wretham Hall Estates Co. Ltd which ploughed up 40 acres to grow potatoes. However, the W. D. was consolidating its case. A White Paper on Services' Land Requirements published in Dec. 1947 stated the Government accepted the fact that pledges were given or understood to be given to the people - it wasn't necessary to press the issue of the broken promise - but the W. D. needed a large training area. To keep its pledge to allow people to return would require requisitioning a fresh training area somewhere else in the Eastern Counties.

THE THETFORD PUBLIC INQUIRY: On the 26th Jan. 1948 the Ministry of Town & Country Planning published notice to hold an Inquiry at Thetford on March 9th into the effect on the public interest of the Army's retention of the Battle Area. Those seeking return of the area were also concerned that the W. D. did not take any more land. They felt the best argument was the potential value of agricultural land

and food production. Having admitted its broken pledge, after all circumstances change, the W. D. saw no point in arguing any further about it; it was void. Moreover the demand for land was cut from 28,000 to 26,878 acres of which 3000 acres SW of Thetford would be cultivated under licences.

According to the E.D.P. 11th March, it was something of a stormy meeting which led to some blunt speaking and occasional sharp exchanges. *The War Office case for permanent acquisition and sterilization of 15,751 and the use of a further 11,431 acres for deployment was presented with soldierly brevity.* The objectors put up a strong defence; the local case for a return of the land *took two days of impressive and voluminous evidence, Landowners and farmers were armed with facts and figures and they had vigorous support from the County Council and rural councils.* It was argued that food production was more important than military manouevres - *the disparaged land of Breckland can be made of permanent value and produce crops of corn, sugar-beet, and potatoes above the national average as well as being very good for dairying and stock breeding.* Claims were made that most of the former inhabitants *passionately desired to return to their homes* - something of an exaggeration - and Lady Walsingham stated that the women of Norfolk were "*not likely to forget should any Government permit this despotic and unwarranted aggression*" , "*We . . . . . want our homes back, the homes where our children were reared and their fathers before them*". A Mrs Halls, whose first husband was buried in the area, demanded the right to see the grave. Major P. G. Roberts M.P. who was farming 2000 acres around Swaffham complained that *he had received compensation at the rate of £1 an acre from the War Office.* Mr. Meyrick said, "*During the war some of the troops had behaved like a rabble looting everything they couild lay their hands on*". Lord Walsingham stated that when the takeover was announced in 1942 *the general attitude of the residents was very hostile and some talked of refusing to move; "I feel very largely responsible for getting them to go quietly. I understood the promise was that the land would be released".*

However all this was to no avail. The War Office spokesmen had no power to change the Government's decision and their assurances, *that strict measures would be taken to minimise the damage and prevent depredations by troops, did little to allay the fears of farmers.* As the E.D.P pointed out; *It is now becoming "this year, next year, sometime" until they begin to fear it may be "never".* Another Meeting at Thetford (13th July) between Mr. Silkin and the Stanford Area representatives discussed aspects of further land use. Invitations were sent out to all

Council officials and persons chiefly concerned with the B.A. Unfortunately none of the past tenants were invited not even the second largest landowner, Mr. J.C.T. Mills of Hillborough who wrote to the E.D.P. claiming that he received a "curt refusal" when he requested an invitation. During these discussions, Mr. H.R. Boileau of the N.C.C. claimed that the retention of the B.A. deprived a 1000 people of their homes and livelihood and denied them use of 22 farms, 140 cottages, 5 churches, 4 schools, parish rooms and public houses. He estimated that the cost of repairs to houses would be about £14,000 but to rehouse the people would eventually cost the R.D.C. well over £280,000. The Ministry had asked those assembled to release the Government from its promise to return the land but *the people present would not do this.* Lord Walsingham said: *the Elvedon area is just as good for a B.A.. It could have been used with much smaller displacement of population . . . . such farm buildings there are ruinous and the land has not been cultivated for a long period.* Furthermore, *"the military have never bothered to go into the matter from the point of view of the people concerned. . . . . . more facts should have been put before the people. They were given a pledge and they believed it. There is a real principle at stake".* He felt that the Public Inquiry was a farce . . and people had had a very raw deal.

Mr. Silkin, announced in the House of Commons (19th July) that the W.O. claims in Stanford B.A. were upheld. He said that it was essential for proper training in the event of war and for the Territorial Units of Eastern Command: *"The Government would be failing in their duty to the nation were they to abandon the Stanford Area without finding an alternative."* The W.O proposed to purchase the 15,731 acres then held under requisition, but Training Rights were required over a further 9,731 and facilities for gun sites on 1700 acres - 27,000 acres altogether (2000 of which were suitable for agriculture). As the E.D.P. commented, *in the 'Guns and Butter' argument the government's answer was guns.*

Lord Walsingham was reported as saying *"the blow has fallen and it is difficult to see what we can do".* Mr. C.R.F. Allen Meyrich of Wretham felt the people of Stanford had been treated in a most disgraceful manner; *"I think they never had the slightest intention of giving up the area otherwise they would have approached the people differently. There has been no attempt to make out a case in detail. we have never been told why this training could not be done on Salisbury Plain, Catterick or elsewhere".* Mr. J.C.T. Mills wrote to the Eastern Daily Press: *"I consider we have been tricked into spending thousands of pounds in engaging cousel and preparing our defence, etc, for nothing. I suggest that this Government which appears to think nothing of breaking pledges and promises either returns our money or satisfies us that our fight was a genuine one".*

One extreme view was expressed in an anonymous letter published by the E.D.P. 24th July 1948:*"We refugees do not loyally accept this decision. We protest most vehemently against it. Our villages were as loyal and patriotic as any in England but our loyalty was flung in our faces and destroyed in the Thetford Inquiry. We gave up our homes to save the homes of others and eventually, we believed, our own. Now our homes are to be torn from us by force and by our own countrymen. . Our churches stand on the threshold of destruction; our churchyards are damned to complete obliteration and the villages we loved to everlating death . . . Few people of whom such tremendous sacrifices were demanded can have been called upon to accept so bitter a reward."*

This caused some comment, particularly a letter to the E.D.P. on the 28th July, from Miss Lucilla Reeve: *"I challenge your correspondent to find a dozen people who have moved in 1942 who either act or speak disloyally about this matter. . . . No more loyal people exist. Although a Petition was sent to his Majesty in 1942, there were many who did not sign and many others who did so under protest. It is a slur on these people to suggest that they have sat moaning by the wayside these past three years. They haven't done anything of the sort. They have been working and making new homes elsewhere cultivating other gardens and behaving with some loyalty to their country . . . Their hearts may be broken but their courage isn't".*

Mr Silkin reported to the Wayland R.D.C. (E.D.P. July 27th) that he felt the Thetford Inquiry *had gone very much in favour of its return to civilian usage*; however the W.O. had decided otherwise. Lord Walsingham accused him of *"batting on a sticky wicket"* and being prepared to do anything to soften the blow in order to bargain for the release of the pledge. *"These people were kicked out and cannot get back. We have got to take it that 'it's a done job'."* The minister had promised that alternative housing would be provided for those who were displaced and could not return. The Council decided that people dispossessed should be settled in similar circumstances to those they had left; new houses were to built by the local authorities at the expense of the government and not the ratepayers.

COMPENSATION: The Stanford Resettlement Committee (composed of representatives from the N.C.C., the Swaffham and Wayland R.D.C.s, the NFU and NUAW, government Departments, and Lord Walsingham and Miss Noble) worked on three categories under which compensation was to be offered to former residents: (a) cash for lost vegetables and belongings; (b) money to farmers for machinery and lost income; (c) rehousing. These were assessed on a value as at Jan. 1st 1946 and adverts were issued inviting people to apply (instead of contacting people, so naturally some former residents lost out). There were 177 claims and £100,000 was paid out in sums ranging from £5 to £9000 (up to £50 was given for the loss of free firewood and garden produce, and one sum of £1000 for the loss of reveniue on a sugar beet crop). Nine claims were not established as actual losses. 74 applicants were entitled to rehousing but it proved impossible to place dispossessed farmers and small holders into similar farms. Lack of records made the accounting process difficult and hindered payments; land was valued at 1938 prices and paid at £25 an acre.

Grandparents' house in Tottington, 1956

Tottington Terrace was built at Merton for former tenants on the understanding that rents were no more than the small amount paid to the last Lord Walsingham, but not until 30th September 1954 was the last person who applied to the Resettlement Committee given his keys as a tenant; that being my cousin Mr. Cyril Spragg. In general new homes at old rents (often only 1s. a week) were offered by the local councils but not always. The Mitford and Launditch R.D.C. at Yaxham voted 26 - 6 in refusing to carry out a Ministry request to build Council houses for an evacuated family and charge 1s 9d. Mr. T. C. Yule said, *"The promise was that they were to be returned. It should not be our responsibility to house them."* This materialistic approach overshadowed any thought or discussion of the other aspects which this book has tried to commemorate. The landowners and farmers were keen to repossess the area for farming and shooting. The buildings were valuable as property; Lord Walsingham even wondered whether it would be possible to salvage some of the building materials - floor boards, window frames, gates and such like. The villagers, their feelings and emotions, were ignored; they were given nothing for inconvenience, the breaking up of extended families, the stress and strain of relocation, re-employment and re-housing. Nowadays compensation for such personal and communal loss would be considered automatic.

Eastmere Fibua village, 1993

EPILOGUE

By 1950 it was all over and there was no going back - the area was subject to a Compulsory Purchase Order at 1938 prices. *'The Promise'* of a return was broken. The relationship to the land and animals, to work and home, was destroyed and could not be re-established. Families had settled elsewhere and many had no wish to return. A writer in the EDP stated: *The houses I saw showed little outward damage other than broken window panes . . . and tiles and thatch slightly misplaced.* Despite such reports the fabric of Tottington as a village was decaying and the military made no provision for preserving even the large buildings. By August 1953 another article in the EDP said: *I visited Tottington about this time but instead of seeing the lovely village I had once known I found it in ruin and desolation. Tanks had made large holes in the roadside hedges, brambles had spread their tangles masses over the pretty flower gardens and the cottage windows, where red and pink geraniums had blossomed, were smashed thus allowing the ravages of winter weather to enter and bring about total destruction. A deep silence hung over the whole village. "Rambler"*

As the rain entered, roofs and walls collapsed, buildings were flattened by shellfire and eventually the Army bulldozed them over to clear the ground. Any return was impractical: *'much of the timber full of lead and unsaleable; all the land presenting a colosal problem of clearing mines, dud shells, UXBs, dannart, and all the metallic junk an Army produces: farms blotted out, villages blotted out, no farm house, no cottages, no drains - who could hope to restore this wilderness marked only by the lonely forms for four medieval churches as a lasting reproof of man's inhumanity to man?'* *A Farm Owner's View* by Hon.R.P.de Grey (Stanford B.A. Booklet 1979).

More than half-a-century has passed since the creation of the Battle Area ended Tottington's existence. During that time few of the previous inhabitants bothered to go back for visits; they were busy creating new lives in other places (see *Appendix:Where the Villagers went to*). After leaving London in 1953 we moved to the village where my parents relocated ten years earlier, Hingham, just east of Watton and about 15 miles from Tottington. That would seem close enough for periodic returns but we were too busy running a grocery shop and bringing up two young boys, to bother with trips to see what was rapidly falling into ruin. During the late 1950s we paid one visit but only half of Eastmere Cottage was still standing along with a small part of the farm (Westmere Farmhouse had been removed to Merton Woods in 1942)

My young sons found empty shell cases lying around the wreckage. It was a sad sight and we never went back. Mother died in 1957, we moved to East Dereham. Father died in 1963 by which time the business had been lost and we were living in Costessey just outside Norwich - there wasn't the time to think about the past. Others, like my cousins, Dolly and Tommy Spragg, living in the nearby village of Thompson, did go onto the Battle Area, sometimes secretly, but I don't believe they visited Tottington much.

Fifty years have passed so quickly with little of real consequence to report about Tottington or the Battle Area itself. In that time four related elements have been important: Army manouevres; sheep farming; the natural environment and an increasing number of visitors. Apart from numerous land and parachute exercises, the Army has continued to seek expansion of what has become known as the Stanford Training Area. Periodically this has brought them into conflict with the local residents of nearby villages such as East Wretham and Gt.Cressingham. The present Lord Walsingham has carried on a ceaseless war of words concerning the use of the 8000 acres of land for which his Father was paid £25 an acre. In 1990 he estimated the Army owed him about £10 million, plus a extra £250,000 for another 500 acres leased for 60 years (1950 - 2010) at a peppercorn rent of one shilling a year.

Hilda and son, James Perry in Fibua village, Eastmere

In 1986, the Army chose Eastmere Farm from seventeen possible sites as a Fibua (fighting in built up areas) mock-up. It consisted of 16 houses, a church, a public house and various outbuildings, resembling an East German village. The plans were submitted to the Breckland District Council in 1988 and cost £4 million to complete. In July 1990 Lord Walsingham wrote to the EDP: *The whole of the Stanford Training Area could be returned to habitation for the same amount of government money easing rural housing in the Breckland district and even providing ample room for the starter homes at £25,000 we have tried unsuccessfully to build locally for the free market* . Whilst this might seem a sound idea particularly in the light of the increasing congestion caused by ever-expanding housing estates in central Norfolk, the Army maintain that the S.T.A. is a dangerous area with much unexploded ammunition: in 1981 twenty acres were cleared revealing 800 pieces of ordnance, 150 of which were still live.

Much criticism has been levelled particularly about the underuse of the S.T.A. In 1990 Mr. Garrett, MP for Norfolk South, asked that this part of the Breckland be given up. In July, Lord Arran from the Ministry wrote to him, *"In view of its importance and the continuing need for training we have no plans to relinguish the Stanford Training Area"*.

In 1992 the National Audit prepared a Report on Managment and Control of MOD lands which stated that the area was used for less than 80% of the time, and mostly in May. However the Army insists the STA is essential for training of troops from all over the world. In November 1993, ten old Chieftain tanks worth £3 milion each were blown up in a two-day arms reduction exercise attended by Nato personnel and representatives from Russia.

Some land has been returned to sheep farming. Mr. Arthur Collins, moved from the West Country in the 1950s, leased 9,300 acres, bought. 1000 Cheviot ewes and crossed them with Suffolk Border, Leicester and Cheviot rams. He introduced Beulah sheep from Wales in the mid 1960s and created Norfolk Sheep Ltd. which was bought up in 1981 by Strutt and Parker Farms from Essex, now with 5000 Beulah ewes and altogether some 15,000 sheep and lambs. The lack of cultivation has led to a unique cnvironment; the largest lowland site, 23,000 acres of special scientific interest. In 1976 a Conservation Committee was established to care for the flora and fauna of the area: 600 different flowers and plants, 23 rare species, 331 moths, 28 butterflies, 137 species of birds and 26 types of mammal. Whilst there has been a lot of woodland restoration, some areas of mature coniferous forest have been turned into heathland by sowing native grass and flower species. There is a huge rabbit population but keepers control the foxes and other vermin. Unfortunately the Breckland Meres seem to be disappearing: Bagpit has dried out and Fowlmere now resembles a bog rather than a lake of fifteen acres.

In the 1950s and 1960s most of the Battle Area roads were closed to the public which didn't make access straight forward and easy. Interest in the Training Area as a Naturalist's paradise and people wanting to visit ruins of where they or their ancestors lived, led to the demand for greater access and more information. During the 1980s coach trips for visitors became a regular feature arranged by the West Tofts Training Centre. After my husband Geoff, died in 1988, my sons and I began to participate in these guided tours. About 1990 we went back with my sister-in-law, Kathleen Worby, catching a coach from Thompson Chequers and meeting up with the Spraggs. We were shown around the old village and the Church yard but nothing much was left except for a few shells of council houses in Church Lane plus the school house. There seemed no life in them, no meaning except in the memories of those who lived there. On another occasion, with the Bone family, we drove around to see Eastmere Cottage and Farm but these had disappeared replaced by the Fibua village for the training of troops in house to house fighting. The mock buildings were more empty, lifeless, concrete shells, surrounded by rubble, barbed wire and wrecks of vehicles. We walked down into the pit we called 'the Hills' and took some photographs, but it was a strange and rather alien place. Beautiful Mortimer had gone but many of the trees remained as do the stately firs of Merton Park. The planting of new saplins has created a lovely nature reserve but as the soldiers use live ammunition people are not allowed to roam about freely. A few cultivated fields could be seen and there were a considerable number of sheep as well as innumerable rabbits.

In November 1990 the Breckland Recreation and Tourism Committee agreed to drop plans for a £5000 Exhibition at the Old Forge at Home Farm, West Tofts, as funds did not stretch to providing portable toilet facilities, but the go ahead was given for a permanent Exhibition costing £1000 in one of the nissan huts at West Tofts Camp. Lt. Col. I. K. MacKinnon began a collection of photos and postcards of buildings and villages in the 1980s which was carried on by Mrs Anne Webster. These were on display in the Conference Room which had been turned into a photo gallery in remembrance of the five villages. We gave over a large selection of old photographs from our Worby family album. These have been copied and added to the walls under the Tottingtom section.

On July 25th 1993 a Reunion was held for all those (and their descendants) who had lived in the villages of Tottington, Sturston, Stanford, Longford, and West Tofts. It was organised by Major Eller, Adjutant of West Tofts Camp and Mrs Anne Webster. About two hundred people attended for a buffet-lunch at the Camp. Afterwards photos were taken of the different groups each of which then boarded a coach to take them round the B.A. to their respective villages. Tottington people were given red badges so we could identify one another which was rather difficult in certain cases especially since many people were only children in 1942. A few of the over- 80s attended and it was wonderful to meet them again. Our coach trip was greatly appreciated but the commentator clearly didn't know anything about the village. He only commentated on all the Army had done whereas people were clamouring to see the old places and talk about the past. When we stopped at Eastmere I was dying to tell everyone about this farm which had employed many of the Fathers and relatives of those seated on the coach. We passed through the village so quickly that it was rather disappointing. I don't suppose the bus driver realised how much Tottington meant to everyone - the shop, the old school, the River Wissey, and all the cottages where everyone had lived.

Hilda and Edmund Perry standing in 'the Hills' Eastmere Fibua Village.

We went up the lane to St. Andrew's Church but the weather turned cold. Several people did get out to wander around the churchyard but it started to rain. Later the EDP published a photo of the Church with Albert Bishop standing near the gates and behind him, my son Edmund talking to a man called Don Sutton. The shower passed and the sun came out for the rest of the journey but as we reached the Camp the heavens opened and the rain fell down. After a cup of tea and biscuits we were invited to the Photo Gallery where Anne Webster had put on display some of the Church Registers, from the Norwich Library Record Office, containing births, marriages and deaths. I was able to hand over the 'old school' bell used in the early 1900s which my Mother had inherited from her Aunt. Most people seemed loathe to leave and were keen to order duplicates of photographs as well as sign a register leaving names and address: the gathering went on until after 6 p.m. The EDP took photographs and interviewed several of us about how we felt and I wrote a short piece for the local newspaper, 'The Mercury' to express our appreciation and how much everyone had enjoyed the occasion. Since then many of the villagers met for a service at Buckenham Tofts Church to commemorate the Fiftieth Anniversary of D-Day, and Carol Services are held there each Christmas. In August 1995 I went back again on a visit arranged for a group from our village of Hethersett. That time Anne Webster gave a proper history talk with photo slides, and I was able to tell everyone on the coach, about Eastmere Farm and some of my experiences. It was another memorable day out.

Unfortunately each year, fewer and fewer of the original inhabitants survive as old age catches up with us. Once we are gone only stories handed down to children and grandchildren will exist to keep the memory of a village like Tottington alive. No doubt our descendents and other visitors will continue to tour round the Battle Area and look at the photographs but without the written word so much will be irretrievable. I hope this book goes some of the way to avert that loss and leave for posterity a tangible record of the village and the people who lived there rather than the epitaph of a name and crumbling ruins.

Reunion of Tottington Villagers, 25th July, 1993 at West Tofts Camp

APPENDIX

The following is a list of the places, the villagers went to when they left Tottington in 1942.

From Eastmere Farm:
Albert and and Alice *Bishop* and sons, Joseph and Albert, moved to Illington Hall near Wretham
Albert and Alice *Worby*, and daughter Hilda, moved to Gurney's Manor Cottages, Hingham.
Ted and Violet *Williams*, and their children, Lily, Gladys, Fred, Sylvia and Shirley moved to Carbrooke.

From Westmere Farm:
Lord and Lady Walsingham had their house taken down and rebuilt in Merton Woods on Watton Road. Their children were Lavender, John, Catherine, Margaret.
George and Alice *Leeder* and their children, Phylis, Cyril, Lena, Douglas, Iris and Billy moved to Watton.
Vic and Florrie *Leeder* and their children Kahleen. Pauline, and John moved to Merton.
Mr and Mrs Jock *Thompson* and daughter Betty, moved to Watton.
Mr *Newstead* and son Reggie moved to Saham Toney.

From the Crossways:
The School Teacher, *Miss White* moved to Bircham Wells.
Miss Lisa *Lefley* and adopted son Douglas *Bell*, went to Eccles.
Edward and Mabel *Bone*, with sons Allan and Fred, moved to Tuddenham St. Mary.
Eliza *Oldfield* and daughter Alice, moved to Griston.

From the Madhouses:
Mable *Nash* and her daughter Hilda, moved to Saham Toney. Jack and Edna *Thompson*, and children moved to Thompson.

From Water House: Arthur and Rose *Hunt* and son Joby moved to Water End Farm, Thompson.

From Grange Meadows: Will *Macro* moved to Suffolk.

From Grange Farm: Mr and Mrs *Green*

From Green Lane:
Alma *Watson* went into a Home.
Mrs Dolly *Hunt* (husband Frank was in a Japanese prison of war camp) went to Water End Farm.
Mrs Ethel *Moore* to London (all her sons had left home before the War).
Mr and Mrs *Lester* went to Cockney Clay near Holt.
Mrs Violet *Lake* went to Griston.
Mrs Bessie *Williams* moved to Watton.
Walter and Ella *Spinks* moved to Rockland.
Tom and Florrie *Spragg*, with children, Tommy and Dorothy, moved to Thompson.

From the main road: Mrs *Belham* and son Jack went to Merton

From Green Man Yard:
Mrs Laura *Wright* and son Maurice went to Merton.
Mrs Annie *Wright* and adopted son Jimmy *Dunham* went to Yorkshire.
Mrs *Leeder*
Arthur and Lily *Oldfield* and daughter Phyllis went to Merton Grove Farm.

From Hall Farm Meadows:
Mr and Mrs *Clarke*, and a Mr and Mrs *Drake*, moved to Griston.

From Hall Farm:
Joe and Hilda *Childerhouse* and their children went to Weeting.
Dan and Rosie *Fisher* went to Griston.

From the Working Man's Club House: Mr and Mrs Walter *Wyett* and children Betty, Peggy, and John, moved to Watton.

From the Shop: Mrs Edith *Balls* and daughter Gladys went to Eccles.

From Pearson's Meadows: Mr. Joe *Balls* and four sons moved to Eccles.

From Church Farm: Mr and Mrs *Page*, their children Betty, Bridget and John moved to Carbrooke.

From Keymer's (Tuddenham's) Corner: Mr. and Mrs. Blanche.

From Church Lane Council Houses:
Mrs Annie Macro and her son Leslie moved to Carbrooke
Mr and Mrs Rand (plus several children) moved to Hochham
Cyril and Winnie spragg and children moved to Cranworth near Hingham
Albert and Ivy Oldfield and children moved to Shropham
Mr and Mrs Hovell and children moved to Croxton
Mr and Mrs Buttle and children moved to Watton
Mr and Mrs Lester and children moved to Cockney Clay
One other teacher moved to Hockham

From the two semi-detached Cottages:
Jack and Maud *Williams* and son George moved to Watton.
Mrs *Thompson* and son Peter and daughter Eleanor moved to Thompson.

From Tottington Vicarage: *the Noble sisters*; all five moved to Saham Toney.

From the House by the Church: Tom and Daisy *Jessup* with several children went to Watton.

From the Houses on Church Meadows: George and Olive *Smith* and daughter Audrey and a lodger, Don *Sutton*, moved to Watton Smith.
Freddie and Meg *Spragg* went to Carbrooke.

From Sturston Farm: Mr and Mrs *Mansfield* moved to Merton.

From Sturston Cottages: Mrs Spinks moved to Merton.
Bill and Evelyn *Hancock* and several children moved to Garveston.
Bob *Woods*

From Mortimer's Farm: Mr and Mrs Bob *Childerhouse* moved to Weeting.

From Icky buildings: Harold and Ethel *Spinks* moved to Tuddenham St. Mary.

From Waterloo Farm: Captain *Johnson* -

From Bagmere Farm: Miss Lucilla *Reeve* who had the Estate Office at Eastmere, bought the large plucking hut and had it moved to Merton Woods.

From Curlew near Stanford Watering:
Mr Arthur *Spinks* plus Mr and Mrs *Curson* (Dolly) moved to Hillborough.
Tom *Cook* the gamekeeper -

Dolly Spragg, Ethel Spinks, Hilda Perry, Hilda Wallace

ACKNOWLEDGEMENTS

Eastern Counties Newspapers for cuttings
from the Eastern Daily Press (1940 - 1996)
Norwich Central ,Hethersett ,Wymondham and Thetford Library
West Tofts Conference Centre (photos)
Norfolk Central Records Office
Kirby House, Norfolk and Norwich Genealogical Society
Church of Jesus Christ of Latter Day Saints, Cringleford
Chigwell School and Mr. Richard Bracewell
Sir John Leman High School (reprographics)
Hilda Wallace, Ann Webster, James Perry
Dolly Spragg, Ethel Spinks
Tim Smith and Brian Seager at Geo. R. Reeve Ltd.
and to all authors quoted.

Tottington re-union, 29th July, 2000